BROOKINGS-WHARTON

PAPERS *on* FINANCIAL SERVICES

2004

ROBERT E. LITAN

and

RICHARD HERRING

Editors

BROOKINGS INSTITUTION PRESS
Washington, D.C.

BROOKINGS-WHARTON

PAPERS *on* FINANCIAL SERVICES
2004

THE BROOKINGS-WHARTON PAPERS ON FINANCIAL SERVICES is an annual publication containing the articles, formal discussants' remarks, and highlights of the discussions from a conference held at the Brookings Institution and arranged by the editors. This year's forum and journal are financed in part by grants from Morgan Stanley, St. Paul Travelers Companies, and the USAA Foundation.

The annual forum and journal are the products of a collaboration between the Brookings Institution and the Financial Institutions Center at the Wharton School of the University of Pennsylvania. All of the papers and the discussants' remarks represent the views of the authors and not necessarily the views of the staff members, officers, or trustees of the Brookings Institution or the Wharton School of the University of Pennsylvania, or of the institutions affiliated with the authors.

Ordering Information

Standing order plans are available by calling 1-800/275-1447 or 202/797-6258. Send subscription orders to the Brookings Institution, Department 037, 1775 Massachusetts Avenue, N.W., Washington, DC 20042-0037. Or call 202/797-6258 or toll free 1-800/275-1447. Or email bibooks@brookings.edu.

Visit Brookings online at www.brookings.edu.

Brookings periodicals are available online through both Online Computer Library Center (contact the OCLC subscriptions department at 1-800/848-5878, ext. 6251) and Project Muse (http://muse.jhu.edu).

Editors' Summary

RICHARD J. HERRING
ROBERT E. LITAN

IMAGINE A SOCIETY where no one could insure against the costs of being treated for a life-threatening disease; where drivers could not insure against the costs of accidents, to themselves or third parties; where homeowners could not protect themselves against the financial costs of fires and windstorms; and where firms and professionals could not protect against the financial costs of liability for harm to third parties. Without the ability to transfer these types of financial risks to insurers, members of such a society would be much less willing to take risks in consumption and investment decisions that are critical to the dynamism of capitalist economies. And consequently, such a society would be far less productive than the one in which we now live.

Yet as important as insurance is to the functioning of modern economies, it is probably the least well understood of all the financial services commonly sold in the marketplace today. Various events in recent years, however, have focused public attention on the insurance industry. Controversy surrounding the system of medical malpractice insurance has again surfaced, with insurance rates for certain specialties skyrocketing in some states and critics charging that the current approach compensates victims poorly, entails enormous overhead costs, and fails to discipline malpractitioners effectively. Recently, even homeowners' insurance has raised public policy concerns as insurers attempt to limit their exposure to new types of litigation, such as that over toxic mold in homes, as well as to catastrophic losses. And, most notably, the terrorist acts of September 11, 2001, prompted the U.S. Congress to enact legislation providing federal reinsurance to private insurers for losses caused by terrorist acts beyond a certain threshold. This legislation will expire next year, unless Congress takes action.

Thus it seemed appropriate for insurance to be the focus of the seventh annual conference on financial services issues sponsored by the Brookings Institution and the Wharton School of the University of Pennsylvania, held at Brookings in January 2004. This summary presents the key findings and conclusions contained in the six papers prepared for the conference. All of the papers stimulated lively discussions among the experts who attended the conference, and these discussions are summarized following each paper.

The Theory and Practice of Insurance: Why the Disjunction?

Economists and insurance experts have studied the industry for many years and have developed a series of theoretical concepts to explain how insurance markets function. This view of the demand for insurance was summed up by one conference participant who noted that an economically rational consumer would understand that, apart from certain tax benefits, when you buy insurance, you are making a bet with an insurance company, which the insurance company wins, on average, because it must cover administrative costs and earn a competitive return for its shareholders. From this perspective, it makes sense to insure only against very large potential losses that would make a difference in your standard of living.

But that is not how consumers behave in many circumstances. For example, one of the fastest-growing insurance markets is repair or replacement insurance for relatively inexpensive electronic products that seldom fail. Usually the insurance is priced as if the risk of failure were much higher than it actually is. Nonetheless, for some products nearly 80 percent of consumers opt for insurance, even though the loss would not have an appreciable impact on their standard of living. Similarly, consider the case of a seventy-year-old widow with three children, all of whom are richer than she. The greatest risk she faces is loss of income, and thus she should buy annuities rather than life insurance. But if the widow behaves like her peers, she is seven times more likely to buy life insurance than annuities.

Just as the demand for insurance seems to diverge from the theoretical, rational paradigm, the supply of insurance also seems to depart from the standard model. For example, in most markets, an increase in demand raises the price and increases the supply. But when the perceived risk of a terrorist incident went from negligible to plausible in the wake of the tragedy on September 11, 2001, demand for terrorist coverage surely increased, but the voluntary supply of such insurance virtually disappeared.

Professors David Cutler and Richard Zeckhauser of Harvard University use these conundrums to argue, in a comprehensive and thought-provoking paper, that there is a systematic tendency for practice to diverge from theory in insurance markets. One consequence is that insurance is often purchased when theory suggests it should not be (life insurance among the elderly), while many substantial risks that should be insured (terrorism) are not. A second consequence is that there are significant mismatches between entities that should bear risk (financial markets) and those that actually do (governments and private and mutual insurance companies).

The authors explore several reasons for the discrepancy between theory and practice. On the demand side, they suggest that the standard model of utility maximization needs to be extended to take account of some of the findings of behavioral economic research. For example, individuals appear to have an aversion to any loss and will pay far more than the expected loss to protect against even small losses. Similarly some evidence shows that individuals significantly overestimate the magnitude of the negative experience from a loss.

On the supply side, they argue that insurers are often risk averse and feel unable to diversify their risks, as in the case of terrorism (where events may be hugely costly and highly correlated) and long-term health care (where it is not possible to diversify the risks cross-sectionally). As a solution to this supply problem, they argue that risk spreading should be encouraged beyond the "narrow confines of primary insurance and reinsurance" to include financial instruments that tap the enormous pool of insurance dollars in global financial markets.

The Crisis in Medical Malpractice

In several states, medical malpractice insurance has become either prohibitively expensive or totally unavailable. This experience follows a relatively quiescent period in the market, when such insurance was broadly available, but seems to echo an earlier crisis in malpractice insurance in the

1970s. Then, many states changed their tort laws to make it more difficult to sue physicians and to cap awards for noneconomic damages suffered by patients. Insurers also took steps to limit their own risks, most prominently by replacing the "occurrence" policy (which covered malpractice as long as it occurred during the policy period) with a "claims-made" policy (covering only those claims filed during the policy period). Moreover, doctors began to self-insure by forming their own mutual companies and "risk retention groups" to cover their malpractice liabilities. And some states adopted measures to assure the availability of insurance and reduce its cost to physicians. These measures included joint underwriting associations for physicians who are unable to obtain coverage in the voluntary market and patient compensation funds that limit the physician's liability at some threshold but provide additional compensation to the patient up to a higher threshold.

In view of these reforms, it is somewhat surprising that the malpractice insurance crisis has recently reemerged. But the fact that the symptoms of the crisis—high insurance rates and unavailability of insurance—vary so widely across states suggests that it may be possible to evaluate the earlier reforms, which also varied across states. For example, malpractice insurance rates for general surgeons increased 75 percent in Dade County, Florida, but only 2 percent in Minnesota, for similar levels of coverage. In the second paper presented at the conference, three experts in medical malpractice insurance from the Wharton School—Patricia Danzon, Andrew Epstein, and Scott Johnson—wrestle with these issues, focusing primarily on the reasons for the cross-state variations.

The authors reach several conclusions, which they take pains to characterize as "tentative" given the paucity of appropriate data. They report that, while "shocks to insurer capital"—or high payouts—have not contributed to premium increases, they have induced some insurers to exit the market. The authors also find evidence that malpractice insurers did not set aside sufficient reserves against losses in the late 1990s and that subsequent revisions of loss forecasts have been positively associated with premium increases. Consistent with general evidence of underwriting cycles (discussed by Scott Harrington in the third paper in this volume), it appears that "excessive competition" during the "soft market" of the 1990s contributed to the "hard market" of recent years, with smaller insurers, especially recent entrants, leaving the market.

Finally, what impacts did various tort reforms have on the malpractice insurance market? Based on their statistical analysis, the authors conclude that states that capped noneconomic damages and limited joint and several liability had significantly lower premium increases than states without these reforms. In contrast, joint underwriting associations and patient compensation funds did not halt the rise in premiums or reduce the probability that insurers will leave the market. In fact, these mechanisms perhaps tended to increase costs. Two of the states with joint underwriting associations— Pennsylvania and South Carolina—had among the largest cumulative rise in premiums over the period.

In a dinner speech to conference participants, Jay Fishman, chief executive officer of St. Paul Travelers, the largest company to withdraw from the medical malpractice insurance market, provided an important perspective on the authors' somewhat puzzling result that shocks to insurer capital (higher payouts) lead to exits from the market rather than to higher premiums. He explained that St. Paul Travelers' decision to exit the malpractice market stemmed from an analysis concluding that the firm could break even only if it raised premiums 30 percent annually for three years consecutively. In the company's view, such premium increases would lead to a "death spiral" of adverse selection, in which only the highest-risk physicians would purchase the insurance, thus raising future losses and requiring still higher premiums in the future. Fishman also cautioned that caps on pain and suffering awards were not the appropriate solution to the malpractice problem. In his view, a more realistic definition of malpractice is needed that takes account of the fact that, even when physicians take all reasonable precautions, the innovative and experimental treatments that modern medical science makes possible and patients demand do not always produce the desired result.

Tort Liability, Insurance Rates, and the Insurance Cycle

Medical malpractice is only a subset of larger concerns about the tort system generally and its relation to insurance rates and availability. In the next paper, a leading analyst of liability insurance markets, Scott Harrington of the University of South Carolina, reexamines these controversial issues.

It is common for analysts of insurance and participants in the market to characterize the business as going through a regular "underwriting cycle"— fluctuations between "soft" periods when premiums are stable or falling and coverage is readily available and then "hard" markets when premiums soar and coverage is less available. Harrington notes that the most infamous example of a "hard" market is the liability insurance crisis of the mid-1980s. More recently, the market for commercial property and casualty insurance has hardened in the wake of September 11, while markets for general liability and medical malpractice are harder than in the past.

Harrington analyzes the various theories that have been advanced in the literature to explain the insurance cycle. Clearly, much of the variation in rates and availability reflects changes in the discounted value of expected claims (the so-called perfect markets hypothesis). But capacity constraints on the supply of capital available to insurers may also play a role. Mixed evidence supports this explanation in the case of hard markets. But evidence of the role of capacity constraints in soft markets is much weaker.

Nonetheless, taking all factors into account, there is good reason for believing that, as the tort liability system expands (both in the type of situations in which damages are awarded and in the amount of damages themselves), insurance rates will increase in the long run. Yet, as Harrington concludes, the case for tort reform does not rest solely on the impact of the tort system on insurance markets. The fundamental issue is whether the current system efficiently deters undesirable behavior.

Insuring against Terrorism: The Policy Challenge

No single event during the past several years has focused public attention on the importance of insurance as intensely as the terrorist attacks on the United States on September 11, 2001. That disaster led virtually all insurers to withdraw or seek to withdraw coverage for terrorist-related events, outcomes that were sanctioned in most states. At the same time, insurers and real estate developers, among others, urged the federal government to provide reinsurance to the primary insurers so that they could again offer terrorism coverage without the fear that another large-scale event could wipe them out. Eventually, Congress responded and the president signed into law the Terrorism Reinsurance Act (TRIA) of 2002, which set up a system of reinsurance under which insurers would pay premiums to the government ex post—or after another such event. Under TRIA, the federal government agreed to pay for 90 percent of an insurer's losses after the insurer first absorbed losses up to 7 percent of its earned premiums (the so-called "retention" level, which rose to 10 percent in 2004 and will increase to 15 percent in 2005). Since TRIA is set to expire next year and there are calls to extend it, this seems an appropriate time to review the act. Kent Smetters is particularly well qualified to undertake this review because he worked on the legislation at the Treasury Department while on leave from the Wharton School.

Smetters is highly skeptical of the need for government-provided reinsurance for terrorism and argues that other sorts of government policies contributed to the scarcity of terrorism insurance after September 11 and indeed to the inadequacy of insurance coverage for other sorts of large catastrophes. Tax policies that prevent insurers from setting aside tax-deductible reserves for catastrophes are one major factor.

The second major factor is regulatory and accounting policies that inhibit the ability of insurance companies to securitize large risks. Smetters believes that, in the absence of these restrictions, investment banks and insurers would develop capital market instruments that would diversify the risks of terrorism and other catastrophic losses. He notes that even losses ten times larger than the $40 billion loss that occurred on September 11 are not uncommon in world capital markets. Indeed, U.S. capital markets alone routinely gain or lose $100 billion on a daily basis and often several trillion dollars on a monthly basis.

Smetters argues that, if either or both of these factors were dealt with effectively, there would be no need for government-provided terrorism reinsurance. He believes that both unfettered insurance and capital markets could absorb large, even catastrophic, losses without undue stress.

Smetters reviews the most common arguments in favor of direct government intervention into the terrorism insurance market and finds most of them deficient because they fail to explain why the private market solution is inefficient. These include the difficulty of forecasting future losses, the magnitude of potential terrorist losses, asymmetric information between the government and private sector, and the fact that many people rationally forgo insurance because they believe the government will bail them out after a major loss. He does concede, however, that *mandatory* coverage might be justifiable for certain risks that are difficult to diversify in capital markets and that are borne by groups, such as homeowners and farmers, that the government is likely to bail out after a significant loss.

Brokers and the Insurance of "Non-Verifiable Losses"

Although insurance contracts are tightly worded documents, in the real world disputes often arise over whether coverage applies and, if so, to what extent. Indeed, according to Neil Doherty and Alexander Muermann of the Wharton School, insurers seem more prone to contesting large claims than they were in the past. They call such contested situations "non-verifiable losses" and seek to explain how insurance brokers play a role in resolving the disputes or in preventing them in the first instance.

Insurers often try a number of prevention techniques themselves. Because insurers make an investment in acquiring information about their larger customers and do not want to lose them, they have incentives to make reasonable offers to pay non-verifiable losses and thus avoid disputes. In addition, some insurers might assist their customers in controlling losses by providing engineering or risk reduction services.

Doherty and Muermann point out, however, that because the insurance brokerage market is highly concentrated—three brokers dominate the market—insurers who derive business from them have strong incentives to avoid the reputation of being unwilling to pay claims. Otherwise, the insurers may lose not only future referrals but some of their existing book of business as well. In addition, insurers that acquire a reputation as being an unwilling payer may have to accede to the demands of brokers for more compensation to steer business in their direction.

In short, the highly concentrated nature of the brokerage industry tends to work in favor of those who are insured if and when they experience non-verifiable losses. This may be the rare exception where a highly concentrated market structure works in favor of customers rather than producers.

Consolidation in the European Insurance Industry

With the development of a single European market, much consolidation among firms, both within European countries and across them, has taken place over the past decade. The insurance business has been no exception to this pattern. In the final paper presented at the conference, David Cummins of the Wharton School and Mary Weiss of Temple University examine whether these European mergers create value for shareholders.

In similar studies of mergers in the U.S. market, principally among banks, various authors have found a predictable pattern: while the stock prices of acquiring companies typically rise after a merger proposal is made, the prices of stocks of acquired companies generally remain unchanged or even drop. Does this pattern hold up for European insurance mergers?

Cummins and Weiss conduct an event-study analysis of stock prices before and after the mergers and confirm that this pattern generally holds. The results of the study show that, while insurance mergers across borders do not change shareholder value for acquirers one way or another, on average, mergers within the same country actually produce significant shareholder losses. In contrast, target companies see their shareholder value increase in both cross-border and within-country mergers, but more so for transactions where the two companies do business in the same country. Cross-border mergers clearly appear to generate net gains to shareholders (acquirers and targets combined), but within-country mergers seem more likely to destroy than to create shareholder value.

These results are relevant to policymakers, especially those concerned with market structure. For example, where shareholder gains arise from entrenchment of market power rather than from efficiencies, antitrust intervention may be warranted. Because insurers in cross-border deals probably are not direct competitors to begin with, their combinations should pose fewer antitrust concerns than within-country mergers (especially where insurance markets may already be concentrated). In contrast to the banking sector, where national bank regulators have often discouraged cross-border mergers, national insurance regulators have seldom intervened to protect national champions. These results are also useful to investors and managers of insurance companies as they consider which kinds of mergers are most likely to produce efficiencies and to enhance market opportunities and thus shareholder gains.

Conclusion

If any common lesson emerges from this conference, it is that insurance is too important to the fabric of the American economy—and indeed to our society generally—to be ignored. If individuals and businesses could not obtain insurance against various causes of financial misfortune, the economy would be much less productive and consumption choices would be much more constrained. These papers represent the most sophisticated and best-informed economic analysis of the key policy issues concerning the insurance industry currently available. Yet the authors have been careful to underline the limits of their analysis. Many aspects of the behavior of insurance markets remain difficult to explain in terms of conventional economic analysis.

Economists, therefore, need to develop richer models to explain the actual behavior of insurance markets. But, even in the absence of new break-throughs in economic analysis, current research provides a strong rationale for policymakers to reexamine the tax and regulatory policies that impede the performance of insurance markets and the allocation of public and private responsibility for the efficient provision of insurance.

Extending the Theory to Meet the Practice of Insurance

DAVID M. CUTLER
RICHARD ZECKHAUSER

*Doth not the wise merchant in every
adventure of danger give part to have the rest assured?*
NICHOLAS BACON, to the Opening of Parliament, 1559

Formal insurance arrangements date back at least to ancient Greece. Marine loans in that era advanced money on a ship or cargo that would be repaid with substantial interest if the voyage succeeded but forfeited if the ship were lost, much like the structure of contemporary catastrophe bonds. The interest rate covered both the cost of capital and the risk of loss.[1] Direct insurance of sea risks, using premiums, probably started around 1300 in Belgium. The first known life insurance policy was written in 1583. By the end of the seventeenth century, sea risk insurance had evolved to a competitive process between underwriters

We are grateful to Anda Bordean and Anna Joo for research assistance, James Ament for thoughtful comments, and Dan Gilbert for helpful conversations. We thank the participants at the Brookings-Wharton Conference on Public Policy Issues Confronting the Insurance Industry for thoughtful comments.

1. Such arrangements are known as bottomry or respondentia bonds. Early insurance arrangements reflected poor understanding of insurance theory. For example, in 1692, England offered life annuities for sale at a fixed price, independent of age. Not surprising, healthy young people bought the policies, and the treasury lost heavily. Mortality tables had not yet been conceived. Indeed, Edmond Halley (from Halley's comet) produced the first life table in response to this event. Still, many of the modern problems had been anticipated. Understanding of moral hazard dates back to second-century Roman Palestine. For more on this and a detailed description of insurance as understood 100 years ago, see the famed eleventh edition of the *Encylopaedia Britannica* (1910).

1

evaluating risks in meetings at Lloyd's coffee house, the precursor to Lloyds of London.

Today, insurance is a major worldwide industry. It moves progressively into new fields. For example, health insurance was virtually unknown in the United States prior to 1929 and now pays for more than 10 percent of the U.S. GDP. Risks ranging from a camcorder breaking down to being sued for sexual harassment are all insurable events.

In recent decades, economic attention has caught up with the remarkable burgeoning of the insurance industry. This is largely attributable to the explosion in attention being paid to information in economics. Indeed, insurance so well illustrates this area that it is a major topic of introductory discussions about the role of information in economics. Moreover, the core insurance topics of moral hazard and adverse selection have been transplanted to fields such as labor economics and finance.

This sounds like a happy confluence of theory and practice growing up alongside one another: theory improves by studying practice, and practice effectively draws on the results of theory. Yet a principal theme of this paper is that perception is fundamentally wrong. We believe that there is an increasing divergence between the theory and practice of insurance. Consider the following quiz about optimal insurance.

> Suppose that a risk goes from negligible to possible—for example, the increased probability of a terrorist accident on U.S. soil after September 11, 2001. Would you expect the private market to provide (a) more insurance or (b) less insurance?
>
> A seventy-year-old unmarried woman has three children, all of whom are comfortably middle class. Would you expect her to be more likely to hold (a) an annuity or (b) life insurance?
>
> A consumer buys a $620 camcorder and is offered insurance in case it breaks. The insurance is for three years and costs $120, supplementing the one-year warranty on parts and labor that comes with the camcorder. The probability of a camcorder needing a repair over three years is 8 percent (mostly in the first year), with average repair costs of $125. Would you expect the person to (a) decline the insurance or (b) accept the insurance?[2]

In each case, optimal insurance principles suggest that (a) is the right answer. But (b) is the answer we often see in the world. Coverage for terrorism risk plummeted after the attacks in September 2001, despite greater demand. About seven times more elderly people have life insurance than

2. Repair costs and frequencies are from *Consumer Reports* (1998).

annuities, in spite of the fact that the incomes of their children are rising over time. And insurance against small-cost consumer durables is among the most profitable items sold by commercial electronics stores. For almost all products, one in five customers purchases the insurance; for some products, four in five do so.

We argue in this paper that these examples are not minor anomalies but reflect a systematic tendency for insurance in practice to differ from insurance in theory. We discuss and grade a number of insurance settings: (a) mortality, health, and property risk for individuals and (b) property, liability, environmental, and terrorism risk for businesses. In the vast majority of cases, we argue, insurance in practice diverges from insurance in theory.

The divergence is of two forms. First, insurance purchases do not match theoretical predictions. Many risks that are insured—sometimes at excessive prices—should not be, and many significant risks that should be insured are not. The case of life insurance among the elderly or insurance for minor consumer durables are examples of the former. The lack of coverage for terrorism insurance is an example of the latter. Second, there are significant mismatches between parties who should bear risk and those who actually do. Risks can be borne by public entities, by private (for-profit and not-for-profit) firms, and through financial markets. In practice, the allocation of risk across these entities seems suboptimal. Governments insure risks that the private sector might better bear, and financial markets, despite their vast resources and wide participation, are not a major bearer of large private risks.

The divergence between theory and practice is not a result of moral hazard or adverse selection. In many settings with failures, information is as close to symmetric as it is possible to be—for example, in the risk of a terrorist attack—and moral hazard is extremely implausible. Rather, we argue that the divergence of insurance theory and practice results from three phenomena: the first on the supply side, the second on the demand side, and the third a true joint product.

The first is highly incomplete diversification on the part of insurers. Investors in insurance companies may be nearly risk neutral for virtually all insurance decisions, but managers of insurance companies are not. This outcome, we believe, arises due to contracting problems on the supply side of insurance. Risks that are hard to predict, or are correlated across the insured, may lead the insurance company to lose significant amounts of money, with some executives being blamed and losing their job.[3] We argue that this is an important reason why large but nontraditional risks—for example, terrorist attacks or long-term health care—are not insured.

Contracting difficulties also help to explain why financial markets, with assets in the trillions, as opposed to billions for insurance companies, have not played a more significant role in insurance. One challenge is to secure collateral from investors—the ideal source to cover claims—in case a claim arises. Catastrophe bonds are a small step in this direction, but there is no reason to use only fixed-income investments as collateral.[4] In time, we expect, individuals will be able to participate in insurance pools by pledging such assets as stocks and real estate. A second challenge is to marry insurance expertise with ready pools of capital. Such marriages have been highly successful in areas such as venture capital and hedge funds.[5] The standard financial arrangement for such contracts (a management fee and a share of profits) may not be sufficient insurance, since recorded profits on insurance may be large until an adverse event occurs, even though expected profits are small or negative. Still, there is plenty of money to write insurance and ample expertise to write the insurance effectively, even if bringing the two together will require innovative institutions and creative contracts.

The demand side contributes its share to the poor performance of insurance relative to theoretical par. The central problem is that people have severe difficulties making decisions where small probabilities and significant stakes are involved. These difficulties have been discussed in the burgeoning literature on behavioral economics and behavioral decision-making, which was pioneered by Amos Tversky and Daniel Kahneman and for which Kahneman shared the 2002 Nobel Memorial Prize in Economics. People seem (irrationally) fearful of uninsured losses. They overly project their unhappiness and regret were a bad event to occur, and they misjudge probabilities. As a result, people often insure when theory would say they should not: they insure against small risks; they take deductibles that are way too small; and they insure against events that, though tragic, do not change the marginal utility of income.

3. Insurance executive James Ament notes as well that the stock market is unforgiving of insurers that post a bad quarter.

4. Such bonds have claimed a smaller share of the market than many observers, including Warren Buffett, expected. In part, this may be the relative lack of familiarity with this instrument and the demand for high returns from the limited pool of catastrophe bond investors.

5. We judge by money raised, not investment results.

The third problem is what we refer to as probability monopoly. It arises when sellers of insurance know risks much better than buyers and when there is limited competition. Sellers then set prices well above actuarial and administrative cost so as to capitalize on the buyers' potential misestimates. Buyers who overestimate the risk of breakdown purchase insurance, at a profit for the insurer. In settings where insurance naturally follows a particular event—buying a consumer durable, for example—this possibility is magnified.

In the remainder of this paper, we develop these themes about the operation of insurance markets in theory and practice. We introduce areas where we think the theory of insurance should be extended if it is to explain practice, such as understanding what benefits actual purchasers believe they get when they purchase insurance. We start with some basics on when we expect insurance to be widespread and then turn to an evaluation of insurance markets in practice.

This is a thought piece. Thus it tries to present neither rigorous theory nor detailed empirical analysis. It draws data from many sources and arenas to illustrate its themes. And it is speculative in part to be provocative. Thus, for example, we provide our own grades for the functioning of insurance markets across many areas.

Insurance in Theory

In many arenas insurance works well. We begin by examining what we might think of as par performance for insurance markets and then grade various insurance areas on how they do on these criteria.

The principal goal of insurance, as assessed by economists, is to transfer resources from states where the marginal utility of income is low to those where the marginal utility of income is high. If insurance is actuarially fair, this process will continue until the marginal utility of money is equal across states. If it is unfair, insurance will be partial, but it will be greater, the greater is risk aversion.

Insurance is most effective when losses are common enough to be of concern but not frequent enough to be routine. Neither asteroid strikes nor car scratches make for good insurable events. Insurance for routine events requires frequent administrative expense that makes the insurance less valuable; the benefits of spreading risk are also low. Insuring extremely rare risks also involves reasonable expense, with little compensating gain.

Similarly, transaction costs make it important that risks be relatively well defined and assessable once they happen. Otherwise, the assessment and litigation of claims can be exceedingly expensive. For most familiar risks—for example, a house burning down—this condition would be met. However, the recent experience with the one- or two-incident World Trade Center catastrophe makes it clear that there are important exceptions, even with burning buildings. Such ambiguities are more likely where new classes of risk come into play.

Effective insurance also requires that unobservable actions—that is, moral hazard—not be too significant. Fortunately, major aspects of nonmonetary, uncovered loss often assure that this is the case. Thus, for example, rational drivers are not likely to drive at unsafe speeds simply because they are insured, and people are unlikely to smoke because they know that, if they get cancer, they will receive treatment. The potential for death and disability in these cases influences actions at least as heavily as covered losses. Monitorable actions (for example, determining whether a building is kept in safe condition) and risks due to an external source (for example, earthquakes) also diminish the moral hazard problem.

These important attributes for effective coverage are generally positively associated with the demand for and volume of insurance. The supply side also determines how well insurance works. Two critical questions are how diversifiable is the risk and whether an entity is capable of bearing it. Most familiar insured risks—for example, the risk of death—are readily diversified cross-sectionally, since the experiences of members of large pools of the insured are effectively independent. There are, however, many critical risks—for example, the costs of common events many years into the future, such as long-term care for current sixty-year-olds—where expected costs for different individuals are strongly correlated; they are so-called aggregate risks. Cross-sectional diversification is not possible with these risks, and other risk-sharing arrangements are needed.

Concerns about the supply side may seem misplaced in an industry like insurance, where there are many firms, and barriers to entry seem relatively modest. Still, competition in insurance seems far from perfect. As one demonstration of this, consider a fundamental attribute of perfectly competitive markets: the law of one price. In a competitive market, the same good should sell at the same price everywhere.

Table 1. Medigap Monthly Premiums for Plan C in Denver, Colorado, by Age
U.S. dollars

Firm	Age 65	Age 70	Age 75	Age 80
AARP	129	129	129	129
Equitable Life	96	113	123	134
5 Star Life	52	78	58	88
Union Banker	204	230	271	326

Source: www.centuraseniors.org. Information was collected in December 2003.

Table 1 shows the price of Medigap insurance—supplemental insurance coverage that pays for the cost sharing required by Medicare—for seniors in Colorado. Medigap is an interesting market to study because the policies that can be offered are absolutely standardized, being set by the federal government. Thus there are no hidden provisions to account for. Still, the price of insurance varies by a factor of four across companies.[6] Even more unusual is the obvious difference in pricing strategies that firms follow. The American Association of Retired Persons (AARP) has a uniform price by age, while none of the other insurers does. In a situation where consumers shop around regularly, this would not occur.

Even businesses find it hard, or seem reluctant, to shop for the best insurance deal. Warren Buffett, one of America's shrewder insurance purveyors, announces periodically in his Berkshire Hathaway report that he will not be writing various types of business coverage this year because the rates are too low.[7] Buffett suggests that, despite expected losses, his competitors are writing insurance to keep their old customers, expecting these customers to stick with them when prices rise.[8] His competitors, at least, think cross-elasticity of demand is low for insurance.

In this section we consider a large number of potential individual and business risks and evaluate them on our criteria, effectively seeing how well they are likely to be spread. Table 2 shows our assessment. In each case that we consider, there is a disparity in marginal utility across states of nature. This is why insurance is valuable, at least from an economic standpoint. The other criteria differ in applicability across the risks.

6. Mitchell and others (1999) show a large divergence in the price of annuities across companies.

7. The insurance price cycle is one of the many divergences between theory and practice that must await future study.

8. Warren Buffett remarks that his competitors sometimes sell insurance when the premiums plus earnings from them are below expected losses. "The most important thing to do when you find yourself in a hole is to stop digging" (Buffett 1990).

Table 2. Assessment of Insurance Possibilities

		Criteria for insurance[a]				
Type of risk	Example	Disparity in marginal utility	Frequency of event	Well-defined loss	Importance of moral hazard	Ease of diversification
Individual risks						
Survival	Life, annuities	+	+	+	+	+
Health	Short-term care	+	−	+	−	+
	Long-term care	+	+	−	−	−
Property and casualty	House, auto, consumer durables	+	+	+	0	+
Business risks						
Property and casualty	Short-term risks	+	+	+	0	+/−
	Long-term risks (pollution)	+	+	+	+	−
Employment	Harassment, unfair hiring practices	+	+	+	+	−
Obligations	Pensions	+	+	+	−	−

a. + indicates that the risk is favorable for insurance; − indicates that it is unfavorable for insurance; 0 indicates that it is neutral for insurance or unknown. The assessments are provided by the authors. See text for more discussion.

Consumer Risks

We analyze three major consumer risks. The first is mortality. Although death is certain, its timing is not. Family-oriented breadwinners would like to insure against early departure. Thus we expect term life insurance to be a common asset in working years. At retirement, the demand should tip to annuities that guard against outliving one's assets.

Mortality risk is a classic case where we expect insurance to perform well. On the demand side, the event is obviously infrequent, so that administrative costs relative to ultimate payouts are not high. The loss is also well defined, and moral hazard is contained.[9] On the supply side, it is relatively easy to diversify mortality risk across people, since aggregate death rates are generally fairly stable.

The second risk is to health—more specifically, the danger of incurring medical conditions that are expensive to treat. We divide health risks into two categories. The first is short-term health risks. People have variable health needs in the current year, which conventional health insurance covers. Health risk is somewhat less conductive to insurance than is mortality risk. In part, the need for medical care is not ideal. While some health

9. Some have speculated that people live longer because they have an annuity, although we suspect that this effect is relatively minor in aggregate.

needs are truly random, others are routine, such as an annual physical or well-baby care. The costs of running payments for such services through insurance may be high. In addition, moral hazard is an issue in health care. People may (or may not) take much worse care of themselves when they have health insurance—termed ex ante moral hazard—but they certainly use more care when insured than when uninsured (ex post moral hazard); they come in more frequently for minor aches and pains. Health insurance is not run like a contingent claims market. Whatever your health condition, the more you spend, the greater the cost you impose on the insurer.[10]

Some health risks are also long term. Future long-term care expenses provide a salient case. About one-third of the elderly will use nursing home care on a sustained basis, and this care can be expensive: current costs are upward of $40,000 a year.[11] Because a lot of the gains from long-term care insurance involve pooling people who die without using a nursing home with those who do, this care needs to be purchased before significant morbidity sets in. Risk about future health is related to long-term-care risk. Health insurance for individuals, or the groups they purchase with, is usually experience rated. Should an individual's health decline, should the health of the average member of the group decline, or should the expenses for treating particular conditions rise, the premium will increase. Thus one might expect people to insure against the risk of becoming high cost in the future.[12]

Adverse long-term health events are sufficiently infrequent, but not too much so, that insurance makes a good deal of sense, at least in theory. But these risks challenge conventional insurance in three other ways. As with short-term health insurance, moral hazard is likely to be an issue in long-term insurance: if grandma is insured, move her to the nursing home. In addition, the loss is poorly defined. When does a person need long-term care, and when is she capable of functioning on her own? What does an individual's health today signal about her potential future spending? These information problems undermine the viability of long-term insurance. On the supply side, there is a substantial concern about diversifying these

10. Medicare diagnosis-related group payments, which make fixed payments to providers dependent on condition, are an exception.

11. National Center for Health Statistics (2003).

12. Pauly, Kunreuther, and Hirth (1995); Cochrane (1995); Cutler (1996). Indeed, since declines in health lead earnings expectations to diminish and earnings cannot be insured, long-term health insurance is that much more valuable.

risks. When future medical costs increase for some people—for example, because expensive new medical technologies become available—they increase for others as well. Similarly, if new medical knowledge extends survival at older ages, it yields such benefits to millions. The unhappy side effect is that a much greater percentage of the population will spend a fair amount of time in a nursing home, assuming that vitality does not increase apace with survival. Such properties of long-term health risks imply that cross-sectional diversification is not entirely possible.

The final individual risk that we address is property and casualty risk. People own homes, cars, and consumer durables that may burn, crash, or break. Consequently, they may want to insure them. Property and casualty insurance has many attributes that are favorable to insurance coverage. The major exception is moral hazard. One might imagine that when people are insured, they drive faster or take less care of their house or other durables. Some evidence suggests that this is the case, although the evidence is far weaker than for moral hazard in medical care utilization.[13]

While mortality, health, and property-casualty risk are the major individual risks that we consider, there are other risks we are not discussing. Most people owe money on a house and face a choice between an ostensibly risky debt payment (an adjustable-rate mortgage) and a fixed, insured payment (a fixed-rate mortgage). However, it is not obvious which form should be preferred—that is, whether the borrower should protect the bank against interest rate movement or vice versa. We might analyze this financial choice in the same way as other forms of insurance. People might also like insurance for their human capital: for example, to guard against depreciation of their skills—think travel agents—or prolonged unemployment. There is public insurance for some of these risks, via unemployment insurance, workers' compensation, and disability insurance. But many risks—for example, lost productivity—are insured by no one. Moral hazard is clearly a substantial issue for many of these risks. In the interest of brevity, however, we do not consider the entire range of risks that individuals face.

Business Risks

Many business risks are similar to individual risks. Businesses own property, for example, and uncertainty is associated with damage to that

13. See Cohen and Dehejia (2003) for a summary.

property. Businesses are also liable for damages if someone is injured on their premises, if they are found to cause health harms, or if their employees are mistreated. As with health risks for individuals, we divide property and casualty risks for businesses into two groups. Short-term risks are the most common type of business risk. They encompass most damage to property and exposure to litigation. Most of these risks involve relatively infrequent events (but not too infrequent) and generally have well-defined losses (the World Trade Center being a notable exception). There may be some moral hazard in these actions, but we suspect that it is not large.

Most, but not all, short-term business risks can be diversified cross-sectionally. The most prominent exception is terrorism risk, where the potential losses are so large (due to correlation in losses across the insured) that even having a substantial insurance pool does not drive the variability of losses particularly low. As a result, we note ease of diversification as being either favorable or adverse.

Long-term property and casualty risks are those risks that will not be realized for some time. Firms may discover only years later that the chemicals in their product increase the risk of cancer. In the same fashion, obstetricians may be sued years after a birth for complications that were only realized (or alleged) later. One can think of the liability revolution in the 1970s and 1980s as a bad realization of a long-tailed risk. Once again, this long-tailed risk makes diversification difficult, since new knowledge-increasing claims against one business are often correlated with increases in claims against another. Difficulties with diversification are a major problem in many long-tailed litigation risks.

Firms also face risk about employment decisions. Firms may be sued for sexual harassment, unjust dismissal, or unfair hiring practices. This risk has many of the attributes of long-term property and casualty risk. The event is not very frequent and is well defined, but it may not be diversifiable cross-sectionally. The same legal changes that made liability for pollution or medical harms greater than were thought also increased the potential losses from employment issues.

Finally, businesses have risky obligations for the pensions and health care of retired workers. Many large firms have defined-benefit pension plans, which obligate them to a specific payment based on the age of the retiree and number of years of service. Retiree health insurance payments may work the same way. If pension costs rise more rapidly than expected or a firm's earnings fall substantially, the firm may be unable to meet its pension obligations. Moral hazard is of clear importance in this risk. Firms that are doing poorly will underfund their pensions, knowing that if the firm fails it will not have sufficient assets to pay out its pension liabilities.[14] Diversification issues are also important, since pension and health costs tend to rise jointly across firms. For this and other reasons (perhaps the political imperative of caring for penurious retirees), pension obligations are generally insured through the public rather than the private sector.

As with individuals, businesses might like to insure other financial risks as well. They can often do this by using sophisticated financial instruments. Companies selling abroad can hedge exchange rate risk, and businesses can insure interest rate risk through appropriate derivative securities. To keep our analysis manageable, we avoid consideration of such financial risks.

Bundling Insurance and Other Services or Attributes

Many products that are officially sold or presented as insurance provide more than just financial protection; they bundle other services with risk-spreading benefits. These additional benefits are important in evaluating the insurance policy.

In some arenas, insurance products have integrated backward into purchasing services or at least procuring them. This enables insurers to purchase products at substantially reduced rates. Health insurance is the most prominent example.[15] When insurance is coupled with provision, the combination may yield significant advantages in exerting leverage as a buyer. Such a

14. In a related situation, one of the authors worked for Equitable Life in the early 1960s. One task was to determine when a company had incurred a catastrophe in an accident. Excess losses would be written off, lest dividends never be paid in the future. Our naïf inquired, "Why don't our policies indicate that there will not be a payoff in case of nuclear war?" The answer was basically: "It does not matter what we say. Given a war, our losses will be too great, and our asset base significantly destroyed. We will not pay." Our second story is at a less monumental scale and in keeping with the early winter of 2003–04. The roommate of one of the authors created a company in high school to shovel snow for a flat fee for the winter, thus offering insurance to its customers. There was a big snowstorm early in December. The company announced it was going out of business and returned the money.

15. Differences in bargaining power produce significant results. Altman, Cutler, and Zeckhauser (2003) find that, for a common pool of the insured (government employees in Massachusetts), the indemnity plan pays prices 35 percent more than health maintenance organizations for the same procedure. The gap with uninsured individuals would surely be much greater. Health plans frequently pay less than half as much for prescriptions from the same pharmacy as uninsured customers. If anything, the administrative costs for insured patients are higher, since two parties have to be charged.

buying consortium should not be thought of as exclusively or even predominantly as an insurance product—that is, as a risk-spreading device.

Many insurance products couple insurance with a tax shield. The buildup in whole life insurance is not taxed, for example, making that product an excellent vehicle for saving. Health insurance that pays for the costs of routine care is also a tax haven, saving the taxation that would be associated with wage and salary payments. The primary motivation for such policies is not the financial risk per se, but the combination of risk reduction and tax rewards.

Still other insurance programs, especially in the public sector, have a strong redistributional element. Government "insurance" programs, such as Social Security and unemployment insurance, almost always have an intended redistributional role. That is, judged ex ante, some participants are hurt, while others are helped. But even in the private sphere, we see redistribution at play. Thus young workers usually subsidize older workers in employer-provided health insurance.

Alas, there is no way to discuss insurance without referring to instruments that work as a buying consortium and significantly redistribute income. These instruments are not strictly insurance. This caveat should inform our discussion below.

Insurance in Practice: Consumer Risks

In this section, we evaluate how insurance for consumer risks fares in practice. Because we consider a number of risks, our analysis is necessarily impressionistic. We rely on conclusions of detailed research studies where possible and on analysis of aggregate data in other cases. For many types of risks, we conclude that insurance performs substantially less well than is anticipated by theory. Table 3 shows our summary.

Mortality

As Yaari first noted, life insurance and annuities cater to mutually exclusive circumstances: living too long and living too short. One would not expect the same person to want both instruments in force at the same time.[16]

---

16. Yaari (1965). Davidoff, Brown, and Diamond (2003) extend this analysis to the case of incomplete markets, with relatively similar results.

Table 3. Evaluation of Insurance Markets

Risk	Example	Issues noted	Other factors	Overall evaluation
Individual risks				
Mortality	Life	Underinsurance of widows; overinsurance of elderly	Tax-free buildup	Fair
	Annuities	Too little purchase		Poor
Health	Short-term care	Too much coverage for small risks	Tax subsidy	Fair
	Long-term care	Too little coverage for large risks		Poor
Property and casualty	House	Too much coverage for small risks		Good
	Auto	Too much coverage for small risks		Fair
	Consumer durables	Why do people buy?		Poor
Business risks				
Property and casualty	General	Good for most industries (major exception is medical malpractice)		Fair
	Long-term risk (pollution)	Inadequate coverage of large risks; market dries up with new knowledge		Poor
	Terrorism	Inadequate coverage of large risks; market dries up with new knowledge		Poor
Obligations	Pensions	Underfunding of pensions	PBGC reinsurance	Poor

Source: The assessment is based on the authors' beliefs. See text for details.

In practice, life insurance is very common, and annuitization is fairly rare. The 2001 Survey of Consumer Finances estimates that two-thirds of families have life insurance, including about 80 percent of two-adult families. In total, families have $16 trillion of assets in life insurance.[17] Annuities, by contrast, are owned by only a small share of the population, usually as one option in a retirement plan, for example, with an IRA rollover. Only 8 percent of the population ages seventy and older has an annuity, while 78 percent of that group has life insurance.[18] Annuity reserves total less than $2 trillion.

Without knowing individuals' preferences exactly, despite knowing their assets, earnings, and family and health status, we cannot tell what

17. American Council of Life Insurers (2003).
18. Brown (1999).

insurance arrangement is optimal for them. A married worker might skip life insurance if he does not value highly the consumption of his non-working spouse. Similarly, a couple may not want an annuity in old age if it is penurious relative to assets or if they can deal with a declining consumption stream. Still, one suspects that such cases are rare and that the large changes in consumption that individuals might experience due to lives cut short or stretched long are not intended. The research literature takes this perspective in evaluating the adequacy of annuitization and life insurance: it examines whether these products are purchased in sufficient quantity to minimize changes in consumption in the event that bad outcomes are realized. Because of the centrality of life insurance and annuities to the lively debates about social security reform, their use has been considered in detail.

LIFE INSURANCE. The spread of life insurance is expected, valuable, and important as a source of savings as well as security. Still, two aspects of life insurance have drawn attention as being suboptimal. The first is the substantial rate of life insurance holdings among the elderly.[19] Some of the elderly—a group whose children are presumably independent—would rationally want life insurance protection (if pensions depend on the survival of one spouse, for example), but three-quarters is a very high share. Even many elderly without dependents have life insurance.

Some work has examined this puzzle. One proposed explanation is that Social Security provides too much annuitization, and people offset that by purchasing life insurance. Brown finds evidence that this is not the case, however; term life insurance is not more likely to be held by people with larger Social Security payments.[20] He suggests that other explanations are more important: tax policy that allows for tax-free buildup in whole-life insurance or tax-free payment of burial costs and inertia from purchasing life insurance earlier in life. The exact share attributable to each is not entirely known, but the nontax explanations such as status quo bias are surely important.[21]

The extent of life insurance during the working years seems broadly appropriate, although concerns linger. In particular, some authors worry about whether people in their working years are sufficiently insured. Recent studies suggest that too few families have life insurance, and many

19. See Brown (1999) for a review.
20. Brown (1999).
21. Samuelson and Zeckhauser (1988).

families that have insurance are underinsured. Bernheim, Forni, Gokhale, and Kotlikoff use data on family income, assets, and demographic characteristics for people ages fifty-one to sixty-one (from the Health and Retirement Survey) to examine the consumption consequences should they die.[22] They estimate that 30 percent of wives and 11 percent of husbands would suffer a decline in consumption of 20 percent or more if their spouse passed away. This is a large enough reduction to rule out the explanation of rational preferences, apart from the joint explanation of little concern for and insufficient bargaining power of the dependent spouse. The shortfall in insurance coverage is more surprising given government tax subsidy for employer-paid premiums and investment earnings during the life of a policy.

Work by Bernheim, Carman, Gokhale, and Kotlikoff suggests that two-thirds of poverty among widows and one-third of poverty among widowers results from a failure to purchase sufficient life insurance.[23] The extent of underinsurance varies with socioeconomic characteristics. After correcting for income and assets, underinsurance is more common among lower-income families and among couples with very asymmetric earnings (for example, one-earner couples). In the latter families, the death of the higher-earning spouse would often pose severe hardships for the surviving spouse.

Adverse selection could explain the underpurchase of insurance among some families, but the literature does not suggest that this factor is important in life insurance. Cawley and Philipson document that prices decrease with additional purchases, where adverse selection would imply the reverse.[24] They also find that individual forecasts of mortality probabilities do not predict the purchase of life insurance. Life insurance is also estimated to have very low administrative expense. More likely is that these families are simply not planning adequately for adverse events that may occur: they do not forecast the extent of consumption declines should death occur, life insurance never becomes a conscious decision the family makes, or the male decisionmaker does not weigh the utility of his spouse very highly.

ANNUITIZATION. The central question about annuities is why so few people purchase them. As noted, less than 10 percent of people ages sev-

---

22. Bernheim and others (1999).

23. Bernheim and others (2001).

24. Cawley and Philipson (1999).

enty and older have a private annuity, although essentially all elderly have Social Security and many elderly have defined-benefit pension plans.

The administrative load in annuities provides a partial explanation. Mitchell, Poterba, Warshawsky, and Brown estimate that the load on annuities is about 15 to 20 percent.[25] About half of that results from adverse selection; the remainder is marketing costs, processing costs, and insurer profit.

The low rate of annuitization remains puzzling, even in light of these administrative costs. First, the investment returns in annuities are strongly tax favored. Second, concerns about risk spreading make annuities worthwhile. In a utility-based simulation model of the annuitization decision, Mitchell and his coauthors estimate that people should be willing to pay an administrative fee of 25 percent to annuitize their assets. That is far above the cost that we see in practice. Conceivably, strong bequest motives could explain low rates of purchase.[26] But annuities are one way to insure the size of the bequest. The literature does not explore the degree or nature of the bequest motivation. We expect that few of these results could stand up to rational economic scrutiny.

The literature speculates more about "behavioral" explanations for the low rate of annuitization. Anecdotal evidence suggests that many elderly may not be aware of or understand annuities, and many fewer have priced them (further undercutting the high-administrative-cost explanation for modest use). Other potential customers may fear paying money to an insurance company only to die shortly thereafter without much return. Along the latter lines is the seemingly inexplicable preference that some people have for annuities that guarantee a payment for a certain number of years, even if the annuitant dies before that time.

SUMMARY. As a means of keeping track of the evidence, we provide our net assessment of the various insurance markets we consider. To keep the analysis simple, we use a three-point scale: good, fair, or poor. We recognize that this assessment is highly subjective; readers may take issue with particular values or even the scale that we use. On the basis of the evidence, we grade life insurance as fair and annuities as poor. Life insurance earns a higher grade because it functions well for many people. But in both cases

---

25. Mitchell and others (1999).

26. But that leaves the puzzle as to why big asset holders give away so little during their lifetime. Such gifts cut the estate tax by a third, since the gift tax, which comes out of the estate, escapes taxation within the estate.

there is some underinsurance and, in the case of life insurance, some overinsurance as well.

Health

Health risk is the second major type of risk for individuals. We divide health risks into two categories: short-term risks and long-term risks.

SHORT-TERM HEALTH CARE. About 85 percent of people in the United States have health insurance for their current medical care, according to the U.S. census. Coverage rates are greater in most other major developed nations, usually because of government involvement.

As with mortality risk, there is substantial analysis of the optimality of private health insurance contracts. The fact that not everyone has private insurance has generated policy debate and research attention. There are three typical explanations for lack of coverage. The first is administrative expense. In any market with administrative costs, we would expect less than full coverage. Administrative costs account for only about 15 percent of health insurance, however, so most analysts discount this explanation. Indeed, the true rate of administrative expense in health insurance is likely smaller, perhaps net negative, in many instances when buyer leverage is figured in. Health insurers, with their strong bargaining power in a high-fixed-cost industry, purchase specific health care goods and services much more cheaply than do individuals. Such discounts likely more than make up for administrative costs.[27]

Adverse selection provides a second explanation. Insurance priced for the average enrolled person can lead to an equilibrium where the healthy do not enroll. We know of no simulations about the importance of this phenomenon, but we suspect that this explanation is right for some people. Many of the uninsured are young and relatively healthy. The value of insurance priced at average rates is not very high for this group. One concern about this explanation, though, is that insurance can vary in generosity. Deductibles, services covered, and access to particular providers all vary across policies, and we might expect more of the healthy to segregate into less generous policies than to go without coverage entirely.

The third explanation is crowdout by government insurance programs (for example, Medicaid) and charitable programs (for example, hospital free care). In this theory, people do not purchase private coverage because

27. See note 12.

they know that they can receive care even if they are uninsured. Naturally, there is a loss. Being uninsured is associated with less, and less appealing, access to medical care providers, less use of preventive and acute care services, and worse health outcomes.[28] But it also saves money. For some people, the savings may be worth it.

Empirical evidence shows that crowdout is a factor in explaining insurance coverage. Increases in the generosity of public insurance and in uncompensated care lead more people to go uninsured.[29] The analysis required to explain what proportion of the uninsured this accounts for has not been undertaken, however.

Even if the level of health insurance were appropriate, one might question the mix of provision between public and private. Insurance has a surprising mixture of such provision: the pattern is hardly in line with notions of comparative advantage across sectors. In the case of health insurance, some argue for public insurance, on the grounds that administrative costs are lower in public programs than in private policies.[30] Others argue for private insurance, for the usual reasons of competition and concern over bureaucracy. And within the private sector, there are arguments for both for-profit and not-for-profit entities. The United States has a mixture of both public and private provision, often in the same narrow sector, with adverse interactions between the two (as witnessed by the literature on crowdout).

Among people who have insurance, economists' greatest concern is not with inadequate coverage but rather with the generosity of coverage for small medical risks. Cost sharing in traditional indemnity insurance policies is relatively low. A typical policy has a deductible of about $400, with 20 percent coinsurance up to a stop-loss of perhaps $1,500.[31] For much of the health spending distribution, cost sharing is very slight; this makes moral hazard a significant concern.

A lengthy literature has explored whether this level of cost sharing is optimal or too small.[32] Generally, the literature concludes that current insurance is too generous, leaving people with too little risk for medical expenses, particularly smaller expenses. The most comprehensive analysis

28. Institute of Medicine (2003).
29. On public insurance, see Cutler and Gruber (1996); on uncompensated care, see Rask and Rask (2000); Herring (2001).
30. Woolhandler and Himmelstein (1989).
31. Kaiser Family Foundation and Health Research and Education Trust (2003).
32. See Cutler and Zeckhauser (2000) for a review.

is from Blomqvist, who finds that optimal insurance should have a declining coinsurance rate ranging from 27 percent at $1,000 of spending (compared to 20 percent in most plans) down to 5 percent at $30,000 of spending (compared to zero in most plans).[33]

The traditional explanation for the low rate of cost sharing is the tax subsidy to health insurance.[34] As with life insurance, employer payments for health insurance are not taxed as income to workers, while wage and salary payments are. Thus there are incentives for people to run more medical payments through employer-paid health insurance than is optimal. This includes having lower cost sharing than would otherwise be desirable. Empirical work shows that this explanation is important in practice.[35] What other factors contribute to a low rate of cost sharing is not known, however.

Behavioral explanations also merit study. Victor Fuchs argues that cost sharing is low, in part, because, in a stressful time of medical need, people do not want to make decisions about whether additional medical care is worth the money.[36] We argue below that prospect-theoretic preferences for outcomes—for example, loss aversion coupled with risk seeking on losses—make individuals eager to avoid small losses.

These types of "behavioral explanations" make normative analysis difficult. Say that loss aversion affects behavior, implying that even small charges per visit strongly discourage use. Would such copayments represent an effective rationing tool, or would they impose noticeable pain without collecting much revenue? Fortunately for us, our analysis has a descriptive, not a normative, purpose.

Finally, given the strong penetration of health maintenance organizations in the private insurance market and their firm supply-side restrictions, it is hard to assess what cost sharing would be appropriate for their members.

LONG-TERM HEALTH CARE. Health also has a component of long-term risk. People may have health needs in the future, which they would like to insure today. Most important here are long-term-care expenses.

A large part of the return to long-term-care insurance is related to early mortality among the elderly. Nearly 20 percent of people over age eighty-five are in a nursing home, compared to about 1 percent of the population

33. Blomqvist (1997).
34. Feldstein and Friedman (1977); Pauly (1986).
35. Cutler and Zeckhauser (2000).
36. Private conversation, April 11, 2004.

ages sixty-five to seventy-four.[37] For long-term-care insurance to be effective, people have to purchase it before they reach an advanced age. Yet most elderly do not have such coverage. Only about 10 percent of the elderly possess long-term-care insurance. The bulk of long-term-care expenses are paid for out-of-pocket or by Medicaid.

Risk about future health is related to long-term-care risk. Health insurance for individuals or for groups is usually experience rated. Should health decline, the premium of the individual or the company will increase. Thus one might expect people to purchase insurance against the risk of becoming high cost in the future.[38] In practice, however, we see virtually no insurance against the risk of becoming sick and facing higher annual premiums in the future.[39]

Adverse selection and moral hazard no doubt contribute to the failure of this market, but we believe the theoretical elegance of those subjects has led economists to give them too much weight. Risk aversion certainly differs across people, and that is not so correlated with health status (many individuals who are in good health but are worried about their future health status want to purchase insurance in addition to those who are currently sick). Ex ante moral hazard is also somewhat deterred because declines in health, even if treated, lead to much worse states, for which compensating payments are not forthcoming.

Attention instead focuses on two alternatives. The first is crowdout of private long-term-care insurance by the public sector. The Medicaid program covers long-term-care expenses for people with no private insurance who have exhausted their income and assets paying for long-term-care services. People may thus rely on Medicaid, if it comes to that, or give away assets to qualify for Medicaid, rather than purchase private insurance.[40] Recent simulation work suggests that these factors explain a significant fraction of the lack of purchase of private nursing home insurance.[41] As

37. National Center for Health Statistics (2003).
38. Pauly, Kunreuther, and Hirth (1995); Cochrane (1995); Cutler (1996).
39. There is some informal insurance for this risk, but it is imperfect. Many large employers, for example, prohibit insurers from experience rating at the individual level, providing a form of intertemporal insurance *if* one stays with the same company. Most states prohibit some forms of experience rating for small groups of people, but these prohibitions are often very limited (see Cutler 2002 for a review). Overall, insurance against the risk of becoming high cost in the future is very limited.
40. Pauly (1990).
41. Brown and Finkelstein (2003).

with short-term health insurance, public and private insurance interact inefficiently.

The second explanation for low insurance coverage is that these risks are nondiversifiable and thus shunned by insurance companies.[42] The dominant driver of changes in long-term-care costs over time is technology that allows people to live longer or higher-quality lives, but at high cost. This technology is common across people and thus cannot be diversified cross-sectionally. We explore how this might affect the supply of long-term insurance below.

SUMMARY. We rate coverage of short-term health risks as fair and coverage of long-term risks as poor. Short-term risks are covered for most people, but, as with mortality risk, there is both underprotection (those without coverage) and overprotection (too generous insurance in indemnity policies). Coverage for long-term health risks is poor, since private insurance is rare and the public sector has substantial inefficiencies.

Property

The third major type of individual risk is damage to personal physical assets. People insure their home, car, and consumer durables against various types of damages. In at least the first two cases, essentially everyone has coverage. Mortgage lenders generally require homeowners insurance, and all states require auto insurance. Fewer people have coverage for consumer durables, but the costs of these goods are far smaller; hence insurance is far less valuable.

The major issue in property insurance is the degree of cost sharing. Most people have relatively low deductibles for home and auto damage. The question is whether these deductibles are too low from the standpoint of the individual and from the standpoint of efficiency. (Efficiency requires avoiding minor claims where administrative costs are large relative to any loss or payment.) There is speculation about this in the literature, but no formal analysis of which we are aware.

As with any evaluation dependent on the parameters of the utility function, we cannot say for certain whether consumers should or should not purchase more generous coverage. But we can evaluate what types of preferences are required to justify current purchases. Suppose that the probability of a loss is p. The loss may be damage to a car or house. For

42. Cutler (1996).

the simple algebra here, we assume that the loss probability is independent of the details of the insurance policy.[43]

People face a menu of insurance deductibles and premiums, where plans with lower deductibles command higher premiums (more is covered and moral hazard is exacerbated). Denoting the insurance premium as π and the deductible as d, the period utility that an individual receives from choosing an insurance policy is:[44]

(1) $$V = p\, U(Y - \pi - d) + (1 - p)\, U(Y - \pi),$$

where Y is income, assumed to be constant.[45]

With the specification of a utility function, we can evaluate which of several possible insurance policies would maximize utility. Considering the calculation another way, we can evaluate what risk aversion parameter would be required to explain the decisions that people make. We suppose that individuals have constant relative risk aversion utility:

(2) $$U(C) = \frac{C^{1-\beta}}{1-\beta},$$

where β is the coefficient of relative risk aversion.

There are no national data sets of insurance premiums and coverage choices. To learn about these issues, we have determined the menu of deductibles and premiums that an individual faces by examining the policies offered by some of the largest home and auto insurance companies. Table 4 shows auto insurance policies in two cities (Boston and Miami) and homeowners insurance policies in two others (Philadelphia and Orlando). The most common policy for both risks, chosen by an estimated 60 to 90 percent of people, has a $500 deductible.

If the deductible is raised to $1,000, the premium savings range from $91 to $264 for auto insurance and $220 to $270 for homeowners insurance. This is a significant share of the extra deductible: 18–53 percent for

---

43. Allowing for moral hazard would only strengthen the conclusions, as the high-deductible policy would look even more attractive.

44. We assume that the utility of money is the same with or without a loss. This seems appropriate in the case of property damage, where the individual is less likely to be permanently harmed.

45. This model assumes no savings. That is empirically close to correct; most people have little savings outside of a house and consume relatively close to their income. We discount borrowing on the house for these purposes. Our simulations assume after-tax income of $20,000.

Table 4. Auto and Homeowners Insurance Policies

U.S. dollars

Type of policy and deductible	Policy 1		Policy 2	
	Premium	Cost relative to common policy	Premium	Cost relative to common policy
Auto[a]				
300	1,487	72	829	47
500[b]	1,415	0	762	0
1,000	1,151	−264	671	−91
2,000	1,064	−351	643	−119
House[c]				
250	3,630	130	n.a.	n.a.
500[b]	3,500	0	1,670	0
1,000	3,230	−270	1,450	−220
1,500	3,100	−400	n.a.	n.a.

n.a. Not available.

a. For auto insurance, policy 1 is offered by Liberty Mutual Insurance in Boston, Massachusetts, and policy 2 is offered by State Farm Insurance in Miami, Florida. In each case, the policy is for a thirty-five-year-old male driving a 2004 Toyota Camry with a clean driving record, good credit, living less than ten miles from work, and with coverage of $25,000 per person / $50,000 per accident and $20,000 per person / $40,000 per accident involving an uninsured motorist. The coverage under policy 2 is the same, with the exception that the lowest deductible is $250, not $300, and the limits for uninsured motorist coverage are $10,000 / $20,000.

b. The most common policy, with an estimated market share of 60 to 95 percent.

c. For homeowners insurance, policy 1 is for a $500,000 home in Philadelphia, Pennsylvania, built of brick structure within five miles of a fire station and 500 feet of a fire hydrant, and with personal property reimbursement included. Policy 2 is for a $300,000 home in Orlando, Florida, built in 1990 of stone structure within five miles of a fire station and 500 feet of a fire hydrant, with a 2 percent hurricane deductible, and with personal property reimbursement included. Both quotations are from AllState.

auto insurance and 44–54 percent for homeowners insurance. Empirically, the probability of an accident is far smaller than this.[46] For auto insurance, the accident rate is estimated to be 4.1 percent and for homeowners insurance the rate is estimated to be 9.3 percent.[47] A risk-neutral individual would thus buy the high-deductible policy over the low-deductible policy.

With risk aversion, it is possible that people will find the lower deductible optimal. But the levels of risk aversion needed are not plausible. In each of the four cases (two cities for auto insurance and two for homeowners insurance), the required β to rationalize the purchase of the low-deductible policy is more than 10. To put this in perspective, econo-

46. The more precise measure is the proportion of people who file a claim. Small damages may not be reported to the insurance company, but this would be true under less generous insurance as well.

47. On auto insurance, see Insurance Research Council (2002); on homeowners insurance, see Insurance Information Institute (2003).

mists are used to working with models of log utility ($\beta = 1$) or perhaps with a somewhat higher $\beta = 2$, but nowhere near $\beta = 10$.[48]

CARVEOUTS. Homeowners insurance does not cover all of the property risks that a typical homeowner faces. Two particular risks are generally excluded: damage from floods and damage from earthquakes. At one time, coverage for floods was included in homeowners insurance. In the 1960s, however, increasing claims from floods, coupled with federal government subsidies to areas affected by floods, led private insurers to pull out of the market.[49] This is the first example of a regular problem: when beliefs about the extent of risk increase and demand for insurance correspondingly rises, insurers often pull out of the market. Today, flood insurance is provided with substantial federal ex ante subsidies and often with ex post federal subsidies (for example, when disaster areas receive assistance).[50]

THE CONSUMER DURABLES INSURANCE PUZZLE. Bizarre levels of excessive insurance are found most acutely with consumer durables. Table 5 shows the menu of warranties a typical consumer faces when purchasing consumer durables. For a number of electronic items, we present the typical manufacturer's warranty, the extra protection offered to consumers, the cost of that extra protection, and the estimated share of customers who purchase that protection.

At face value, the purchase of this insurance seems hard to justify. A typical electronic item has a probability of needing repairs of about 10 to 25 percent (10 percent for a compact disk player; 25 percent for a camcorder or videocassette recorder). The cost of a repair is perhaps $100. Thus the expected value of the warranty is perhaps $15. Since most problems show up very quickly, and are thus covered by the manufacturer's standard warranty, or after many years, after the additional warranty has run out, the actuarial value of these additional warranties is even lower. A guess is $5 to $10. The premium for the insurance, in contrast, is many times that amount, generally averaging $70 to $100.[51] Indeed, even this calculation overstates the value of the warranty for many insured items, since

---

48. As a more intuitive reference, a person with a coefficient of relative risk aversion of 10 would not take a gamble over a $1,000 gain or loss unless the odds of winning were nearly two-thirds.

49. U.S. General Accounting Office (2003).

50. Adverse selection is a serious challenge to flood insurance as it is currently written. In theory, if the market were purely private, insurers would develop methods to better discriminate and price flood risk.

51. This is roughly the equivalent of the plans priced as a share of purchase cost as well.

Table 5. Common Insurance for Consumer Durables

Product	Typical warranty	Extended product protection or replacement plans[a]	Percentage of customers who purchase[b]	Frequency of repairs[c]	Typical repair cost[c]
Camcorders	One year for parts and labor	Extended product protection at $70 for two years, $120 for three years, $300 for five years	30	25 percent within five years, 8 percent within three years	$125
Videocassette recorders	One year for parts; ninety days for labor	Product replacement plan at 15 percent of cost for two years	70	24 percent within five years	$75
DVD players (single)	One year for parts and labor	Product replacement plan at 15 percent of cost for two years	50	n.a.	$100
DVD players (home theater systems)	One year for parts	Extended product protection at $30 and labor for two years, $175 for five years,	50	n.a.	n.a.
Compact disk players	One year for parts; ninety days for labor	Product replacement plan at 15 percent of cost for two years	80	10 percent within five years	$80
MP3 players	Ninety days for parts and labor	Product replacement plan at 15 percent of cost for two years	70	n.a.	$100
Television sets (item cost $80–$180)	Two years for picture tube; one year for parts; ninety days for labor	Product replacement plan at 15 percent of cost for two years	30	7 percent during lifetime	$90
Television sets (item cost $180+)	Two years for picture tube; one year for parts; ninety days for labor	Extended product protection depending on cost of the item, in the range of between $150 for three years and $2,000 for five years	45	20 percent during lifetime	$175
Boom boxes	One year for labor; ninety days for parts	Product replacement plan at 15 percent of cost for two years	60	n.a.	n.a.

	Warranty	Extended protection plan		Repair rate	Average repair cost
Microwaves	One year for parts and labor; ten years for magnitron	Extended product protection at $70 for three years, $100 for five years	5	n.a.	$150
Dishwashers	One year for parts and labor	Extended product protection at $90 for three years, $140 for five years	35	19 percent within five years, 8 percent within three years	$250 (major); $95 (minor)
Washers	One year for parts and labor; five years for transmission	Extended product protection at $100 for three years, $170 for five years	20	23 percent within five years	$300 (major); $100 (minor)
Dryers	One year for parts and labor	Extended product protection at $70 for three years, $140 for five years	20	14 percent within five years	$150 (major); $80 (minor)
Refrigerators	One year for parts and labor; five years for compressor	Extended product protection at $110 for three years, $170 for five years	30	8 percent within three years	$300
Vacuums	One year for parts and labor	Extended product protection at $40 for two years, $70 for five years	40	34 percent within five years	$50
Electric ranges	One year for parts and labor	Extended product protection at $90 for three years, $140 for five years	30	14 percent within five years, 8 percent within three years	$300 (major); $100 (minor)
Digital cameras	One year for parts; ninety days for labor	n.a.	n.a.	n.a.	n.a.
Treadmills	One year for parts; two years for labor; three years for motor	Extended product protection $140 for three years	10	n.a.	n.a.
Laptops	One year limited warranty	Extended product protection $190 for two years, $280 for five years	n.a.	19 percent within five years	$100

n.a. Not available.

a. Common plans offered at Sears and other retailers.
b. Estimates from sales clerks at Sears in Boston, Mass.
c. Information from consumerreports.org and sales clerks in Boston, Mass.

the prices of electronic goods are falling rapidly—over 20 percent a year in many cases—and their capabilities are increasing. Hence, the net benefit of repairing an item when it breaks, as opposed to merely replacing it, is falling substantially over time.

Despite this fact, purchase of comprehensive protection for consumer durables is widespread. An estimated 20 to 80 percent of people purchase extended protection for consumer durables, and such protection is widely perceived as lucrative.[52]

SUMMARY. The major types of property insurance are widespread, being mandated by government (auto insurance) or required by lenders as collateral (homeowners insurance). Underpurchase is generally not a problem in this market. But overinsurance is. Many people have deductibles that seem far too low given price differentials, the size of the risk, and common beliefs about the extent of risk aversion in normal circumstances. For this reason, we rate coverage of home and auto insurance as fair. The magnitude of consumer durable insurance is more problematic, since almost no utility function would justify purchase of insurance for low-cost durables. We assess the function of this market as poor.

Insurance in Practice: Business Risks

Some markets for business risks seem to work well. Businesses own physical property, for example, and most businesses insure at least some portion of that property. The data on the extent of this insurance are poor, but studies of the industry suggest that this insurance is generally believed to work well. This is not surprising, since large businesses have individuals who specialize in the purchase of insurance, and even small businesses usually have some financial expertise. Based predominantly on secondary references, we rate this insurance as good on our scale.

Businesses also have general liabilities associated with damages they may incur in the course of doing business (for example, suits arising from injury to a customer falling in a store or to a patient suffering from a misdiagnosis or a failed operation). The performance of this insurance varies by industry. If we take account of both drama and policy import, the situation is particularly problematic in medical malpractice. There have been three medical malpractice crises in the past twenty-five years: one in the

52. Consumer Reports (1998).

mid-1970s, another in the mid-1980s, and a third in just the past two years.[53] Each crisis occurred when the claims paid increased more rapidly than the premiums collected, precipitated by changes in the social climate, not any upswing in adverse medical incidents. The number of lawsuits filed increased more rapidly than expected, and the awards of liability judgments were greater than expected.

As a result, insurers lost money. In response, premiums rose precipitously, many insurers dropped out of the market, many physicians found insurance difficult to obtain, and some physicians changed their practices (for example, some obstetrician-gynecologists quit doing obstetrics). After only a few years, the market returned to reasonable function, with insurance again available, albeit at higher price. This type of availability crisis, though often without a return to normalcy, is common with many types of business insurance.

Risks with Residual Variability: Environment and Terrorism

In theory, insurance is best equipped to deal with small- to moderate-probability, high-loss risks, where it does the most good. However, it is for precisely those risks that business insurance has failed most recently. Environmental liability is the classic issue here, recently joined by terrorism losses.[54] In each case, private markets worked much less well than anticipated, once the risks eventuated. We discuss these two risks in turn.

Prior to the mid-1980s, insurance provided firms with environmental coverage indefinitely for events that occurred during the policy year (termed an occurrence-based policy). Long-term risk was thought to be small. Events in the 1970s and 1980s, however, highlighted the "long-tailed" nature of risk. Asbestos claims in the 1970s, for example, dealt with exposure to asbestos in the 1940s and 1950s. Total costs of land-based pollution control—predominantly remediation efforts under the Resource Conservation and Recovery Act and Superfund—went from $10 billion to $57 billion (1992 dollars) from 1972 to 2000.[55]

Exacerbating this vast escalation in unanticipated costs was the perception that legal interpretations were changing the provisions of insurance policies. It was frequently asserted that courts ignored restrictions in poli-

---

53. Mello, Studdert, and Brennan (2003).

54. On environmental liability, see U.S. General Accounting Office (1986, 1988); Huber (1988); Zagaski (1992).

55. U.S. Environmental Protection Agency (1990, pp. 8–21).

cies to "sudden and accidental" environmental damage. Moreover, the courts, usually on the basis of jury decisions, imposed liabilities well beyond those the policy was intended to cover.[56] The result was increased uncertainty about the liability of environmental insurers.

In theory, an increase in risk should increase the demand for insurance, increase the price of insurance, and result in greater overall coverage at higher prices. This was not the outcome with environmental risk, however, or with medical malpractice insurance. Rather, the policies themselves changed in a way that made them *less* generous. For example, the occurrence-based policy was dropped in favor of a claims-made policy, which covers damages only if the claim is filed within a certain period of time.[57] Effectively, this eliminates insurance coverage for long-tailed risk, placing that risk instead on the insuring firm, in the form of higher premiums as the extent of damages is realized. Indeed, the reduction in insurance coverage was not limited to primary insurance markets. In 1984 international reinsurance markets began denying coverage for pollution liability reinsurance.

Insurers also imposed aggregate dollar limits on payouts for environmental damage, to limit their overall risk exposure. Of course, this denies protection precisely where it is needed most: for high losses.[58] These changes limited the aggregate risk born by the insurer, with the consequence that more of the risk was retained by the firms at risk. Even two decades after the liability revolution and the initial cutbacks in insurance coverage, the market for environment insurance is substantially less generous than it was.[59]

The "crisis" in terrorism insurance burst onto the scene on September 11, 2001. The attacks that day drastically changed expectations about the likelihood and magnitude of terrorism losses in the future. Unlike nature's

56. A notorious case of jury overreach in damages—not related to the environment—involved a new car that BMW sold without notifying the buyer that it had been repainted after being damaged in shipping. The buyer was awarded $4,000 in compensatory damages and $4 million in punitive damages.

57. Similar changes happened in medical malpractice insurance in the 1970s and professional liability insurance in the 1980s. The stated reasons for the change were similar to those for environmental coverage.

58. There may be a moral hazard justification for limiting coverage for large losses. Insured individuals may have some control over the size of loss, trading off probability and magnitude. Thus a toxic waste release on the ground may be allowed to sit untreated, avoiding a medium loss, but risking a much larger loss should it leach into the groundwater.

59. An implicit part of the coverage for many types of insurance was lost—namely the idea that if you insure today, you will be guaranteed coverage tomorrow.

extreme blows (for example, Hurricane Andrew), which can increase perceived future losses by, say, 100 percent, the man-made loss of September 11 increased future expected terror losses at least by a factor of ten, perhaps much more. The immediate result was a crisis in insurance availability. Insurers claimed that terrorism was "uninsurable" and stopped writing coverage for it. About one-quarter of policies written in 2002—and an even larger share for large firms—excluded terrorist acts.

Although the most dire predictions about the consequences of lost insurance did not come true—buildings got built and buildings traded hands—the potential for severe economic disruption was judged to be high. After several months, the federal government stepped in to stabilize the market. The Terrorism Risk Insurance Act of November 2002 provides coverage related to international terrorism, with the federal contribution rising with the magnitude of loss up through $100 billion of insured losses. Beyond that, Congress decides what additional payments it wants to make.[60] In exchange for taking the back-end risk (without coinsurance), the act requires insurers to write coverage for smaller terrorist losses. The act sunsets at the end of 2005, and it is not clear what will happen in the market beyond that point.

Employment Practice Insurance

Many businesses also have insurance for employment liability resulting from claims such as sexual harassment and race or gender discrimination lawsuits. As the potential liability from employment issues has become more widespread, the cost of this insurance has increased. As table 6 shows, a business with twenty full-time employees and twenty part-time employees, for example, would pay a premium of $5,000 a year and have a 10 percent coinsurance rate.[61] There is also a limit on *insurer* liability, generally $1 million. We do not know of general assessments of this line of insurance, however, so we omit it from the table.

---

60. Thus businesses are protected against attacks that knock things down, which are highly unlikely to exceed the losses of September 11. However, they are not protected against other risks such as dirty bombs, which make major parts of a city uninhabitable for a sustained period.

61. As with auto insurance, the change in premiums for a change in deductible is highly nonlinear. Moving from a $5,000 deductible to a $2,500 deductible raises the premium by only $26. Raising the deductible to $10,000, in contrast, lowers the premium by more than $1,000. We suspect that adverse selection and some miscalculations by the insurance company are behind these rate differences.

**Table 6. Premium for Employment
Practices Liability Insurance**[a]

U.S. dollars

Deductible	Premium	Difference
2,500	5,357	0
10,000	4,283	−1,074
25,000	4,021	−1,336

Source: Farmers Insurance Group.
a. The premium is for a policy in Massachusetts with a $1 million limit, cap of $50,000, and coinsurance of 10 percent. The firm has twenty full-time and twenty part-time employees.

Pension Obligations

Obligations to retirees represent an important long-term risk to firms. Many firms, particularly large manufacturers, have substantial defined-benefit pension obligations. Firms also have obligations for retiree health insurance. These obligations are risky because retirement experiences and the earnings on pension assets are both uncertain.

Insurance for these risks is affected by a substantial degree of moral hazard. Firms that are doing poorly have the option of declaring bankruptcy and defaulting on their pension liabilities rather than continuing to pay them. As a result of this moral hazard, pension risk is insured by the government. The Pension Benefit Guaranty Corporation (PBGC) requires firms to contribute an annual premium based partly on the number of retirees and partly on the degree of pension underfunding.

Like many government programs, PBGC has difficulty changing prices to guarantee solvency. This is particularly difficult since pension default is a long-tailed risk: premiums taken in today need to be saved for potentially high use in the future. Boyce and Ippolito estimate that PBGC charges premiums that are 50 percent below what equivalent private insurance companies would charge, with unfunded liabilities currently more than $100 billion.[62] For these reasons, the General Accounting Office rates PBGC as high risk.

Because participation in PBGC is mandatory, we lose the yardstick of what private insurance would charge for equivalent coverage. And because it is effectively subsidized, there is little complaint. For these reasons, we rate the operation of pension insurance as poor.

62. Boyce and Ippolito (2002).

Summary

Businesses are much more sophisticated than individuals about the purchase of insurance, with professionals handling the task in large firms. For traditional risks, insurance works well. Recent years, however, have witnessed the rise of risks due to purposeful human activity—for example, the liability revolution or terrorism. These risks are larger than older risks, are correlated across insuring firms, and often are not resolved for many years. For such risks, insurance markets tend to work poorly.

Explanations for Poor Performance

Insurance in practice differs substantially from insurance in theory. Despite rating many insurance markets as likely to work well in theory, only one of the actual markets we evaluate draws a "good" rating—homeowners insurance. Four markets get a fair rating (life insurance, short-term health insurance, auto insurance, and general business property and casualty insurance). The remaining six risks (annuities, long-term health risks, consumer durables insurance, and business environmental, terrorism, and pension coverage) all rate poorly. While some may quibble with our ratings in particular cases, we suspect that none would disagree with our overall assessment of substantial underperformance in actual insurance markets.

The discrepancy between theory and practice is of two types. The first is a mismatch between expected coverage and actual coverage. Some risks that we expect to be covered, such as terrorism risk, long-term health risk, longevity risk, or environmental liability risk, are covered not at all or, at best, are covered poorly. Even risks that are covered well, such as life insurance, are not covered by everyone who likely would benefit from such insurance. In contrast, many risks that theory predicts would be uncovered, such as small losses for automobiles, houses, and consumer durables, are covered by individuals who voluntarily purchase insurance. Assuming rational decision, only excessively high degrees of risk aversion could explain the pattern of property coverage that we observe. Further, many elderly seem overinsured against unexpected death (life insurance), even as they are underinsured against beyond-average survival (annuitization).

In addition, there is little rhyme or reason to the mix between public and private coverage. To be sure, coverage of many of the largest risks, such as terrorism, has made its way into the public sector, as one might expect. But smaller risks are covered publicly as well (flood insurance, for example), and many large risks are left to private insurers (environmental damage).

A common but troubling phenomenon is severe underpricing of risk coverage by the public sector, often because premiums are insufficiently responsive to risk differentials. Savings and loan insurance prior to the multi–hundred billion dollar bailout is a good example. When politics and political pressures intrude, it is often impossible to impose significant differential rates for insurance. Often government just sets a risk standard to be met if one wants to insure. Such standards are often ambiguous, and government denial of insurance is often too much of a nuclear weapon.[63] The interactions between public and private insurance seem unhelpful at best and harmful at worst.[64]

There are a number of complementary explanations for the mismatch between insurance theory and insurance markets in practice. We explore them in the next sections.

Information-Based Explanations

The explanation favored by most economists (casual polls suggest) is asymmetric information. Insurers may not offer particular products because they worry that the product will affect the behavior of the insured (moral hazard) or will be selected by people who have a high likelihood of suffering a loss (adverse selection). Such "bad behavior" cannot be monitored.

These explanations contribute, but we suspect that they are far from sufficient. For many of the risks that are uncovered, such as long-term

63. The 2003 struggle of the Pension Benefit Guaranty Corporation with U.S. Airways is instructive. To enable it to emerge from bankruptcy, U.S. Air argued that it needed to lower its pension obligations substantially. Failing to secure direct legislative relief, U.S. Air terminated its pension plan for pilots. On April 1, PBGC became responsible for this plan. In its last filing prior to termination, U.S. Air reported that the fund was 94 percent funded on a current liability basis. At termination, however, it was only 33 percent funded. This case highlights two problems: many insured companies are underfunding their pension plans, and companies may be able to use Chapter 11 to separate their assets from their pension obligations and put the burden of pensions on PBGC.

64. On pricing, the "sliver solution" deserves attention. With it, a private insurer writes coverage for a small part of a risk. The government insures the rest at a premium proportional to the private insurance. This inserts private market discipline into the price. Government terrorism reinsurance does this to some extent, charging insurance companies roughly 10 percent of their premium.

environmental exposure by firms or the need for long-term care, evidence of moral hazard is at best tenuous. Where we are certain that there is moral hazard is insurance for use at a point in time, such as for short-term health care. This risk is covered, if anything, too well.

Neither is adverse selection much of an explanation. Evidence to date suggests no adverse selection in the purchase of long-term-care insurance, for example.[65] While adverse selection has dominated the theoretical literature, the actual experience of an insurer—what we think of as "adverse experience"—depends on many factors beyond perceived risk. Risk aversion is important: healthy individuals who are worried about their health purchase insurance just as much as high-risk individuals. As a side benefit, this keeps premiums low for those on the margin of purchase.[66] Indeed, risk aversion may be inversely correlated with risk levels, if risk-averse people take better care to avoid putting themselves in risky situations.

Ignorance is also a blessing here. If potential purchasers of insurance do not know their risk levels, there will be no correlation between risk and the insurance decision. More generally, nonrational behavior helps to deter adverse selection. It introduces many new elements that encourage people to insure, without necessarily being correlated with risk.[67]

In many situations, we might expect that insurers would know *more* about risks than individuals. This is likely the case with warranties for consumer durables and possibly with health insurance as well. Variation in price by risk status limits adverse selection, although it may be inefficient in other ways (preventing people from insuring their risk level).

The limited explanatory power of asymmetric information-based explanations shows up most clearly in the analysis of terrorism insurance. By all assessments, there is little to no differential information about the likelihood of terrorists striking any particular object (adverse selection); neither is it plausible that firms would substantially lower their guard against terrorist attack (moral hazard) just because they are insured. (The uncompensable losses, including one's own loss of life, are just too great.) Insurance coverage has dried up for other reasons.

---

65. Finkelstein and McGarry (2003).

66. Market power on the part of insurers cuts in the opposite direction. Prices above marginal cost encourage low-risk people to drop out of the market.

67. From the welfare perspective, the variation introduced by behavioral decision, unlike that generated by varying levels of risk aversion, does not assure that those who do buy insurance are the ones who need it most.

Our more general hypothesis is that, in many markets where adverse selection can be expected to exert a powerful undertow on the market, adverse selection proves to be a mild current rather than a sweeping tide. We propose three alternative reasons why the theory and practice of insurance diverge in the early twenty-first century.

Incomplete Diversification, Supply-Side Contracting Difficulties

The first explanation is insufficient diversification of insurance companies. People may want insurance against a risk, but insurers have to be willing to provide that risk, even at rates far above the best estimates of actuarial cost. If insurers—or, more accurately, insurance executives—are worried about their capitalization, they may be unwilling to write policies for some risks, even if both price and demand are high. The prospect of severe losses, or even bankruptcy with its limited liability, may not scare the diversified investors in an insurance company, who would be happy to write unusual insurance for robust premiums. But insurance executives have to worry about misestimating risks and premiums, with consequent collapse of their career.[68]

In the standard theory of insurance, risks are minimally correlated across the insured. A few people will experience a loss in a period, but the vast majority will not. Insurers use the premiums from those who do not suffer a loss to compensate those who do. Many risks, however, have an aggregate component; many people incur a loss at the same time. Nuclear wars represented the ultimate aggregate risk for many years. Today's aggregate risks include new liability revolutions (as with environmental damage), significant increases in prices (say, for medical care), and major terrorist attacks. Even good developments have a component of aggregate risk. Thus rapid rises in longevity would impose heavy aggregate costs on pensions and other annuities. Long-term-care insurance well represents an aggregate risk. When the expected costs increase for one person—say, because a jump in longevity makes nursing home stays, particularly Alzheimer's stays, more expensive—this factor applies to many individuals with insurance. As a result, the traditional method of risk diversification—pooling independent risks across people—fails.

---

68. The behavior of Warren Buffett, by contrast, shows what happens when an executive has no such concerns.

Risk-neutral insurers do not care about this aggregate risk. The owners of insurance company assets can diversify the risk posed by diversifying their portfolio. But managers and workers in those insurance companies may care. They may lose their job if the company goes bankrupt or if that line of business loses gobs of money. This leads to a classical principal-agent problem. Thus the insurance company itself, under guidance from its executives, may behave in a risk-averse manner.

Ambiguous risks—that is, those whose losses are hard to estimate—aggravate any principal-agent problem. Think of terrorist risks today. Were an insurance company to write substantial coverage, and should there be unexpectedly large and frequent attacks, Monday morning quarterbacks would be likely to demand the heads of those who decided to write the coverage. Thus principal-agent problems strongly discourage the sale of insurance for ambiguous risks.

A moderately risk-averse insurance company will still sell insurance but will impose a higher administrative charge to do so. Administrative loads in long-term-care insurance, which has a large contingent of aggregate risk, are 35 percent at a minimum and reach 50 to 70 percent for some groups.[69] In comparison, administrative costs in short-term health insurance are only about 15 percent, roughly their level for annuities.[70]

An insurer who is more risk averse than the potential insured will refuse to write insurance altogether. We often see this in the nature of risk exposure that is written. When they do write policies, long-term-care insurers limit their exposure to a fixed dollar amount per day of nursing home care; one cannot buy coverage for the actual cost of care received (in contrast to annual health insurance). Similarly, environmental insurers and medical malpractice insurers refuse to cover all claims that result from operations today; instead, they put a time limit on when the claim must be filed.

The cycle of insurance crises shows clearly this problem. When risks increase more than expected—for example, the liability revolution, knowledge of particular chemical harms, terrorist action—insurers respond at first by refusing to cover new risk. That is understandable, as markets digest the new information. Over time, prices rise. That too is predictable. But even after the market "settles down," insurance frequently becomes

---

69. Cutler (1996); Brown and Finkelstein (2003).
70. U.S. Department of Health and Human Services, Health Care Financing Administration (1984); Mitchell and others (1999).

less generous than it was formerly and stays that way indefinitely. That is the economically undesirable part.

While the practice may appear to be irrational economically, the idea of severely curtailing company risk is standard advice in the insurance industry. According to a leading analyst of the insurance industry, insurers should keep the risk of any line of business small: "To provide stability and safety, an insurer should limit its maximum loss exposure on a single risk (or group of related risks) to a small percentage of its policyholders' surplus, normally less than 2 percent."[71] With aggregate risks, insurers face the Scylla and Charybdis of not knowing their market or having too heavy exposure. The outcome is that the insurance industry does not write certain classes of risk.

For some risks the government may step in, as it has with high-cost terrorism risk. But that is a short-term (three-year) solution, it is an adjunct to other private sector insurance, and it is in an area where the government could be deemed to have responsibility for controlling the risk. Government as reinsurer is not a likely solution for many troubling aggregate risks, such as long-term environment or health care risks.

Fortunately, a far greater pool of resources could conceivably absorb such risks: financial markets. Risks that are large even for the world's insurance pool—estimated to be on the order of $1 trillion in the United States and $2 trillion worldwide—are small relative to financial markets.[72] For example, the value of equity markets in the United States alone is more than $10 trillion. One great advantage of financial markets as insurance instruments, apart from their volume, is that they effectively bring together tens of millions of investors, none of whom would have to hold much of an aggregate risk.

There has been recent use of financial markets to diversify aggregate insurance risks. Most prominent have been catastrophe bonds, used to reinsure weather-related housing risks. Interest in these bonds rose with Hurricane Andrew in 1992, the Northridge earthquake in 1994, and the Kobe earthquake in Japan in 1995, all involving losses that were massive relative to historical experience. The market for catastrophe bonds is relatively small, but it is perceived to be successful.[73] One measure of success is the prices charged. Famed investor Warren Buffett underwrote earth-

71. A. M. Best (1991, p. xiii).
72. Insurance Information Institute (2003).
73. U.S. General Accounting Office (2002).

quake reinsurance in California for four years in the early 1990s, earning an 11 percent premium for an estimated 1 percent risk. Buffett recognized what other insurers must have missed: this risk, though unusual, brought neither adverse selection nor moral hazard. Over time, the advantage of this investment became known and premiums fell. "The influx of 'investor' money into catastrophe bonds—which may well live up to their name—has caused super-cat prices to deteriorate materially. Therefore, we will write less business in 1998," Buffett wrote.[74]

Use of these new instruments is not without problems. Participation of insurance companies is likely to be important, since these companies have vital expertise in assessing risk. Possibly, insurance companies will underwrite the risks initially, to provide their assessment expertise for a fee, and investors will then take their share. Reinsurance is already common in the insurance industry, although it is typically done by specialized companies rather than broader financial markets.

Perhaps more important, the nature of the payment needs to be determined. Investment managers are currently paid for assuming risk. The common arrangement with hedge funds, for example, is for the general partner to charge an annual management fee (say, 1 percent) and to receive 20 percent of the profits or excess profits.

With insurance, equivalent arrangements would be hard to structure, since risks are discrete and it is hard to know whether a policy issued has been profitable in expectation thus far. If there is a 3 percent chance of a calamitous event, for example, but otherwise no losses, a general partner paid on the basis of annual "profits" would be expected to do quite well for a period before the odds bring down the house. Further compounding the difficulty, prior management and incentive fees would probably be unrecoverable in the event of a bad loss. Many of the names at Lloyds of London experienced just such a string—many moderate successes followed by a mammoth loss—when the liability revolution hit.

One way around this problem is to have a highly diversified portfolio of risks. But such diversification blunts the value of specialized expertise on the market being insured. Other types of contracts may be needed.

With additional time, we expect that financial instruments will continue to evolve and allow further investors to enter the market. It is possible—perhaps likely—that the first problem we identify has a solution forthcoming.

74. Wettlaufer (1998).

Nonstandard Behavior on the Demand Side

The second reason why theory and practice diverge in the insurance industry is that the potential purchasers of insurance engage in nonstandard economic behavior. In traditional decision theory, people have concave utility functions defined over consumption. Risk-averse people will want to insure against all risks, assuming fair actuarial pricing. They temper this because of moral hazard and administrative costs, which lead prices to exceed expected payouts. In response, people choose to cover large risks, at least substantially, and leave small risks unprotected.

Such preferences may not correspond to reality, however, as the prevalence of insurance coverage for small risks suggests. Several alternatives to standard preferences may explain this type of coverage.

PROSPECT THEORY. A leading possibility is loss aversion: the idea that people significantly dislike any loss, even small ones.[75] Hence, people are willing to pay far above actuarial value to protect against small losses, such as when a stereo breaks.[76]

It seems plausible that this phenomenon could explain some of the anomalous behavior we have documented here, especially the purchase of insurance for small risks. To see how readily this explanation might work, we modify our analysis to allow for simple loss aversion. Suppose that the utility consequence of incurring any deductible is $1 + \theta$, where θ represents the additional utility cost of having to make a cash outlay. With this set of preferences, expected utility is given by:

(3) $$V = p\, U[Y - \pi - d * (1 + \theta)] + (1 - p)\, U(Y - \pi).$$

If we assume a particular utility function, we can use the menu of choices that people face to determine what value of θ is required to explain insurance decisions. Assuming that utility is logarithmic in consumption ($\theta = 1$), for automobile insurance the θ required to explain a preference for a low deductible over a high deductible ranges from 0.5 to 2.5, depending on the policy and the degree of risk aversion. For homeowners insurance, the equivalent value of θ ranges between about 3 and 4. (Such a value would imply that deductibles have a utility-equivalent cost of deductibles of $3 or $4 per dollar; this value is too high to seem plausible.) Thus pref-

75. Kahneman and Tversky (1979).

76. Kahneman and Tversky (1979) hypothesize that people were concave in both gains *and* losses about the certainty point. Additions to wealth were valued with concave utility, as were losses to wealth: small losses had a greater marginal cost than did large losses.

erences of this sort could perhaps contribute to the overinsurance phenomenon, but they cannot explain it all.

AFFECTIVE FORECASTING. Recent work demonstrates that people significantly overestimate the magnitude of the negative experience from a loss. Gilbert and others, for example, attribute this to a durability bias— a belief that the negative aspects of the loss will last much longer than they do—and to a significant overestimate of the regret they will feel after a loss.[77] People who believe their utility will diminish permanently with a loss will want to purchase more insurance coverage than people who recognize that losses will be readily accommodated. It is not surprising that such people are interested in very generous insurance.

ANXIETY AND REGRET. Consider a significant loss: one that would drive down utility considerably but would not affect marginal utility of income. For example, one might have a painting of one's departed grandmother, which is worth a great deal sentimentally but little monetarily. The death of a nonearning loved one would be the same. Rationality-loving economists would say not to insure. But many people do.[78] One reason for this is that insurance reduces anxiety, acting as a form of reassurance for many people. If the heirloom gets stolen or damaged, people reason that at least they will receive some money for their pain.[79]

Regret is similar to anxiety, although it looks backward rather than forward. A person who has rationally chosen not to purchase insurance may suffer lower utility if the bad state of nature arises, both because the risk occurred and because the person did not purchase insurance for the risk. Imagine, for example, that a person buys a new camcorder, rationally chooses not to buy supplemental insurance but then finds that the camcorder breaks in the first week of use. The person will regret not having purchased the insurance. Knowing the possibility of regret later on, the person in the store may choose to buy camcorder insurance.

Purchasing insurance as a means to reduce anxiety or stave off regret is not difficult to reconcile with the standard neoclassical framework. We show the situation for anxiety, although regret is similar. Suppose that an individual is faced with a lottery L, defined by $L = [-d, p; 0, 1 - p]$, where

77. Gilbert and others (2002).

78. The American Council of Life Insurers reports that about 15 percent of people under age eighteen have life insurance (Curry 2003). Although such coverage may be for burial costs in some instances, such costs are trivial relative to the cost of raising a child.

79. It may also be that people do not realize that their marginal utility will not change, perhaps because they are not proficient at forecasting their utility in different states of nature.

$d > 0$ is the loss and p is the probability of loss. An individual determines that her utility for outcomes $V(L) = V(C)$, where $C = [-e, 1]$; that is, e is the certainty equivalent. If insurance is offered at price $f > e$, the person will decline, since for lottery $D = [-f, 1]$, $V(L) = V(C) > V(D)$.

Now allow for a time dimension to the lottery: for example, the camcorder might break down any time in a three-year period. Utility has two dimensions: the lottery L and time t ($t = 0$ is the present). Unresolved risk creates anxiety. We model this as $U(L,t) = V(L) - A(L,t)$. Our interest is in the form of $A(L,t)$. First consider the nature of the lottery. If the lottery is over good states ($d < 0$), and $t > 0$, there might be "joy along the way"— $A(L,t) < 0$—and people will not purchase insurance. If, as with insurance situations, the outcome is significantly adverse ($d > 0$), anxiety is likely to arise. If L involves only a certainty outcome, C, we normalize to no anxiety.[80] The time dimension is also important. Without significant dispute (we suspect), we assume that $A(L,0) = 0$ and $\partial A / \partial t > 0$.

Assume that the insurance purchase is for a year and that the lottery is resolved at the end. Our potential insured experiences anxiety. Then we might have:

(4) $$U(L,0) = V(L) > V(D),$$

but $U(L,1) = V(L) - A(L,1) < U(D,1) = V(D) - A(D,1) = V(D)$. This can happen since $A(L,1)$ is positive and $A(D,1)$ is 0. Thus the person may reject the insurance if the lottery is resolved immediately but accept it if resolution is delayed sufficiently.

SALIENCE. Many insurance policies pay double if someone dies in an accident as opposed to natural causes. When asked whether they want to purchase such coverage, many individuals, particularly young individuals, say yes. Insurance theory would say the individual should insure for the same amount, no matter how he dies. (If anything, dying in an accident is likely to be cheaper than, say, dying from cancer.) But the accident becomes salient as a way to die, and individuals purchase such insurance. We suspect a form of "availability heuristic" is playing a role here.[81] We see this in other contexts as well, such as Kunreuther's finding that people purchase flood insurance after a flood and purchase supplementary insurance before taking an airplane trip.[82]

---

80. People might get anxious about a bad event they know will occur (a borrowed car must be returned), but we abstract away from this.
81. Tversky and Kahneman (1974).
82. Kunreuther (1978).

HYPERBOLIC DISCOUNTING. Some insurance that we think should be purchased, such as annuities when elderly, are not bought. One possibility is hyperbolic discounting: people value today more than proportionately over the future. A hyperbolic discounter knows that purchasing an annuity is a good idea but always wants to delay the purchase to the next year—either because consumption is particularly valuable today or because it is easier to delay decisionmaking until tomorrow. Empirically, people who are forced to make financial decisions by a specified date choose to save more than people who are free to make such decisions at any time.[83]

SUMMARY. Almost certainly, one theory cannot explain all the phenomena we seek to explain. As a starting point for future research, we provide some of our own speculation about theories of likely importance on the consumer side of the market, shown in table 7. Future research is needed to test these theories more completely and possibly to develop others.

We have principally been interested in improving descriptive theory. Usually when economists, including the authors, find normative (or prescriptive) theory and practice diverge, they proselytize for the former.[84] However, studying insurance is a sobering prospect. Unlike our standard models, most insurance decisions involve future contemplation and backward reflection. Thus, for example, given the importance that consumers attach to minimizing regret and anxiety, there is strong argument that such concepts should be given a role in our normative theories. This is a task for future efforts.

Probability Monopoly

There is considerable market power for some forms of insurance. At the high end, only the electronics store can realistically sell you an extended warranty at the time you purchase a camcorder or DVD player. Much life insurance is sold by salesmen calling on buyers rather than vice versa. Even standardized Medigap insurance shows considerable price variability, a sign of market power.

Given market power, the sale of insurance introduces an element of monopoly pricing. People have some idea of expected loss probabilities,

---

83. Choi and others (2002).

84. Prescriptive theory tells what a particular individual should do to maximize his or her own welfare. Normative theory tells what is desirable for a group of individuals and requires some notion of social welfare.

Table 7. Examples of and Possible Explanations for Insurance Phenomena

Phenomenon	Example	Possible explanation
Insurance against small risks	Appliance insurance, low-deductible insurance	Prospect theory, regret avoidance
Insurance against risks that do not affect marginal utility	Single elderly with life insurance; family heirlooms	Affective forecasting, regret avoidance, anxiety
Insurance against salient risks	Purchase of flood insurance after flood	Salience, anxiety
Lack of insurance for big risks	Underpurchase of annuities, life insurance	Hyperbolic discounting

but this information is not complete.[85] Indeed, the loss probability might be aided by salespeople (once the device has been safely purchased, so as not to imply that its quality is low).[86] Potential insurers can thus price above marginal cost, knowing that those with low risk assessments will choose to forgo coverage, while those with high assessments will buy. The markup on the population with high loss probabilities can make this a profitable strategy. We refer to this situation as probabilistic monopoly and believe that it helps to explain the purchase of vastly overpriced insurance in a range of situations.

Consider a specific example: a store faces risk-neutral consumers with different probabilities of needing repairs. The likelihood distribution is triangular, with density of 8–32y for probability y ranging between 0 and 25 percent. The implied mean breakdown probability is 8.33 percent. The store knows that the true likelihood is 2 percent, the same for all customers.

The store will set a price of insurance that maximizes expected profits, knowing the distribution of perceived risks. Normalizing the price of the good to 1, the solution is the value x that maximizes

---

85. Unlike the situation with adverse selection, it is possible that people have differences in their perceived loss probabilities that are not true in reality. A person might think he is clumsy with electronic devices but not know that the devices are designed with clumsy people in mind.

86. High-priced extended warranties undermine a product's presumed reliability. Thus we now have many auto companies offering extremely long warranties. Electronics stores only offer extended warranties once a sale seems firm, and it is the electronics store, not the manufacturer, that is offering them. Such bundling with a sale has the additional advantage of rolling the two costs into one price. Raising the cost of a $620 item to $690 is more likely to get a sale than setting a new $70 price for the warranty, for example, of a camcorder.

$$\int_{x}^{.25} (8 - 32y)(x - .02)dy.$$

The optimal price is 0.097, or nearly 10 percent of the purchase price. This is nearly five times above actuarial value and well above the mean value in the population.

Monopoly pricing will not work if the buyers draw appropriate inferences from the situation. People who ask why the store is willing to sell insurance will conclude that it is only because the warranty makes money, and real sophisticates will recognize the monopoly situation. Hence they will decline the offer. Fortunately for electronics stores, even relatively informed people are poor at drawing appropriate inferences.[87]

Monopoly pricing also will not work if people underestimate the risk probability. We suspect this occurs in some situations where insurance is not sold. But as we learn from prospect theory, most people overestimate the risk of small-probability events.

Summary

We posit three explanations for the poor performance of insurance markets beyond the traditional explanations surrounding moral hazard and adverse selection: contracting difficulties on the supply side, leading to incomplete diversification; nonstandard behavior on the demand side; and probability monopoly. Given the vast divergence between the theory of insurance and actual practice, students of insurance must extend current theory, often in unfamiliar directions. We believe these are promising paths for the future.

Conclusions

The U.S. government recently enacted the largest expansion in health insurance coverage in a generation. The Medicare program, set up in the 1960s and largely the same today as then, was enriched in 2003 by the addition of an outpatient prescription drug benefit.[88] In many ways, adding

87. In a somewhat parallel situation, few bidders correct sufficiently for the winner's curse.

88. Prescription medications used on an inpatient basis are already covered in Medicare hospital payments. For simplicity, we refer to the new benefit as prescription drug coverage, leaving implicit the restriction on medications taken on an outpatient basis.

prescription drugs to Medicare represented a triumph of economic reasoning. The fundamental principle of insurance demand is that coverage becomes more valuable as the variability of potential outcomes grows. In the 1960s, prescription drug costs were low, and little risk was associated with buying medications. It made little sense to include prescription drugs in coverage. By 2003, the risks for the elderly were much greater. Even though the costs to the government were high, the potential risk-spreading value made offering the new benefit worthwhile.

Unfortunately, effective risk sharing was not fully enshrined in the new legislation. Indeed, the cost sharing in the new legislation is, by economic considerations, somewhat bizarre. Elderly enrolling in the new program face a $250 deductible. After that, the government pays 25 percent of the bill up to $2,250 in total spending. The government then ceases payment until total spending reaches $5,100 ($3,600 of individual costs). Above that amount, the government pays 95 percent and the individual 5 percent. There is no upper limit on individual spending.

From a risk-spreading perspective, a far more valuable insurance policy would have individuals cover more of the up-front costs and leave the government to take more of the back-end liability. Politics no doubt helps to explain the benefits structure, complemented perhaps by the type of utility anomalies discussed above. A certainty equivalent benefit of $110, where the actual monies go to 10 percent of the elderly population, may be politically less effective than a certainty equivalent benefit of $100, where a large share of the money is spread broadly across the population.

The new legislation also considers the issue of public and private insurance, but here too the answer seems strange. Why does the private sector not offer insurance for prescription drugs if that coverage is so valuable? The answer is that drug benefits are almost a poster child for adverse selection. The elderly with high drug needs know who they are, and they would raise the cost of private drug coverage beyond what the vast majority of elderly would consider paying.[89] Given sufficient skewness in expenditure, the market unravels.

---

89. There is substantial evidence of adverse selection for prescription drug coverage in the Medigap insurance market, which sells supplements to the standard Medicare package (see Atherly 2002). Pauly and Zeng (2003) simulate a private market for prescription drug coverage allowing for reasonable degrees of adverse selection and conclude that such a market is not feasible.

Still, the new legislation envisions the majority of the elderly obtaining coverage through private insurance companies offering stand-alone pharmaceutical coverage. The classic economic solution to adverse selection—single-payer health insurance—was explicitly rejected as being too regulatory a solution. To partly offset the selection incentives induced, the legislation includes a substantial sum for employers already providing drug coverage—28 percent of costs between $250 and $5,000 per person. It is not known if this subsidy will prevent crowdout.

Unfortunately (for economists), the seeming anomalies in the Medicare drug benefit are more common than we would care to admit. Exploring a number of insurance policies in practice, we argue that the conventional theory of insurance misses reality in two respects. First, it assumes near risk neutrality on the supply side of the market, when in fact strong risk aversion is more appropriate, particularly given the agency concerns of insurance decisionmakers. Second, we show that many attributes of insurance outcomes can best be explained if people's behavior diverges from the rational model, meaning that they have nonstandard preferences: for example, they care about even tiny losses; they seek to equate utility across states, not marginal utility; they disproportionately buy coverage for risks that are "available."

We also identify possible solutions. Encouraging greater risk spreading beyond the narrow confines of primary insurance and reinsurance is a central one. Government and private firms sometimes collaborate in this venture, as in terrorism insurance, where the government is a reinsurer. More generally, financial markets represent an enormous pool of largely untapped potential insurance dollars.

The future, we are confident, will confront significant new risks and will develop new mechanisms for spreading them. Unfortunately, neither the invisible hand nor sophisticated theories of insurance will assure that the right entities write the right coverage for the right group of insured. Our theories of insurance must be elaborated to capture realities on the ground, including the factors that motivate entities to insure. Insurance practice should be adjusted to meet realistic expectations of how risks can be spread effectively. This ongoing minuet of adjustments—perhaps a dance over decades—should allow the theory and practice of insurance to reunite.

Discussion

This paper generated a lively discussion among many of the conference participants. Howard Kunreuther of the Wharton School opened the discussion by calling for a broader view of errors in judgment within the demand and supply framework when dissecting reasons for the divergence between insurance theory and practice. On the demand side, consumers seem to view insurance as an investment rather than a contingent claim. This view creates a strong preference for low deductibles and rebate schemes so that the insured can "get something back." Also on the demand side, paying a premium over and above the expected value is rational for consumers who derive peace of mind from the risk transfer. On the supply side, only a principal agent problem or some ambiguity in coverage can explain the decision not to offer coverage at a certain premium.

Insurers buying reinsurance share the view of insurance as an investment. Joan Lamm-Tennant of the General Reinsurance Corporation criticized insurance companies for focusing on margins rather than volatility issues when they buy reinsurance at dangerously low attachments. Seeing combined ratios on their net business worse than those on their gross business, insurers should realize that reinsurers do charge a margin for their capital.

Scott Harrington of the University of South Carolina asserted that there is less evidence than intuition refuting rational models of how insurance markets work. Low deductibles operate as effectively higher claims thresholds than their nominal values since the insured does not generally make claims for small losses, fearing future rate increases or even cancellation of their policy. On the supply side, high uncertainty requires significant capital to preserve franchise value. This leads to higher tax and agency costs, which in turn raise the supply price of insurance. This can help to explain a lack of transactions in certain markets. Alex Muermann followed up with further comment on the disutility of regret as an explanation for otherwise irrational behavior, which would explain why consumers buy seemingly expensive warranties for inexpensive electronics products.

Jim Ament of State Farm suggested that even though consumers and suppliers may be acting rationally, their behavior may be confounded by third-party constraints. Lenders wanting to protect their collateral and federal examiners seeking to maintain banking stability both effectively impose caps on maximum deductibles.

Patricia Danzon offered two explanations for the anomalies of Medigap coverage. First, the law of one price only applies in a market of truly homogeneous risk, which does not characterize this market. Second, Medigap coverage for the coinsurance and deductibles of Medicare creates the moral hazard of overuse, a cost that is passed on to Medicare.

Zeckhauser responded by reiterating that his paper was about discrepancies between elementary economic analysis and observed practice. He urged a reevaluation of current rational theories to include backward reflection and future contemplation. Normative theory should incorporate these tendencies if consumers do seek to minimize regret and anxiety. For the future, an examination of how best to disentangle and define more clearly the public and private role in government would serve the industry well. Ensuring transparency and preserving some vestige of private provision of insurance, if only as a guideline for pricing, are both critical in framing a market in which the government is the primary supplier.

References

Altman, Daniel, David Cutler, and Richard Zeckhauser. 2003. "Enrollee Mix, Treatment Intensity, and Cost in Competing Indemnity and HMO Plans." *Journal of Health Economics* 22 (1): 23–45.

American Council of Life Insurers. 2003. *Life Insurance Fact Book.* Washington.

Atherly, Adam. 2002. "The Effect of Medicare Supplemental Insurance on Medicare Expenditures." *International Journal of Health Care Finance and Economics* 2 (2, June): 137–62.

Bernheim, B. Douglas, Katherine Grace Carman, Jagadeesh Gokhale, and Laurence J. Kotlikoff. 2001. "The Mismatch between Life Insurance Holdings and Financial Vulnerabilities: Evidence from the Survey of Consumer Finances." NBER Working Paper 8544. Cambridge, Mass.: National Bureau of Economic Research, October.

Bernheim, B. Douglas, Lorenzo Forni, Jagadeesh Gokhale, and Laurence J. Kotlikoff. 1999. "The Adequacy of Life Insurance: Evidence from the Health and Retirement Study." NBER Working Paper 7372. Cambridge, Mass.: National Bureau of Economic Research, October.

A. M. Best. 1991. *Best's Insurance Reporter.* New York.

Blomqvist, Ake. 1997. "Optimal Non-Linear Health Insurance." *Journal of Health Economics* 16 (3, June): 303–42.

Boyce, Steven, and Richard A. Ippolito. 2002. "The Cost of Pension Insurance." *Journal of Risk and Insurance* 69 (2): 121–70.

Brown, Jeffrey. 1999. "Are the Elderly Really Over-Annuitized? New Evidence on Life-Insurance and Bequests." NBER Working Paper 7193. Cambridge, Mass.: National Bureau of Economic Research, June.

Brown, Jeffrey, and Amy Finkelstein. 2003. "Why Don't People Purchase Long-Term Care Insurance?" Unpublished ms. Cambridge, Mass.: National Bureau of Economic Research.

Buffett, Warren. 1990. "Shareholders Letter." In *Berkshire Hathaway, Inc. Annual Report.* Omaha, Neb.

Cawley, John, and Tomas Philipson. 1999. "An Empirical Examination of Information Barriers to Trade in Insurance." *American Economic Review* 89 (4): 827–46.

Choi, James, David Laibson, Brigitte Madrian, and Andrew Metrick. 2002. "Defined Contribution Pensions: Plan Rules, Participant Decisions, and the Path of Least Resistance." In James Poterba, ed., *Tax Policy and the Economy,* vol. 16, pp. 67–114. Cambridge, Mass.: MIT Press.

Cochrane, John. 1995. "Time-Consistent Health Insurance." *Journal of Political Economy* 103 (3): 445–73.

Cohen, Alma, and Rajiv Dehejia. 2003. "The Effect of Automobile Insurance and Accident Liability Laws on Traffic Fatalities." NBER Working Paper 9602. Cambridge, Mass.: National Bureau of Economic Research, April.

Consumer Reports. 1998. "When It Breaks: A Smart Guide for Getting Things Fixed." *Consumer Reports* 63 (5, May): 12–18.

Curry, Pat. 2003. "Life Insurance for Kids?" Bankrate.com, September 23. Available at www.bankrate.com/brm/news/insurance/kids-life1.asp?prodtype=insur [May 6, 2004].

Cutler, David. 1996. "Why Don't Markets Insure Long-Term Risk?" Unpublished ms. Harvard University.

———. 2002. "Public Policy for Health Care." In Alan Auerbach and Martin Feldstein, eds., *Handbook of Public Economics,* vol. 4. Amsterdam: Elsevier.

Cutler, David M., and Jonathan Gruber. 1996. "Does Public Insurance Crowd out Private Insurance?" *Quarterly Journal of Economics* 111 (2): 391–430.

Cutler, David, and Richard Zeckhauser. 2000. "The Anatomy of Insurance." In Anthony Culyer and Joseph Newhouse, eds., *Handbook of Health Economics,* vol. IA, pp. 563–643. Amsterdam: Elsevier.

Davidoff, Thomas, Jeffrey Brown, and Peter Diamond. 2003. "Annuities and Individual Welfare." Unpublished ms. University of California, Berkeley, May.

Encyclopaedia Britannica Company. 1910. *Encyclopaedia Britannica,* 11th ed., pp. 656–80. New York.

Feldstein, Martin, and Bernard Friedman. 1977. "Tax Subsidies, the Rational Demand for Insurance, and the Health Care Crisis." *Journal of Public Economics* 7 (2): 155–78.

Finkelstein, Amy, and Kathleen McGarry. 2003. "Private Information and Its Effect on Equilibrium: New Evidence from Long-Term Care Insurance." NBER Working Paper 9957. Cambridge, Mass.: National Bureau of Economic Research, September.

Gilbert, D. T., E. C. Pinel, T. D. Wilson, S. J. Blumberg, and T. P. Wheatley. 2002. "Durability Bias in Affective Forecasting." In Thomas Gilovich, Dale Griffin, and Daniel Kahneman, eds., *Heuristics and Biases: The Psychology of Intuitive Judgment,* pp. 292–312. Cambridge, U.K.: Cambridge University Press.

Herring, Bradley. 2001. "Does Access to Charity Care for the Uninsured Crowd Out Private Health Insurance Coverage?" Unpublished ms. Yale University.

Huber, Peter W. 1988. *Liability: The Legal Revolution and Its Consequences.* Basic Books.

Institute of Medicine. 2003. *Hidden Costs, Value Lost: Uninsurance in America.* Washington.

Insurance Information Institute. 2003. "Facts and Statistics on Homeowners Insurance." New York. Available at www.iii.org/media/facts/statsbyissue/homeowners [December 20, 2003].

Insurance Research Council. 2002. *Trends in Auto Injury Claims, 2002 Edition.* Malvern, Pa.

Kahneman, Daniel, and Amos Tversky. 1979. "Prospect Theory: An Analysis of Decision under Risk." *Econometrica* 47 (2, March): 263–91.

Kaiser Family Foundation and Health Research and Educational Trust. 2003. *Employer Health Benefits: 2003 Annual Survey.* Washington.

Kunreuther, Howard, and others. 1978. *Disaster Insurance Protection: Public Policy Lessons.* Hoboken, N.J.: Wiley Interscience.

Mello, Michelle M., David M. Studdert, and Troyen A. Brennan. 2003. "The New Medical Malpractice Crisis." *New England Journal of Medicine* 348 (23, June 5): 2281–84.

Mitchell, Olivia, James Poterba, Mark Warshawsky, and Jeffrey Brown. 1999. "New Evidence on the Money's Worth of Individual Annuities." *American Economic Review* 89 (5, December): 1299–318.

National Center for Health Statistics. 2003. *Health United States.* Hyattsville, Md.: Centers for Disease Control and Prevention.

Pauly, Mark V. 1986. "Taxation, Health Insurance, and Market Failure in the Medical Economy." *Journal of Economic Literature* 24 (2): 629–75.

———. 1990. "The Rational Nonpurchase of Long-Term Care Insurance." *Journal of Political Economy* 98 (11): 153–68.

Pauly, Mark V., Howard Kunreuther, and Richard Hirth. 1995. "Guaranteed Renewability in Insurance." *Journal of Risk and Uncertainty* 10 (2): 143–56.

Pauly, Mark V., and Yuhuj Zeng. 2003. "Adverse Selection and the Challenges to Stand-Alone Prescription Drug Insurance." NBER Working Paper 9919. Cambridge, Mass.: National Bureau of Economic Research, August.

Rask, Kevin, and Kimberly Rask. 2000. "Public Insurance Substituting for Private Insurance: New Evidence Regarding Public Hospitals, Uncompensated Care Funds, and Medicaid." *Journal of Health Economics* 19 (March): 1–31.

Samuelson, William, and Richard Zeckhauser. 1988. "Status Quo Bias in Decision Making." *Journal of Risk and Uncertainty* 1 (1, March): 7–59.

Tversky, Amos, and Daniel Kahneman. 1974. "Judgment under Uncertainty: Heuristics and Biases." *Science* 185: 1124–31.

U.S. Department of Health and Human Services, Health Care Financing Administration. 1984. *Long-Term Care Financing and Delivery Systems.* Washington: Government Printing Office.

U.S. Environmental Protection Agency. 1990. *Environmental Investments: The Cost of a Clean Environment.* Washington.

U.S. General Accounting Office. 1986. *Liability Insurance: Changes in Policies Set Limits on Risks to Insurers.* Washington.

———. 1988. *Hazardous Waste: The Cost and Availability of Pollution Insurance.* Washington.

———. 2002. *Catastrophe Insurance Risks: The Role of Risk-Linked Securities and Factors Affecting Their Use.* Washington.

———. 2003. *Flood Insurance: Challenges Facing the National Flood Insurance Program.* Washington, April 1.

Wettlaufer, Dale. 1998. "Berkshire: Part 4, Super-Cat." *Motley Fool*, December 9. Available at www.fool.com/BoringPort/1998/BoringPort981209.htm [May 5, 2004].

Woolhandler, Steffie, and David U. Himmelstein. 1989. "A National Health Program: Northern Light at the End of the Tunnel." *Journal of the American Medical Association* 262 (October 20): 2136–37.

Yaari, Menahem E. 1965. "Uncertain Lifetime, Life Insurance, and the Theory of the Consumer." *Review of Economic Studies* 32 (2): 137–50.

Zagaski, Chester A. 1992. *Environmental Risk and Insurance*. Chelsea, Mich.: Lewis Publishers.

The Crisis in Medical Malpractice Insurance

PATRICIA M. DANZON,
ANDREW J. EPSTEIN,
and SCOTT J. JOHNSON

SINCE 1999, MANY states have experienced a "crisis" in medical malpractice insurance. The median premium increase for internists, general surgeons, and obstetricians-gynecologists increased from 0–2 percent in 1996–97 to 17–18 percent in 2003, climbing to 60 percent in some states in 2001–02, after adjusting for inflation. In December 2001, St. Paul Travelers, which was the largest malpractice insurer operating in forty-five states, announced its decision to withdraw from the market, citing losses of millions of dollars on its medical liability business. Two other major insurers— PHICO and Frontier Insurance Group—exited from the market entirely. Faced with insolvency, the Medical Inter-Insurance Exchange reorganized and restricted its operations to New Jersey. In some states, including Pennsylvania and New Jersey, physicians went on strike, threatened to leave the state, and discontinued high-risk services; however, a recent General Accounting Office study finds no conclusive evidence of widespread, measurable effects of the crisis on the availability of medical services.[1]

This most recent malpractice insurance crisis followed an unusually long period of flat or modest increases in premium rates and widespread availability of insurance, which, in turn, followed a severe crisis of affordability

The authors would like to thank the Wharton Financial Institutions Center for providing financial support and the Huebner Foundation for providing access to data from the National Association of Insurance Commissioners.

1. General Accounting Office (2003a, pp. 5, 12, 13).

in the 1980s and a severe crisis of affordability and availability in the mid-1970s. In response to these earlier crises, many states adopted reforms of tort law that were intended to reduce the level and unpredictability of claims, including caps on awards for noneconomic damages, collateral source offset, and shorter statutes of limitations. At the same time, some states adopted measures to assure the availability of insurance and reduce its cost to physicians. Joint underwriting associations serve as residual market mechanisms for physicians who are unable to obtain coverage in the voluntary market. Patient compensation funds limit the physician's liability at some threshold (for example, $200,000 per claim); additional compensation to the patient up to a higher threshold (for example, $1 million) is financed through assessments on all physicians practicing in the state. By shifting costs from individual defendants to all practicing physicians, with assessments levied on a pay-as-you-go basis, these funds produced short-term relief for physicians facing the highest premiums, particularly specialists in urban areas.

In addition to these statutory changes, malpractice insurance markets adopted voluntary changes to reduce insurer risk and establish more robust sources of coverage. Most insurers replaced the occurrence policy form with the claims-made policy form, thereby shifting from insurer to policyholder the risk related to losses incurred, but not reported, during the policy period.[2] In addition, in many states physicians established their own physician-owned mutuals, reciprocals, and risk retention groups. These physician-directed companies replaced the traditional commercial stock companies, many of which either withdrew or sharply curtailed their malpractice exposure during the crises of the 1970s and 1980s. In theory, physician-owned companies may have informational or risk-sharing advantages over stock companies in writing a line such as medical malpractice insurance.[3]

The most recent malpractice insurance crisis raises the question of whether these tort and insurance market reforms have achieved their goals of moderating premium increases. A General Accounting Office report on the current crisis concludes that, although physicians in most states have

2. A claims-made policy covers all claims filed in the year that the policy is written, provided that the policyholder had coverage with this insurer during the year in which the incident occurred. An occurrence policy covers all claims related to incidents in the year in which the policy is written. Thus if a physician with claims-made coverage switches insurers or retires, he or she generally buys "tail coverage" to cover any future claims that may be filed related to his or her prior practice.

3. Danzon (1984); Doherty and Dionne (1993).

Figure 1. Growth in Premiums for Three Physician Specialties in States with and without Caps on Noneconomic Damages, 2001–02

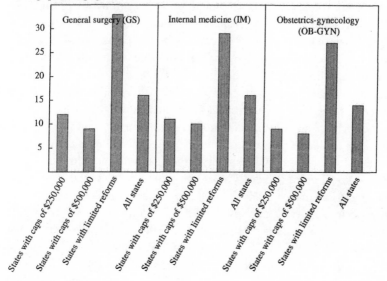

Source: General Accounting Office (2003b, p. 33). General Accounting Office analysis of Medical Liability Monitor base premium rates, excluding discounts, rebates, and surcharges, reported for the specialties of general surgery, internal medicine, and obstetrics-gynecology. Premiums are adjusted for inflation to 2002 dollars.

experienced some increase in premium rates since 1999, the between-state variation has been significant.[4] From 1999 to 2002, the largest writer of medical malpractice premiums for general surgeons in Dade County, Florida, increased premiums 75 percent, while Minnesota's largest insurer for general surgeons increased premiums only 2 percent for a similar level of coverage. Moreover, the rate of premium increase was significantly lower in states that enacted tort reforms, specifically, the placement of caps on awards for noneconomic damages (see figure 1). Although this evidence suggests that caps on awards for noneconomic damages slowed the growth in premiums, such conclusions remain tentative because the analysis is based on only one year of premium increases and does not control for other factors.

4. General Accounting Office (2003b, p. 10).

Viewing the current crisis from a longer-term perspective, the pattern of premium increases over the last decade—flat or falling rates for several years, followed by sharp increases—resembles the typical insurance cycle that has been experienced in other "long-tailed" lines of liability insurance, in particular, general liability (including product liability) insurance. Several theories have been developed to explain these alternating periods of soft markets with intense competition and flat or falling premiums followed by hard markets with sharp premium increases, insurer exits, and restricted availability. The "capacity constraint" theory posits that hard markets are triggered by periodic exogenous shocks to insurer capital, often due to unanticipated shifts in liability rules that apply retroactively and render prior insurer reserves inadequate, or to declines in asset valuations and investment yields that erode capital.[5] Given regulatory constraints on permissible premium-to-capital ratios and costs of adding external capital, the contraction of insurer capital, in turn, leads to a reduction in the supply of insurance and an increase in its price. Cummins and Danzon extend this model to include insolvency risk of insurers and demand for insurance that depends on the firm's financial quality.[6] In this model, a decline in insurer capital leads to a decline in the price of insurance, as measured by the loading charge; premium rates may, nevertheless, increase to the extent that expected loss costs increase.

Less attention has been paid to soft markets. One exception is Harrington and Danzon, who develop and test alternative theories of excessive competition.[7] They hypothesize that if some insurers undercharge, due to either inexperience or excessive risk taking, then other insurers will rationally cut their prices below short-run marginal cost in order to preserve quasi rents on their established business. Clearly, soft-market periods of pricing below short-run marginal cost cannot continue indefinitely. Whether this excessive price cutting ultimately contributes to more-than-corrective price increases (in excess of increases in prospective loss costs) and to insurer exits, especially by insurers with low levels of investment and hence low quasi rents, remains an untested hypothesis.

In this paper, we first document the extent of the recent crisis, in terms of premium increases and insurer exits, and then examine the role of several possible contributing factors. In particular, we examine the contribution

5. Grøn (1989, 1994); Winter (1994).
6. Cummins and Danzon (1997).
7. Harrington and Danzon (1994).

of shocks to insurer capital, inexperience, and excessive risk taking during the soft market. These theories of abnormal pricing are tested against the null hypothesis: that the premium increases simply reflect increases in expected loss costs and declines in expected investment yields. We also examine the extent to which tort and insurance market reforms mitigated—or exacerbated—premium increases and insurer exits over the period 1994–2003. Specifically, we test for the effects of caps on awards for noneconomic and total damages, collateral source offset, limits on joint and several liability, and whether the state has a joint underwriting association or a patient compensation fund. We also test whether physician-directed companies behave differently from commercial companies.

Our data on the level of and increases in medical malpractice premiums are from Medical Liability Monitor, which reports premium rates by state for three major specialties: internists, general surgeons, and obstetricians-gynecologists. Our measures of insurer experience are from the annual statement data reported by all insurers to state regulators, as compiled by the National Association of Insurance Commissioners (NAIC).

The structure of the paper is as follows. The first section describes our data. The second section outlines the evidence on the extent of the crisis in terms of trends in premiums, in insurer losses paid and losses incurred, and in number of exits. The third section outlines a model of insurance pricing, extending the standard actuarial model to incorporate the theories of hard and soft markets. The fourth section reports results of multivariate analysis of premium rate increases and insurer exits. A final section concludes.

Data

Our data on medical malpractice premiums are from Medical Liability Monitor, which reports premium rates by state or territory, for a standard claims-made policy ($1 million per claim; $3 million aggregate for the policy year) for three major specialties: internists, general surgeons, and obstetricians-gynecologists. These data are collected by survey from one or more leading insurers in each state. These premium rates should be reasonably representative of rates for each state; however, the number of physicians written at each rate is not reported.[8] These rates do not reflect discounts and

---

8. In states with multiple rating territories, we included the highest and lowest rates. For analyses that require a single rate per specialty per state, in cases where we have rates from

dividends to policyholders; to the extent that such discounts and dividends became less frequent in the hard market, the rate increases reported in our data may underestimate the real increase in cost to physicians. In a few states, the Medical Liability Monitor rates are for coverage limits other than the standard $1 million/$3 million claims-made policy; possible effects of this on our analysis are noted below. The data on premiums are for select years between 1994 and 2003. All current dollar values are adjusted to constant dollars using the GDP deflator.

Our data on malpractice insurers are from the National Association of Insurance Commissioners database, for the period 1993–2002. This database includes the annual financial reports that all licensed insurers are required to file in each state in which they are licensed. It thus includes many more firms than the Medical Liability Monitor data. For each firm, the NAIC reports state-level data on premiums written and losses incurred for medical malpractice, countrywide data on medical malpractice loss forecast revisions from Schedule P, and countrywide data on all lines of insurer capital, investment yields, and assets. We include all firms that reported at least $100,000 in net medical malpractice premiums written (in 2002 dollars) in at least one state. We categorize a firm as exiting from a state in year t if the firm's direct premiums written dropped below $100,000 in year t and remained below that threshold in that state for the remainder of our observation period, having previously exceeded the $100,000 threshold.

Although the NAIC database includes all licensed insurers, a significant fraction of malpractice insurance is not captured by the NAIC data. In particular, if physicians obtained coverage through self-insurance arrangements of hospitals or health maintenance organizations, and these arrangements were not subject to state regulation, they are not represented in our data. Also excluded from the NAIC data are most state-run pools, including joint underwriting associations and patient compensation funds. Since the NAIC data report each firm's aggregate premium and loss experience, they cannot be disaggregated into changes in premium rates versus number of policyholders or limits of coverage. Our analysis of premium increases therefore focuses on the subsample of firms that are represented in the Medical Liability Monitor data for which we have matching NAIC data on firm characteristics.

---

multiple insurers or multiple rating territories, we calculate a simple average of the rates reported for that specialty and state, since we lack information on the number of physicians by insurer and territory, which is necessary to calculate a weighted average.

Trends in Premiums, Insurers' Losses, and Exits

In this section we document the extent of the recent crisis in malpractice insurance in terms of premium increases and insurer exits to set the stage for the presentation of theoretical models of premium setting.

Premium Levels and Increases

Table 1 shows the median premium rate across states for $1 million/$3 million claims-made coverage, for internal medicine, general surgery, and obstetrics-gynecology for each available year between 1994 and 2003, in constant 2002 dollars. The table also shows the twenty-fifth, fiftieth, and seventy-fifth percentiles and the maximum percentage increase from the distribution of rate increases across states. In 1994 the median premium rates were $6,075 for internal medicine, $22,269 for general surgery, and $39,122 for obstetrics-gynecology. By 2003 the median premium rates were $9,000 for internal medicine, $33,297 for general surgery, and $53,630 for obstetrics-gynecology. Thus for the median state, the cumulative increases over the nine-year period were 52 percent for internal medicine, 47 percent for general surgery, and 35 percent for obstetrics-gynecology, in excess of general inflation.[9] The fact that the increases were concentrated in the last four years rather than spread evenly over the nine years may have limited the ability of physicians to pass on the increases to patients through higher fees for medical services, thereby increasing the burden on physicians and contributing to the sense of crisis. Still, for the typical state, the magnitude of these premium increases does not appear to have constituted a crisis.

However, states at or above the seventy-fifth percentile of annual increases experienced cumulative rate increases over the nine-year period of more than 90 percent for internal medicine and general surgery and more than 74 percent for obstetrics-gynecology, with increases exceeding 10 percent in 2001 and 20 percent in 2002 and 2003, after inflation. The maximum annual increases exceeded 60 percent in 2002. Thus the distribution of premium increases was highly skewed, with a few states facing extreme increases, particularly in the last two years. Presumably, the sense of crisis was greatest in states facing high percentage increases on top of high pre-

9. Our estimates of cumulative percentage increases, by specialty and state, are approximate because the Medical Liability Monitor insurers surveyed are not necessarily the same in each year. Thus the cumulative percentages may reflect differences in territories or insurer selection policies as well as underlying rate increases.

Table 1. Average Level of Malpractice Premiums and Percentage Increase, by Specialty and Selected Year, 1994–2003[a]

| Year and specialty | Median premium rate (U.S. dollars) | Annual percentage change | | | |
		Twenty-fifth percentile	Median	Seventy-fifth percentile	Maximum
1994					
Internal medicine	6,075	0.0	5.4	9.7	27.8
General surgery	22,269	0.0	2.5	6.5	35.5
Obstetrics and gynecology	39,122	0.0	3.0	6.9	40.0
1996					
Internal medicine	6,367	0.0	2.4	7.1	16.0
General surgery	24,598	0.0	2.2	6.9	34.3
Obstetrics and gynecology	39,502	0.0	0.9	5.0	16.0
1997					
Internal medicine	6,706	0.0	0.3	5.1	34.9
General surgery	24,067	0.0	0.6	5.0	15.0
Obstetrics and gynecology	39,318	0.0	0.0	4.3	15.0
2000					
Internal medicine	6,230	n.a.	n.a.	n.a.	n.a.
General surgery	24,066	n.a.	n.a.	n.a.	n.a.
Obstetrics and gynecology	40,503	n.a.	n.a.	n.a.	n.a.
2001					
Internal medicine	6,970	0.0	6.4	12.5	62.5
General surgery	26,030	0.0	6.1	13.5	62.5
Obstetrics and gynecology	40,569	0.0	5.0	11.5	62.5
2002					
Internal medicine	7,544	6.5	13.0	33.7	59.3
General surgery	27,922	5.0	11.0	29.3	57.5
Obstetrics and gynecology	42,928	6.0	11.2	26.5	60.7
2003					
Internal medicine	9,000	8.5	16.9	25.5	43.8
General surgery	33,297	10.8	18.0	25.2	42.0
Obstetrics and gynecology	53,630	8.9	16.8	23.4	42.0

Source: Medical Liability Monitor annual surveys. Authors' calculations of distribution across states.
n.a. Not available.
a. Rates for $1 million/$3 million claims-made policy, unadjusted for discounts and dividends, by state. Premiums are reported in 2002 dollars except for 2003, which is unadjusted for inflation.

mium levels. In general, however, the rate of premium increase was greater for states that started from relatively low premium levels: the Pearson correlation between 1994 premium level and 1994–2003 premium increase is –0.30 for internal medicine, –0.25 for general surgery, and –0.38 for obstetrics-gynecology.

The highest cumulative increases were 328 percent in Pennsylvania and 301 percent in South Carolina. Both of these states have joint underwriting associations, and Pennsylvania also has a patient compensation fund (formerly the "catastrophic," or "cat," fund, now MCare). In fact, the high premium increase in Pennsylvania is misleading because it reflects in part the increase in the required limits on physicians' basic coverage, from $200,000/$600,000 in 1993 to $500,000/$1.5 million in 2003; thus the increase reported in table 1 overstates the increase for constant limits of coverage. Nevertheless, the surcharge for the catastrophic fund also increased. Summing the base rate and the surcharge in Pennsylvania, and averaging across the companies for which we have Medical Liability Monitor rates, the increase in total premiums between 1993 and 2003 ranged from 209 to 273 percent, depending on specialty and territory. The intra-specialty range of rates across territories also increased.[10] Although South Carolina had the second highest rate of increase, absolute levels were only $18,000 for obstetrics-gynecology in 2003.

Aggregate Trends in Insurer Losses and Premiums

Figure 2 shows trends in aggregate loss paid, loss plus loss-adjustment expense incurred, and direct premiums written, summed over all insurers in our NAIC sample. Loss paid trended up gradually, with sharper increases in 1998, 2000, and 2002. By contrast, incurred loss plus loss-adjustment expense, which reflects insurer estimates of losses on policies written in that calendar year plus any adjustments to reserves for prior years, declined between 1993 and 1994, despite an increase in losses paid in that year. From 1995 through 1999, incurred loss plus loss-adjustment expense tracked paid losses reasonably closely, but for 2001–02 incurred losses far overshot paid losses. Aggregate premiums actually declined between 1993

10. According to the Medical Liability Monitor data, the intra-specialty range of premiums charged by the Pennsylvania Medical Society's medical malpractice insurer (PMSLIC) for base coverage and the mandatory catastrophic fund surcharge grew from 194 to 250 percent for internal medicine, 184 to 239 percent for general surgery, and 217 to 279 percent for obstetrics-gynecology, from 1994 to 2003.

Figure 2. Aggregate Trends in Premiums and Losses

Billions of 2002 U.S. Dollars

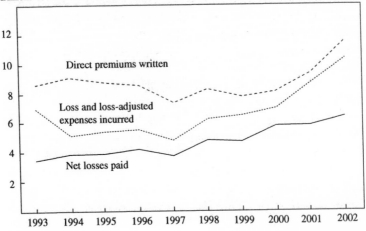

Source: NAIC annual statements.

and 1997, stayed roughly flat through 2000, and shot up in 2001–02. Because all three series reflect changes in volume as well as price or loss per unit of coverage, these trends cannot be interpreted as showing trends in premium rates or loss per policy. However, since any change in volume applies to all three series, comparison between them is informative. This comparison shows that premiums written and, to a lesser extent, losses incurred were more cyclical than paid losses. This is consistent with the hypothesis of excessive price cutting during the soft market, possibly with underreporting of incurred loss in order to conceal inadequate pricing.

Figure 3 shows trends in aggregate initial loss forecasts (loss forecast in year t) and the loss forecast two years later (loss forecast in year $t + 2$). For claims-made coverage, which was the norm for medical malpractice insurance by this time, the number of claims (claim frequency) is known by the end of the policy year, and only the average payment per claim (claim severity) remains unknown, due to lags in the disposition of claims.[11] Nevertheless, initial loss forecasts were quite inaccurate, following a marked cyclical pattern of underestimates in 1991, overestimates in 1992–94, and persistent underestimates through 2000. By contrast, losses incurred as of $t + 2$ trended upward quite steadily, except for a dip in 1996.

11. Insurer risk related to claims incurred but not reported during the policy year was eliminated by switching from occurrence to claims-made coverage.

Figure 3. Aggregate Trends in Loss Forecast and Forecast Error

Millions of 2002 U.S. Dollars

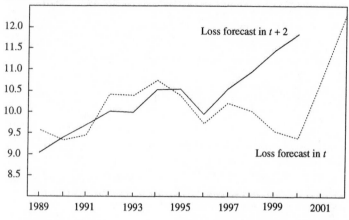

Source: NAIC annual statements.

Remarkably, from 1997 to 2000, the aggregate initial loss forecast declined, despite a steady and sharp increase in losses incurred as of $t + 2$ and in paid losses. This evidence is consistent with initial understatement of loss forecasts, possibly to conceal inadequate premiums. After 2000 a very sharp increase in initial loss forecasts was necessary to bring the initial forecast more in line with subsequent realizations.

The industry aggregate forecast error in figure 3 may understate the full extent of initial under-reserving by some firms, to the extent that negative forecast errors (initial overestimates) by some firms offset positive errors (initial underestimates) by other firms. To provide evidence on this, figure 4 disaggregates the industry aggregate forecast error into its positive and negative components. In fact, although the overall error was near or below zero from 1989 though 1995, this reflects the offsetting of positive errors by negative errors. The theory of competitive price cutting suggests that if some firms in the industry underestimate losses and set low prices, either intentionally or due to ignorance, this may suffice to set off a price war as other firms match price cuts to preserve market share and quasi rents. Between 1993 and 2000, paid losses increased, while aggregate premiums written fell. This evidence of significant positive forecast errors by some firms throughout the period may explain the period of flat or declining premiums, despite steadily rising paid losses.

Figure 4. Aggregate Trends in Loss Forecast and Forecast Error

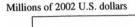

Millions of 2002 U.S. dollars

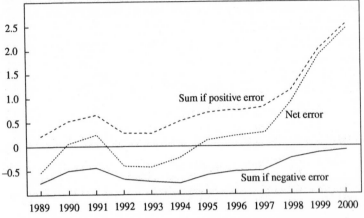

Source: NAIC annual statements.

From the NAIC data, we cannot disaggregate trends in total paid losses into trends in the frequency and severity, respectively, of claims. Limited evidence of this decomposition is available from the Physician Insurers Association of America (PIAA) for its member companies and from Bovbjerg and Bartow.[12] Claim frequency (number of claims per physician) countrywide reportedly rose little after the mid-1990s, although some states saw increases. By contrast, claim severity increased dramatically. National data from the *Jury Verdict Reporter* show that the median verdict in cases taken to trial where the jury finds in favor of the patient more than doubled between 1995 and 2000, reaching about $1 million per case. The mean verdict was even higher. However, because *Jury Verdict Reporter* relies heavily on voluntary submission of information by trial attorneys, levels of and trends in payments may be upward biased if attorneys tend to report only the largest cases that they wish to publicize.[13]

More representative data on total claim payments, including jury verdicts and out-of-court settlements, are available from the PIAA Data Sharing Project. This shows that median claim payments, in nominal dollars, increased from $50,000 in 1990 to about $175,000 in 2001, more than a threefold increase, while mean claim payments increased from roughly

12. Bovbjerg and Bartow (2003, pp. 25–27).
13. Bovbjerg and Bartow (2003, p. 26).

Figure 5. Trends in Mean and Median Payment per Claim, 1988–2001

U.S. dollars

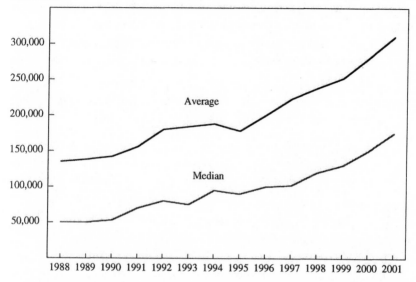

Source: Physician Insurers Association of America Data Sharing Project in Smarr (2003, p. 15); Bovbjerg and Bartow (2003, p. 27).

$145,000 in 1990 to $315,000 in 2001 (see figure 5). Moreover, these upward trends were steady, except for a one-year drop in 1995. Claims exceeding $1 million were about 8 percent of all claims paid for individual practitioners; the percentage doubled in the past four years.[14] Assuming that these trends in claim severity for the PIAA companies are reasonably representative of experience for all malpractice insurers, the decline in initial loss forecasts from 1994 through 2000 was at odds with available evidence on trends in paid claims.

Since competitive premiums reflect the discounted value of expected losses, trends in expected investment income may have contributed to this apparent failure of premiums and initial loss forecasts to increase with paid losses. The General Accounting Office reports that a significant source of loss for medical malpractice insurers has been the relative decline in their bond-weighted investment portfolios due to declining bond yields since 2000. Although equity values increased through 1999, PIAA reports that 79 percent of its insurers' assets were in bonds.[15] If this is typical of most insur-

14. Smarr (2003, p. 19).
15. General Accounting Office (2003b); Smarr (2003, p. 8).

ers, the increase in equity values in the 1990s would have had only a modest effect on the portfolio of malpractice insurers. Declining bond yields may have contributed but surely cannot fully explain the average increase in premium rates after 2000 or the extreme experience in some states.

Insurers and Insurer Exits

Since the extent of the crisis varies significantly across states, our analysis of insurer exits is at the state level and uses the firm-state as the unit of observation. Recall that our NAIC sample includes all firms that reported at least $100,000 in net premiums written in at least one state over our 1994–2002 sample period. Our sample includes more than 300 firms per year and 1,619–1,945 firm-states per year. The majority of these firms write a very low volume of premiums, and some may be "shells" that exist mainly to keep active a state license. However, for medical malpractice, many of these small firms are physician initiated, quasi self-insurance arrangements that play an important role in the malpractice insurance market.

The NAIC data characterize firms as stock, mutual, risk retention group, or other type of company. Unfortunately, this categorization does not reliably identify physician-directed firms. Many physician-owned companies started out as mutuals or reciprocals but by 2002 had converted to stock companies and hence cannot be reliably distinguished from commercial firms in the NAIC database. In 2002 sixty-four of the 309 firms (20.7 percent) writing medical malpractice policies were categorized as mutuals, reciprocals, or risk retention groups; these firms accounted for 35 percent of the volume of premiums. By contrast, PIAA reports that physician-owned firms accounted for about 60 percent of the market.[16] To provide a more accurate measure of physician-directed companies, we augment the NAIC designation of mutual, reciprocal, or risk retention group with a listing of physician-directed companies provided to us by PIAA. Using this combined categorization, eighty firms (26 percent) were physician directed, and these firms accounted for 47.4 percent of the direct premiums written. Because the PIAA list only includes firms with premiums over $1 million in 2002, we almost certainly undercount physician-directed small firms. The percentage of premiums written by physician-owned firms varied widely across states, from almost 12 percent in Wyoming to 85 percent in Oklahoma.

16. General Accounting Office (2003b, pp. 2, 5).

Given the large number of firms that write a very low volume of premiums, the definition of an insurer exit is somewhat arbitrary. Here we define a firm as exiting a state in year *t* if its direct premiums written fell below $100,000 in year *t* and did not exceed that threshold during our period of analysis. We define a firm as entering in year *t* if its net premiums written in a state exceeded $100,000 for the first time in year *t*.

In table 2, the first panel shows entries and exits by firms at the state level (firm-states), and the second panel shows entries and exits by firms writing any malpractice insurance countrywide (national firms), for 1995–2002. For these firm-state-year exits, there was clearly a trend toward more exits from 1999 onward, with more than 200 exits in three of the four subsequent years, compared with 60–136 in the previous years. At the same time, other firms entered the market, with the largest number of entries in 2002, such that the total number of firm-state-years tended to increase over the period. Two caveats are in order in reviewing these data. First, the results are sensitive to the definition of entry and exit. Second, entry by small, new firms does not necessarily indicate a healthy insurance market, to the extent that the new firms are quasi self-insurance arrangements adopted to fill a void left by the exit of larger, more diversified firms.

If we restrict the analysis of exits to large firms, defined as firms that wrote at least $1 million in direct premiums in at least one state during our sample period, there were 6,445 large firm-state-years over the 1996–2002 period. Of these, 378 firms, or 6 percent, exited during the period, and of these 207, or 55 percent, exited in 2001–02. The number of large firm-state-years increased from 862 in 1996 to a maximum of 963 in 2001 and declined to 938 in 2002. Thus the exiting large firms were not fully replaced by entering large firms, resulting in a reduction of twenty-five in the number of large firm-state-years in 2002.

In order to distinguish the exit of a firm from an individual state from the exit of an insurer countrywide (national exit), table 2 also reports the number of exits and entries by year with firms aggregated to the national level. Thus a national exit occurs when a firm withdraws from all states. There was at most a slight increase in the number of national exits in the hard market of the early 2000s; however, conclusions are tentative due to the small sample size.

Another measure of the disruption caused by insurer exits is the share of direct premiums written by the exiting firms. Table 3 reports the mean and

Table 2. Annual Entries and Exits of Medical Malpractice Insurers, by Firm-States and National Firms, 1995–2002

Year	Firm-states			National firms		
	Firms	*Exits*	*Entries*	*Firms*	*Exits*	*Entries*
1995	1,619	60	195	227	9	17
1996	1,665	110	203	229	12	10
1997	1,624	136	170	218	22	17
1998	1,728	112	214	219	12	13
1999	1,699	204	183	209	24	16
2000	1,772	157	178	201	22	9
2001	1,802	246	198	198	18	11
2002	1,945	311	339	206	25	25

Source: NAIC annual statements. Authors' calculations.

Table 3. Direct Premiums Written by Exiting Firms, 1994–2003[a]

Millions of U.S. dollars

Year	Direct premiums written		Percentage of premiums		
	Mean	*Median*	*National*	*Mean state*	*Maximum state*
1994	3.51	0.59	25.0	29.0	49.5
1995	3.69	0.21	3.1	1.6	42.3
1996	0.50	0.24	0.8	2.0	30.5
1997	2.94	0.21	6.0	5.0	34.7
1998	0.39	0.20	0.7	1.2	4.7
1999	1.62	0.23	5.0	3.7	42.0
2000	0.92	0.25	2.3	3.3	27.6
2001	3.48	0.42	13.0	10.2	51.2
2002	1.17	0.38	4.8	6.2	24.0

Source: NAIC annual statements.
a. Premiums in $t-1$ by firm-states exiting in year t.

median direct premiums written in year $t-1$ by firm-states exiting in year t, the percentages of national and state premiums written by exiting firms, and the maximum market share of exiting firms for any state. The mean premium share of exiting firms clearly was higher in 1999–2002 than in the preceding four-year period, reaching 13 percent of national premiums in 2001, the year in which St. Paul Travelers withdrew. The maximum premium share of exiting firms also reached a peak of 51 percent in 2001 and tended to be higher in the 1999–2002 period than in the previous four years, but with significant year-to-year variation. Thus the availability of medical malpractice insurance was severely disrupted by the exit of firms but was limited to a small number of states.

Theoretical Model of Malpractice Premium Setting

In the standard actuarial model of insurance rate setting,[17] the premium rate for a policy with specified limits of coverage in a given specialty-state-year reflects the discounted expected losses plus loss-adjustment expense in that state, which may depend on tort and insurance market reforms, plus adjustments for taxes and overhead. Ignoring taxes and overhead, this may be written as follows:

$$(1) \qquad P_{stm} = \alpha_1 EL_{stm} (Z_{it}) + \alpha_2 EV_{tm} + u_{stm},$$

where s is the state; t is the year; m is the medical malpractice line; P is the premium rate for a policy with given limits of coverage; EL is the expected loss plus loss-adjustment expense; Z is a vector of tort and insurance market reforms that affect expected losses; EV is the expected rate of return on invested assets; and u is a random error.

This standard model predicts that premium increases will parallel increases in expected losses and move inversely with expected investment income. It cannot explain the observed cycles and crises in markets for liability insurance, including medical malpractice. Several theories have been developed to explain, respectively, the hard phase of insurance cycles, with overshooting on prices and insurer exits, and the soft phase, with undercharging relative to discounted expected loss costs.

Capacity Constraints

The "capacity constraint" theory of hard markets starts off by noting that insurance risk for liability lines is imperfectly diversifiable due to factors such as socioeconomic trends that affect all policyholders similarly.[18] Raising external capital to pay unexpected losses is costly due to taxes and other factors. Insurers therefore hold capital reserves to ensure that they can pay claims that exceed expected values. For reasons of both internal solvency and regulatory requirements, insurers have a target ratio of capital to premiums. In this model, a shock to insurer capital, due to factors such as an unexpected increase in claim liabilities for prior policy years, leads to a contraction of capacity, reflected in a leftward shift of the short-run supply of insurance. This can lead to a premium increase in excess of any increase

17. For example, Myers and Cohn (1987).
18. Grøn (1989, 1994); Winter (1994).

in expected losses and, in the extreme, to insurer exit. However, the empirical tests of this model, using industry aggregate data, are inconclusive: the evidence supports the prediction of an inverse relation between the price of insurance and capitalization for cycles prior to 1980, but not for the liability crisis in the 1980s.[19] Other evidence confirms the theory for short-tail lines but not for long-tail lines.[20]

Cummins and Danzon extend this model to incorporate insolvency risk of insurers and policyholder demand for insurance that is positively related to the firm's financial quality—that is, insurance is viewed as risky debt.[21] This model predicts a positive relationship between a firm's financial quality and the price that policyholders are willing to pay for the insurance. The empirical analysis of firm-level data for the period 1980–88 is consistent with this model of insurance as risky debt. Note that although these studies measure the price of insurance by the loading charge (ratio of premiums to discounted losses), this measure is positively correlated with the absolute level of premium rates, controlling for expected losses. Thus the capacity constraint model predicts a negative relationship between the premium rate for given limits of coverage and the (lagged) capital-premium ratio, whereas the risky-debt model predicts a positive relationship.

Underpricing due to Moral Hazard or Inexperience

Harrington and Danzon find some evidence to support the hypothesis that price cutting during the soft market may reflect moral hazard or inexperienced forecasting that can cause some firms to price too low, leading to matching price cuts by other firms in order to protect their market share and quasi rents in the short run.[22] This analysis does not test whether undercharging during soft markets contributes to hard markets, as these risky firms either exit or raise premiums. Here we provide rough tests for the hypothesis that underpricing during soft markets may contribute to the premium increases and firm exits that characterize hard markets. Specifically, we test for the effects of loss forecast errors on prior policies as well as the firm's experience and indicators of moral hazard or risk taking.

19. Winter (1994).
20. Grøn (1994).
21. Cummins and Danzon (1997).
22. Harrington and Danzon (1994).

Industry Structure and Corporate Control

A question of considerable research and policy interest is the extent to which physician-owned firms, which were formed in response to prior crises, behaved differently from commercial firms during the most recent crisis. Theory suggests that mutuals may have informational advantages in selecting and disciplining their policyholders. They may also be better bearers of nondiversifiable, socioeconomic risk,[23] for example, if they are able to assess their members if prior reserves prove to be inadequate due to unanticipated trends in legal rulings. However, physician-owned companies take many forms and may have different strategies. Some are highly selective, whereas others are not. Moreover, many have become stock firms. For other lines of insurance and other types of financial institutions, such conversions have raised questions of expropriation of policyholders. Thus it is an open question whether physician-directed companies now behave differently from stock companies.

Premium rate increases are sometimes blamed on insurer market power. We therefore test for effects of insurer concentration, as measured by the Herfindahl index of premium volume, at the state level.

Tort Reforms and Insurance Pooling Mechanisms

Many states enacted tort reforms in response to prior crises. Previous studies have found that caps on awards for noneconomic damages did reduce claim severity in the 1980s, and the bivariate analysis of the General Accounting Office suggests that states with caps under $300,000 experienced lower premium increases in the 1990s.[24] Caps on awards for total damages may plausibly have a similar or greater effect, depending on the threshold. Collateral source offset is also found to reduce the frequency and severity of claims;[25] however, at most it constrains payments for economic loss, so the effects on growth in total premiums are uncertain. Limitations on joint and several liability could reduce physician premiums by limiting the plaintiff's ability to shift liability to the deepest-pocket defendant, who may be only tangentially related to the incident.

---

23. Danzon (1984); Doherty and Dionne (1993).
24. Danzon (1984); Zuckerman, Bovbjerg, and Sloan (1990); General Accounting Office (2003b).
25. Danzon (1984).

Joint underwriting associations, like any residual market mechanism, may solve an availability problem in the short run. But because the premiums of joint underwriting associations are usually flat rated or at most roughly differentiated by specialty and territory, such arrangements may ultimately increase total malpractice payouts by subsidizing the highest-cost doctors; depending on incentive structures, pooling arrangements may also weaken incentives for optimal cost control in managing claims. In many states, joint underwriting associations were set up on a pay-as-you-go basis, which bought short-term relief at the cost of creating unfunded liabilities that would have to be paid in the future. To the extent that these accumulated unfunded liabilities now necessitate assessments on physicians currently in practice, premium increases may be higher in states that established joint underwriting associations in the past.

Similarly, patient compensation funds shift liability for the highest tier of losses to pools that are funded on a pay-as-you-go basis, with premium surcharges that are differentiated across physicians at most by broad specialty and territory designations, not by other measures of experience. Like joint underwriting associations, such pools shift rather than reduce claim payments. In fact, such pooling arrangements may ultimately increase total losses, to the extent that the pooling of losses weakens incentives for high-risk physicians to avoid losses or reduces the incentives for the entity running the pool to manage claims, and hence may result in the assessment of larger surcharges on current physicians than would occur in the absence of pooling.

The standard premium model in equation 1 can be modified to test these various hypotheses. First differencing and dividing by the lagged value give a model of the percentage increase in premium rates per physician.[26] Our estimating equation for percentage change in premiums is thus:

$$
\begin{aligned}
(2) \quad \Delta P_{stmf} &= \alpha_1 \Delta L_{s(t-1)f} + \alpha_2 \Delta V_{(t-1)f} + \alpha_3 \Delta R_{s(t-1)f} + \alpha_4 Z_{s(t-1)} \\
&+ \alpha_5 \Delta KP_{(t-1)f} + \alpha_6 EXP_{(t-1)f} + \alpha_7 NPG_{(t-1)f} \\
&+ \alpha_8 \Delta REIN_{(t-1)f} + \alpha_9 M_f + \alpha_{10} \Delta F_{(t-1)f} + \alpha_{11} G_{(t-1)f} \\
&+ HHI_{s(t-1)} + X_{(t-1)f} + Y_t + SPEC_m + e_{stmf},
\end{aligned}
$$

where ΔP_{stmf} is the percentage change in the premium rate in state s between years $t-1$ and t for specialty m for firm f; $\Delta L_{s(t-1)f}$ is the percentage change in losses plus loss-adjustment expense incurred between $t-2$ and $t-1$;

---

26. The percentage change in any variable V is calculated as $[V_t - (V_{t-1})] \,/\, \mathrm{abs}(V_{t-1})$.

$\Delta V_{(t-1)f}$ is the percentage change in the rate of return on assets between $t-2$ and $t-1$; $\Delta R_{s(t-1)f}$ is the percentage change in losses paid between $t-2$ and $t-1$; $Z_{s(t-1)}$ is a vector of state-specific tort and insurance market reforms; $\Delta KP_{(t-1)f}$ is the percentage change in the ratio of capital to net premiums written between $t-2$ and $t-1$; $EXP_{(t-1)f}$ is firm experience equal to the quadratic of number of years since 1988 with premiums greater than \$3 million; $NPG_{(t-1)f}$ is the percentage growth in net premiums written countrywide between years $t-3$ and $t-1$; $\Delta REIN_{(t-1)f}$ is the percentage change in the ratio of reinsurance recovered to net admitted assets between $t-2$ and $t-1$; M_f is a dummy variable for a mutual or other physician-sponsored company; $\Delta F_{(t-1)f}$ is the change between $t-2$ and $t-1$ in average percentage forecast error for policy years $t-6$ through $t-4$; $G_{(t-1)f}$ is the average forecast error; $HHI_{s(t-1)}$ is a statewide Herfindahl index; $X_{(t-1)f}$ is a vector variable controlling for expected loss, yield, and availability of capital; Y_t is a dummy variable for year; $SPEC_m$ is a dummy for physician specialty; and e_{stmf} is a random error.

In equation 2, we include loss plus loss-adjustment expense incurred and loss paid in year $t-1$ as proxies for expected loss in year t. As a measure of the expected yield on invested assets, we use the actual investment gain (net investment income plus realized capital gains, net of tax) divided by total assets in year $t-1$ to test for the effects of firm-specific returns. Economywide changes in asset yields are captured by year fixed effects.

As a measure of the availability of capital, relative to exposure, we use the ratio of surplus to total net premiums written. This ratio is used in the NAIC's Financial Analysis Tracking System (FATS) developed in the early 1990s for solvency screening and was also used in the earlier Insurance Regulatory Information System (IRIS). Since it measures total surplus and all-lines national net premiums written, it reflects capital shocks from losses on all lines of insurance written by the firm, not just medical malpractice, and any unrealized capital gains and losses on invested assets.

We use two measures of loss forecast error. The average forecast error for policy years $t-6$ to $t-4$ measures the absolute reserve shortfall for these three years. The average percentage forecast error for years $t-6$ to $t-4$, differenced, is the growth in this forecast error between years $t-2$ and $t-1$. Since these forecast errors could reflect both unintended prediction error and intentional understatement of initial losses, we include other proxies for these characteristics. Growth in net premiums written between $t-3$ and $t-1$ is a measure of riskiness (premium growth is one of the FATS measures of risk). As a measure of experience in writing medical malpractice, we use the number of years since 1984 that this firm wrote more than $3 million of net premiums for medical malpractice. The ratio of reinsurance recovered to net admitted assets is included as a measure of risk taking, assuming that firms that grow unduly rapidly may hide this growth from regulators by reinsurance, some of which may be of dubious value.

We include indicator variables for four types of tort reforms: a cap on noneconomic damages at less than or equal to $500,000 and a cap greater than $500,000, a cap on total damages, collateral source offset, and modification of joint and several liability. These tort reform variables indicate whether a particular reform was enacted and not repealed in the state in year $t - 1$. If caps and collateral source offset limit the absolute level of awards, they should constrain the growth of premiums. We do not attempt to measure the effects of changes in tort reforms because very few states enacted changes during our sample period. Indicator variables are also included for states with joint underwriting associations and patient compensation funds.

We include a Herfindahl measure of market concentration at the state level. Standard models of concentration imply that firms in more concentrated markets have greater market power and hence may be able to raise premiums and should be less likely to exit. However, malpractice insurance markets are contestable—that is, the ability of policyholders to form self-insurance arrangements limits the market power of established firms. In contestable markets, concentration measures based on established firms provide an inaccurate measure of market power. Moreover, in states with joint underwriting associations, concentration may be high due to regulation of rates to levels deemed inadequate by voluntary insurers, in which case concentration would indicate inadequate rather than excessive rates.

We use the identical set of explanatory variables for both the exit equation and the premium equation. This tests the underlying hypothesis: that the same factors that lead to premium increases by financially solid firms may trigger exit by firms in financial distress.

Estimation Methods

The premium change equation is estimated using ordinary least squares with robust standard errors. We also estimate results adjusted for clustering of residuals across specialties and territories within firm-state-year. The exit equation is estimated using maximum likelihood complementary log-

log regression, with robust standard errors. The coefficients from this procedure reflect the underlying proportional hazards of exit, and taking the antilog of the coefficients yields hazard ratios. Results are also reported with standard errors adjusted for clustering by firm.

Several of the firm financial variables from NAIC had extreme values. The results reported here reflect the exclusion of outliers using two thresholds applied to the key explanatory variables: three standard deviations from the mean and the highest and lowest percentile values. Because of the large number of missing and outlier values for the percentage change in losses paid, we include an indicator variable for outlier or missing values of this variable. Using both screens reduces the number of state-year-firm-specialty observations for the premium change equation from 1,320 to 1,170. Results are very similar using either the three-standard-deviations screen alone or both screens. Results are also generally robust to excluding the top and bottom fifth percentile of observations. We report results here excluding outliers based on the two screens.

All dollar-denominated variables are adjusted to 2002 using the GDP deflator.

Empirical Results

This section reports the results of multivariate analysis of premium rate increases and insurer exits.

Premium Increases

Table 4 reports the analysis of premium increases. The dependent variable is the percentage increase in the premium rate for a specific firm-specialty-state-year. Significance levels are based on robust standard errors adjusted for clustering of residuals within firm-state-year to reflect possible correlation of a given firm's change in rates for different specialties and territories within a given state. The first specification omits year fixed effects, which are added in the second equation.

ACTUARIAL MODEL. The standard actuarial model, at least as proxied by our data, cannot explain the pattern of premium increases for medical malpractice insurance. Premium increases are unrelated to state-specific growth in lagged loss plus loss-adjustment expense incurred or paid, our proxies for

Table 4. Annual Percentage Change in Malpractice Premiums, Selected Years, 1994–2003[a]

Variable	Year fixed effects not included	Year fixed effects included	Variable	Year fixed effects not included	Year fixed effects included
Percentage change in losses and loss-adjustment expenses ($t-2$ to $t-1$)	0.002 [0.416]	0.002 [0.357]	Years since 1984 with total medical malpractice net premiums earned $\geq$ \$1 million	−0.001 [0.944]	0.038* [0.060]
Percentage change in losses and loss-adjustment expenses paid ($t-2$ to $t-1$)	−0.001 [0.423]	−0.001 [0.522]	Years since 1984 with total medical malpractice net premiums earned $\geq$ \$1 million squared	0.001 [0.345]	−0.002* [0.057]
Percentage change in losses and loss-adjustment expenses paid is an outlier dummy	−0.003 [0.505]	−0.005 [0.227]	General surgery specialty dummy	−0.003 [0.481]	−0.002 [0.550]
Percentage change in investment gain ($t-2$ to $t-1$)	0.033 [0.286]	0.03 [0.326]	Obstetrics-gynecology specialty dummy	−0.013* [0.070]	−0.012* [0.085]
Noneconomic damage cap $\geq$ \$500,000 dummy	−0.008 [0.754]	−0.023 [0.366]	Average forecast error $t-6$ to $t-4$ ($t-1$)	−0.025 [0.691]	0.03 [0.626]
Noneconomic damage cap < \$500,000 dummy	−0.054*** [0.001]	−0.057*** [0.001]	Average difference in forecast $t-6$ to $t-4$ ($t-2$ to $t-1$)	0.447 [0.212]	0.453 [0.214]
Total damage cap (any size) dummy	0.01 [0.785]	0.015 [0.657]	Forecast error variables are missing dummy	0.009 [0.825]	0.014 [0.734]
Collateral source offset in effect dummy	0.003 [0.842]	−0.001 [0.941]	Log of net medical malpractice premiums written (in millions of dollars) ($t-1$)	−0.013 [0.169]	0.002 [0.816]
Joint and several liability in effect dummy	−0.056*** [0.001]	−0.041** [0.101]	Log of state direct medical malpractice premiums written (in millions of dollars) ($t-1$)	0.002 [0.620]	0.004 [0.401]

Variable	(1)	(2)
Joint underwriting association dummy	0.034 [0.105]	0.027 [0.165]
Patient compensation fund dummy	-0.025 [0.327]	-0.028 [0.250]
Percentage change in capital / net premiums ($t-2$ to $t-1$)	0.01 [0.763]	0.011 [0.719]
Percentage change in direct medical malpractice premiums written ($t-3$ to $t-1$)	0.076** [0.022]	0.009 [0.768]
Percentage change in reinsurance recovered / assets ($t-2$ to $t-1$)	0 [0.926]	0.001 [0.761]
Firm is physician-directed dummy	0.042** [0.035]	0.029 [0.119]
State-year Herfindahl-Hirschman index ($t-1$)	-0.211** [0.012]	-0.163** [0.038]
Intercept	0.05 [0.710]	-0.17 [0.186]
Year 1997 dummy		0.009 [0.620]
Year 2001 dummy		0.121*** [0.001]
Year 2002 dummy		0.216*** [0.000]
Year 2003 dummy		0.268*** [0.000]
Number of observations	1,438	1,438
R^2	0.265	0.306

Source: NAIC annual statements; Medical Liability Monitor annual survey; authors' calculations.

* Significant at 10 percent.
** Significant at 5 percent.
*** Significant at 1 percent.
a. Robust p values in brackets, clustered by state-firm-year.

the firm's expectation of future loss growth, assuming that current loss forecasts are based on immediate prior experience. Reported calendar-year loss plus loss-adjustment expense is an inaccurate measure of policy-year losses to the extent that calendar-year losses include revisions to reserves in prior policy years. However, these reserve adjustments are roughly controlled for through the two measures of countrywide change in forecast error. The finding that premium increases are unrelated to changes in state-specific losses incurred may reflect the considerable variability in year-to-year growth of losses at the state level, particularly for small firms whose loss experience has low credibility.

The change in investment yield is positive but insignificant, rather than negative, as predicted under the hypothesis that a firm's prior yields are a reasonable proxy for its expected future yields and that these rates are passed on to policyholders through lower premiums. Finding no significant effect of firm-specific yields on pricing is consistent with the alternative hypothesis: that pricing is based on economywide investment yields, such as Treasury bill rates, and that deviations of firm-specific yields from these economywide averages accrue to firms, not to policyholders, in competitive markets.

Testing for the effect on premiums of changes in economywide yields is problematic because the effects of yields cannot be distinguished from other time-varying but firm-invariant factors, which all are subsumed in the year variables. The significant year fixed effects imply average premium rate increases of 12.1, 21.6, and 26.8 percent, for 2001, 2002 and 2003, respectively, after controlling for increases in losses paid, losses incurred, and revisions to prior-year reserves. This pattern is consistent with the hypothesis that the decline in expected asset yields contributed to premium increases; however, the average effects seem too large to reflect yield effects alone. Moreover, changes in countrywide yields cannot explain the differences in premium increases and insurer exits across states and firms.

CAPACITY CONSTRAINT HYPOTHESIS. The change in the capital-premium ratio is also insignificant. Thus these data prima facie provide no support for either the capacity constraint hypothesis, which posits a negative relationship between prices and the capital-premium ratio, or the insurance-as-risky-debt hypothesis, which posits a positive relationship between prices and the capital-premium ratio. It is possible that this finding of no effect of the premium-capital ratio on premiums reflects the fact that our dependent variable—the percentage increase in premium levels—does not directly measure the price of insurance, which is measured more appropriately by the loading charge or economic loss ratio. However, since our estimating equation controls for percentage change in loss plus loss-adjustment expense incurred, the change in premium rate controlling for change in $L + LAE$ should measure the change in loading.

It is possible that the finding of no significant association on average between premium increases and an insurer's financial capacity may conceal differential effects, depending on the financial condition of the firm. For example, a financially sound firm that experiences a modest decline in its capital-premium ratio may be able to raise prices in the short run, assuming that policyholders would incur costs in switching insurers. However, if the shock to capital is sufficient to threaten insolvency, then the risky-debt hypothesis may dominate: the firm is unable to raise premiums, and policyholders may switch to other insurers, thereby increasing the risk of exit. This is a subject for future research.

MORAL HAZARD AND INEXPERIENCE. Premium increases are positively related to the growth in the forecast error on prior policies. This effect is highly significant when we exclude the fifth percentile outliers and is economically significant. A 10 percentage point increase in the forecast error is associated with a 63 percent increase in premiums, controlling for year effects. The effect is smaller and only significant at the 21 percent level in the specifications reported, which use a more parsimonious definition of outliers. This evidence is consistent with the hypothesis that firms that underestimate prior losses and undercharge, due to either inexperience or intentional risk taking, must eventually raise premium rates disproportionately if they are to stay in business.

Premium rate increases are positively related to prior growth in a firm's premiums written for years $t - 3$ to $t - 1$, which is prima facie also consistent with the hypothesis that firms that undercharge and grow relatively rapidly during the soft market must eventually raise premium rates to stay in business.[27] However, this effect becomes insignificant once we control for year effects, which suggests that it reflects industrywide correlation of premium increases over time rather than variation across firms in response to their differential rates of prior premium growth. Premium increases are also unrelated to growth in reinsurance, another proxy for prior risk-taking behavior.

27. Growth in premiums written is positively correlated with growth in volume if demand is elastic.

Premium increases are significantly positively related to the firm's experience writing medical malpractice insurance, measured by the number of years since 1984 that the firm's net malpractice premiums written exceeded $1 million. However, premium increases are unrelated to the firm's volume of malpractice premiums in $t - 1$, at either the state or the national level. This evidence suggests that willingness and ability to raise rates are related more to years of experience in the market than to the volume of a firm's current malpractice business.

TORT REFORMS. Noneconomic damage caps with thresholds at or below $500,000 have slowed the growth in premiums, controlling for other factors. States with such caps have 6 percent smaller premium increases, on average, than states without such caps. By contrast, there is no evidence of significant effects of caps on awards for noneconomic damages at higher thresholds or of caps on awards for total damages. Limits on joint and several liability also appear to slow the rate of growth of premiums: states with such limits, on average, have 4.1 percent lower annual premium increases than states without such limits. Collateral source offset laws, on average, appear to have no effect. It is possible that the more stringent laws do indeed have an effect, even though the average effect is not significant.

The presence of a joint underwriting association or a patient compensation fund has no significant effect on premium increases in the specifications reported here. However, the effect of the joint underwriting association is significantly positive in some specifications, depending on outlier screens. As noted earlier, two of the joint underwriting association states, Pennsylvania and South Carolina, had the largest cumulative premium increases during the period studied. Thus it seems reasonable to conclude that joint underwriting associations at best do not reduce premium growth and, at worst, perhaps exacerbate premium increases.

MARKET STRUCTURE AND CORPORATE CONTROL. The Herfindahl measure of insurer concentration is negative and significant, indicating that premium increases are smaller in states with more concentrated insurance markets. This is inconsistent with allegations that malpractice premium increases reflect the market power of insurers that remain in the market after other firms exit. Rather, the evidence suggests that, in the context of malpractice insurance, insurer concentration is an indicator of inadequate rates, possibly due to rate regulation, which makes the market unattractive to new entrants. More generally, given the ease of entry to and exit from the malpractice insurance market, market power of established insurers is unlikely to be significant.

Rate increases appear to be significantly higher for physician-directed insurers; however, this effect becomes insignificant after controlling for year effects. Thus to the extent that physician-directed firms do assess their members, this must be in the form of special assessments, not premium increases.

Insurer Exits

Table 5 reports the complementary log-log regression estimates of determinants of firm exits over the period 1996–2002.[28] Recall that exit is defined at the firm-state level as a reduction in net premiums written below $100,000 for the duration of our sample period. This measure designates firms as exiting if they become insignificant participants in a state, even if they remain solvent. In table 5, columns 1 and 3 omit year fixed effects, which are included in columns 2 and 4. Adjusting for year fixed effects may over-control for some variables that are highly correlated across firms over time, such as loss shocks or financial yields. Columns 3 and 4 include interaction terms, to test for differential effects for small insurers, defined as firms with under $1 million direct premiums written in the state. Columns 3 and 4 report the average or large-firm effect; columns 5 and 6 report the small-firm interaction effect, with *p* values on the tests for significant differences between small and large firms. Columns 7 and 8 report the net effects for small firms; the *p* values indicate whether these net effects for small firms are significantly different from zero. All *p* values use robust standard errors. We also estimate significance levels adjusted for within-firm clustering of standard errors; if this adjustment changes the significance level, the new level is indicated in parentheses. The effects reported are $e^{\beta} - 1$, where ß is the vector of estimated coefficients from the complementary log-log regression. These reported effects represent the percentage change in the hazard ratio for a one-unit change in the independent variable.

ACTUARIAL MODEL. Exits are unrelated to growth in lagged incurred or paid losses. Together with the similar finding of no effect of incurred or paid losses on premium increases, this evidence suggests either that recent state-specific loss experience is a poor proxy for expected future losses or that

---

28. The need for lagged explanatory variables eliminates from the regression sample exits that occurred in 1993–95.

Table 5. Determinants of Firm-State Exit by Malpractice Insurers, 1993–2002[a]

Variable	Exits no outliers robust effect[a]		Large or average effect		Small interaction effect		Small net effect	
	(1)	(2)	(3)	(4)	(5)	(6)	(7)	(8)
Percentage change in losses and loss-adjustment expenses (t − 2 to t − 1)	0.002 [0.810]	0.000 [0.968]	-0.01 [0.375]	-0.011 [0.351]	0.016 [0.250]	0.015 [0.309]	0.01 [0.211]	0 [1.000]
Percentage change in losses and loss-adjustment expenses paid (t − 2 to t − 1)	0.001 [0.734]	0.001 [0.719]	-0.001 [0.877]	-0.002 [0.741]	0.005 [0.460]	0.006 [0.363]	0.004 [0.423]	0.005 [0.977]
Percentage change in losses and loss-adjustment expenses paid is missing dummy	0.019 [0.153]	0.018 [0.184]	0.014 [0.296]	0.012 [0.374]				
Percentage change in investment gain (t − 2 to t − 1)	0.623*** () [0.000]	0.537*** () [0.003]	0.265 [0.249]	0.163 [0.488]	0.673* [0.069]	0.721* [0.072]	1.116*** [0.000]	1.001*** [0.004]
Noneconomic damage cap ≥$500,000	-0.171 [0.213]	-0.173 [0.211]	-0.191 [0.161]	-0.189 [0.169]				
Noneconomic damage cap < $500,000	-0.046 [0.705]	-0.102 [0.398]	-0.009 [0.940]	-0.07 [0.572]				
Total damage cap (any size) dummy	0.247* (**) [0.082]	0.191 (*) [0.166]	0.301** [0.038]	0.261*[0.066]				
Collateral source offset in effect dummy	0.086 [0.444]	0.129 [0.259]	0.112 [0.329]	0.156 [0.184]				
Joint and several liability in effect dummy	-0.168** (**) [0.050]	-0.15* (**) [0.083]	-0.172** [0.048]	-0.154* [0.078]				
Joint underwriting association dummy	-0.011 [0.923]	-0.008 [0.947]	-0.017 [0.887]	-0.014 [0.903]				
Patient compensation fund dummy	-0.029 [0.815]	-0.015 [0.907]	-0.082 [0.504]	-0.081 [0.510]				
Percentage change in capital / net premiums (t − 2 to t − 1)	-0.321** () [0.026]	-0.24* () [0.051]	-0.429* [0.053]	-0.342* [0.088]	0.237 [0.560]	0.154 [0.638]	-0.294 [0.114]	-0.24 [0.76]
Percentage change in direct med mal premiums written (t − 3 to t − 1)	-0.253*** () [0.005]	-0.271*** () [0.002]	-0.704*** [0.008]	-0.704*** [0.008]	2.416*** [0.009]	2.346*** [0.009]	0.01 [0.881]	-0.01 [0.96]
Percentage change in reinsurance recovered / assets (t − 2 to t − 1)	-0.042** () [0.027]	-0.047** () [0.020]	-0.046** [0.040]	-0.054** [0.034]	0.006 [0.888]	0.015 [0.729]	-0.04 [0.241]	-0.039 [0.341]

Firm is physician directed dummy	(1)	(2)	(3)	(4)	(5)	(6)	(7)	(8)
Firm is physician directed dummy	-0.672*** (**) [0.000]	-0.676*** (**) [0.000]	-0.418*** [0.004]	-0.393** [0.011]	-0.686*** [0.000]	-0.711*** [0.000]	-0.817*** [0.000]	-0.825** [0.013]
Years since 1984 with total medical malpractice net premiums earned ≥ $1 million	-0.071*** ( ) [0.006]	-0.057*** ( ) [0.034]	-0.002 [0.960]	0.025 [0.588]	-0.089 [0.123]	-0.097* [0.098]	-0.091** [0.017]	-0.074*** [0.000]
Years since 1984 with total medical malpractice net premiums earned ≥ $1 million squared	0.000 [0.881]	-0.002 [0.231]	-0.005** [0.015]	-0.008*** [0.001]	0.007** [0.027]	0.008** [0.019]	0.002 [0.317]	0 [1.000]
Average forecast error $t-6$ to $t-4$ ($t-1$)	0.421** ( ) [0.018]	0.422** ( ) [0.019]	0.016 [0.944]	0.094 [0.702]	0.547 [0.195]	0.594 [0.172]	0.573* [0.063]	0.745*** [0.000]
Average difference in forecast $t-6$ to $t-4$ ($t-2$ to $t-1$)	-0.959*** (**) [0.000]	-0.972*** (**) [0.000]	-0.693 [0.180]	-0.892** [0.023]	-0.956** [0.012]	-0.913* [0.065]	-0.986*** [0.000]	-0.991*** [0.000]
Forecast error variables are missing dummy	10.121*** (***) [0.000]	8.813*** (**) [0.000]	15.851*** [0.000]	14.371*** [0.000]	-0.768** [0.022]	-0.787*** [0.019]	2.91*** [0.007]	2.271*** [0.000]
Log of net medical malpractice premiums written (in millions of dollars) ($t-1$)	-0.069* ( ) [0.051]	-0.059 [0.110]	0.048 [0.450]	0.069 [0.299]	-0.178** [0.018]	-0.201*** [0.009]	-0.138*** [0.005]	-0.146 [0.383]
Log of state direct medical malpractice premiums written (in millions of dollars) ($t-1$)	-0.292*** (***) [0.000]	-0.299*** (***) [0.000]	-0.215*** [0.000]	-0.215*** [0.000]	-0.146 [0.225]	-0.197* [0.100]	-0.329** [0.071]	-0.369*** [0.000]
State-year Herfindahl-Hirshman index ($t-1$)	-0.797*** (***) [0.003]	-0.772*** (***) [0.007]	-0.831** [0.020]	-0.807** [0.032]	0.104 [0.917]	0.098 [0.923]	-0.813** [0.015]	-0.788*** [0.003]
Year 1997 dummy		-0.566*** (*) [0.000]		-0.594*** [0.000]				
Year 1998 dummy		-0.533** (*) [0.000]		-0.558*** [0.000]				
Year 1999 dummy		-0.106 [0.399]		-0.152 [0.250]				
Year 2000 dummy		0.011 [0.937]		-0.152 [0.250]				
Year 2000 dummy		0.011 [0.937]		0.01 [0.946]				
Year 2001 dummy		0.536*** ( ) [0.001]		0.533*** [0.001]				
Firm is small dummy		1.522** [0.014]		1.664** [0.011]				
Number of observations	8,163	8,163	8,163					

Source: NAIC annual statements; Medical Liability Monitor annual survey; authors' calculations.
a. Robust p values in brackets. Significance levels in parentheses indicate significance with clustering by firm.
* Significant at 10 percent.
** Significant at 5 percent.
*** Significant at 1 percent.

state-specific loss experience is not a significant factor in a firm's decision to increase premiums or exit from a particular state.

Exits are significantly positively related to investment yield, which is inconsistent with the hypothesis that declining investment yields precipitate exits, at least for realized returns. However, this effect is confined to small firms, and the average effect becomes insignificant with clustering of standard errors within firms.

CAPACITY CONSTRAINT HYPOTHESIS. Exit is significantly negatively related to growth in the capital-premium ratio. The effect is large and significant (with lower significance after adjusting for firm clustering): a one-unit increase in the capital-premium ratio is associated with a 32 percent (24 percent) reduction in the exit hazard without (with) controls for year fixed effects and is not significantly different for small versus large firms. Thus capacity constraints seem more likely to be associated with exits than with premium increases. This is not surprising for malpractice insurance, since physician policyholders are likely to be aware of and concerned about an insurer's financial quality and can switch at relatively low cost to other firms or to self-insurance arrangements rather than buy insurance from financially weak firms. This mobility of policyholders presumably constrains the ability of impaired firms to raise premiums beyond prospectively fair levels to recoup prior losses and restore their capital.

Several factors may have contributed to shocks to insurer capital over this period. The decline in equity values during 2000–02 presumably reduced insurer capital somewhat. However, the effect was limited if most insurers held the majority of their assets in bonds.[29] Unanticipated losses on insurance lines other than medical malpractice may have played a role for larger, multiple-line companies. However, the finding of no significant difference in the capital-premium ratio coefficient for small versus large companies suggests that losses on other lines were not a major contributor and that loss shock effects were more likely attributable to medical malpractice.

MORAL HAZARD AND INEXPERIENCE. Exits are significantly positively related to the average forecast error on prior malpractice policies written countrywide. This average effect is due solely to small firms: a one-unit change in the forecast error for small firms is associated with a 74.5 percent increase in the exit hazard, controlling for year fixed effects.

---

29. About 79 percent of assets of PIAA insurers is in bonds; Smarr (2003).

Exit is also strongly related to the indicator for firms with missing data for the forecast error. Since our estimate of the forecast error requires six prior years of data, firms with missing data have fewer than six years of experience writing malpractice insurance countrywide. The coefficients are bigger for large firms than for small firms; both imply a very large increase in the probability of exit for firms with less than six years of experience. Growth in the forecast error is significantly negatively associated with exit hazard. This is contrary to expectations. It may be influenced by the very large positive coefficient on the indicator variable for missing forecast data.

For small firms, the probability of exit is significantly negatively related to the firm's malpractice experience, as measured by the number of years with premium volume greater than $1 million. A one-year increase in experience reduces the probability of exit 7–9 percent. Similarly, the exit hazard is negatively related to state-specific volume of business (malpractice premiums written), and this effect is greater for small firms than for large firms. A one-unit increase in the (log of) direct premiums written in the state reduces the exit hazard 22 percent for large firms and 37 percent for small firms. This strong evidence—that exit is more likely for firms with little experience or relatively small volume of premiums—is consistent with the hypothesis that firms with relatively little investment of tangible and intangible capital— hence relatively low quasi rents at risk—are more likely to exit.

Exit is significantly negatively related to growth in reinsurance recovered, relative to assets, but the effect is small and applies only to large firms. This suggests that, if anything, reinsurance is successfully used as a device to spread risk. Thus we find no evidence for the joint hypothesis: that firms tend to use reinsurance to conceal intentional risk taking and that this eventually leads to financial trouble and exit.

MARKET STRUCTURE AND CORPORATE CONTROL. Physician-directed firms are, on average, 67 percent less likely to exit than commercially owned firms, with larger differentials for small firms (82 percent) than for large firms (39 percent). This suggests that, although many physician-directed firms change their corporate form from mutual or reciprocal to stock firms, they nevertheless continue to behave more likely policyholder-owned firms than do the commercial stock firms. Whether this greater staying power reflects more conservative strategies, greater ability to assess their members, greater ability to restore inadequate reserves and depleted surplus, or other factors cannot be fully resolved with these data.

Exit is less likely in states with concentrated markets. This is consistent with the hypothesis that competition may be "excessive" in some states, leading to exit by firms with little experience and little tangible or intangible capital at risk. Consistent with this, the probability of exit is more than twice as high for small firms than for large firms, controlling for other factors such as experience.

Conclusions

The most recent crisis in medical malpractice insurance exhibits some of the characteristics of a typical insurance cycle, but with some differences. In the late 1990s, aggregate premiums written and initial loss forecasts remained flat or declined, although insurers were paying out larger amounts on claims and revising upward their loss forecasts and reserves for prior years. This "soft market" was followed by a sharp increase in premiums from 2000–2003, with inflation-adjusted median rate increases of 11–18 percent a year and rate increases of 30–60 percent for states in the top quartile of rate increases. At the same time, the number of firms exiting the market increased, including many small firms with relatively low premium volume and little experience but also several very large firms, including the St. Paul Companies, which had business in more than forty states.

This pattern is typical of insurance cycles, and our analysis of premium increases and insurer exits supports some of the hypotheses that have been developed to explain such cycles. A surprising finding is that state-specific premium rate increases are not significantly related to prior increases in state-specific losses paid or incurred, contrary to standard models of insurance pricing. This may reflect lack of credibility of firm-specific experience, especially for small firms in small states; however, it may also reflect strategic pricing, in particular, intentional undercharging in soft markets to gain market share.

The evidence also provides no support for the capacity constraint theory, in which rate increases are associated with shocks to an insurer's capital-premium ratio. However, such loss shocks are associated with insurer exits. Taken together, this evidence suggests that firms experiencing significant declines in their premium-surplus ratio are unable to increase premiums to restore surplus and hence are more likely to exit. Given the relative ease with which physician policyholders can switch to self-insurance arrangements and, more generally, the apparent ease with which new firms enter the medical malpractice insurance market, it is not surprising that established firms experiencing shocks to their surplus are unable to recoup these losses by raising premiums.

There is considerable support for the hypothesis that some of the problems of the crisis or hard market originated in the prior soft-market period. We find that premium increases were positively related to upward revisions of reserves following initial under-reserving and that firms with large prior forecast errors were more likely to exit. These findings are consistent with the hypothesis that under-reserving in the years of the soft market contributes to the premium increases and insurer exits of the hard market. How far this under-reserving reflects inexperience of new firms versus intentional undercharging to gain market share is not fully resolved here. However, we do find that firms with few years of experience and low premium volume—hence firms with relatively little experience and relatively low tangible and intangible capital at risk—are much more likely to exit. The theory of competitive price cutting implies that undercharging by some firms in the market can lead to matching price cuts by other firms seeking to preserve market share and quasi rents, which may in turn lead to large premium increases and to exit of the weakest firms. The evidence here is broadly consistent with this model; however, conclusions are tentative because our analysis does not incorporate changes in premiums over the 1998–2000 soft-market period.

Although the malpractice crisis is broadly consistent with models of insurance crises more generally, it is mitigated by certain features specific to medical malpractice. In particular, two types of tort reform—caps on awards for noneconomic damages with thresholds at or below $500,000 and limits on joint and several liability—significantly reduce premium increases in states enacting such reforms. By contrast, caps on awards for noneconomic damages at higher levels and caps on awards for total damages appear to have no effect; conclusions are tentative, however, because of the small number of states with such caps.

The finding that caps on awards for noneconomic damages of under $500,000 slow the growth of malpractice premiums is not by itself a sufficient reason for adopting such caps. The policy case for any tort reform, including caps on awards, should be based on whether such reforms improve the efficiency of the malpractice system in deterring medical negligence and providing appropriate compensation to injured patients. These issues are discussed in detail elsewhere.[30] Placing some limits on awards for noneconomic damages is consistent with appropriate compensation. Such noneconomic losses are, by definition, irreplaceable; hence any attempt to place a dollar value on them is likely to be arbitrary and exposed to moral hazard. No form of private or social insurance other than tort law provides compensation for noneconomic damages. Thus, as individuals, we do not choose to buy such compensation for ourselves when faced with the choice and the bill; yet tort law effectively forces us to buy high levels of compensation for noneconomic loss for medical injuries, which we pay for as patients through higher fees for medical services. If some compensation for noneconomic damages is to be retained, economic theory suggests that a schedule of payments related to the severity of the injury and the patient's life expectancy would provide more appropriate compensation than a single cap that is most binding for young, severely injured victims who face a lifetime of disability. In designing an appropriate schedule of payments for noneconomic loss, an important issue is whether limiting the amount payable by the defendant might undermine the deterrence effects of the malpractice system. In practice, since physicians are generally heavily insured for monetary damages, it seems unlikely that reasonable limits on noneconomic loss would undermine any deterrence effects of the malpractice system. Indeed, such deterrence is plausibly derived primarily from the time costs, embarrassment, and other nonmonetary factors associated with being sued; these intangible costs depend on the frequency of claims rather than the severity per claim and so are unlikely to be affected significantly by caps on awards for noneconomic damages. Thus economic analysis supports scheduled limits on compensation for noneconomic damages, on grounds that such schedules improve the efficiency of tort compensation with minimal, if any, loss of deterrence. The fact that caps also tend to reduce malpractice premiums may have the added benefit of reducing disruption in insurance and medical markets; however, this is not the main economic rationale for such reforms.

Insurance market regulations, including joint underwriting associations and patient compensation funds, clearly do not reduce premium increases overall or reduce the probability of exit. Whether these mechanisms tend to increase costs remains an open question. Two states with joint underwriting associations (Pennsylvania and South Carolina) had among the largest

30. Danzon (1984).

cumulative premium increases over the period. This plausibly reflects the lagged effects of these pay-as-you-go mechanisms, which tend to shift losses to future years and may increase total loss payouts, if these pooling mechanisms undermine incentives for loss prevention and for claims management. More detailed analysis of the effects of these mechanisms is warranted but is beyond the scope of this paper.

In contrast to these mandatory pools, the voluntary changes in the insurance market have an effect. In particular, physician-directed firms are much less likely to exit, and this effect is greater for physician-directed small firms than for physician-directed large firms. Thus to the extent that entry, undercharging, and subsequent exit of inexperienced small firms contribute to the problems in this market, the evidence suggests that this problem applies less to physician-directed firms than to commercial firms.

If these tentative conclusions are correct—that the entry and subsequent exit of small, inexperienced firms contribute to the soft- and hard-market periods experienced in medical malpractice—appropriate policy response would have to weigh the competitive benefits of easy entry and exit against the costs, if indeed inexperienced players with little to lose do exacerbate insurance cycles.

Discussion

Henry Aaron of Brookings opened the discussion by asking what impact tort reforms in the various states have had on the malpractice insurance market. Danzon responded that the reforms have had long-lasting effects. While most were enacted in the 1970s or 1980s, effects persist even to the present. Since many caps on damages were set in nominal terms, more claims face the constraint over time. The frequency, rather than the severity, of claims seems to drive claims paid.

Steve Carney of Medical Mutual of Maryland agreed that, although there has not been a major increase in the frequency of claims, there has been an increase in the "embedded frequency," the percentage of claims requiring a payment to be closed. Maryland has seen a shift from 22 percent to nearly 30 percent of claims requiring payment. However in the past two years, the average severity of claims rose from $275,000 to about $370,000. Altogether, Medical Mutual of Maryland's total indemnity payout jumped from $43 million in 2002 to $73 million in 2003.

Neil Doherty of the Wharton School summarized the paper's findings as claiming that the roots of a hard market are in the preceding soft market and that, for lack of experience, some insurers under-reserve and are forced out of the market, but that their presence affects prices as other firms respond to them. Doherty suggested that this result seems to contradict previous work by Danzon and Cummins implying that credit risk is reflected in insurance company pricing. If so, customers should be able to differentiate between the under-reserving risk-taking insurers and the established companies with better credit risk. Doherty wanted to know if this work was based on malpractice insurance; if so that may explain the apparent discrepancy here. Danzon replied that, in revisiting the previous paper, she found that companies financially at risk could not charge high premiums and that consumers appear to have examined surplus rather than claims-specific reserves.

Terri Vaughn, Iowa state insurance commissioner, seconded the conclusion that hard markets may originate in preceding soft markets. She suggested that, in her experience with micro-level data, tracing premiums charged to specific practitioners reveals dramatic fluctuations in rates over time. Although Iowa has avoided the "crisis" designation of the American Medical Association, it saw premiums drop by half and then double in two five-year periods. She also observed that rate changes are correlated across subspecialties because insurers rely on relativity factors over time because losses for subspecialties lack credibility.

The noisiness of the data elicited several comments. Larry Cluff pointed out that the National Association of Insurance Commissioners (NAIC) and Medical Liability Monitor both rely on hospital data, which is a diminishing segment of the market (since less than 50 percent of hospitals are in the traditional insurance market). He also noted that many states have only one or two mostly doctor-owned insurance companies and thus wondered about the applicability of the Herfindahl-Hirschman index, which reported high concentrations of insurers in various markets. Scott Harrington pointed out that NAIC data were taken at the state level and were for calendar-year claims costs, which have been corrected for revisions and forecast errors of years past. As a result, these data may not be well linked to the specific medical specialties that were the subject of the paper. For these reasons, he was not troubled by the statistical insignificance of the cost-growth variable in the regressions reported in the paper. Danzon acknowledged the data difficulties as being unavoidable. She offered two competing interpretations of the higher values of the Herfindahl-Hirschman index: Are they caused by regulation, or is greater concentration insulating the market against the destabilizing influences of smaller inexperienced and overly optimistic firms? Perhaps a moderate degree of concentration is good for stability.

Cluff was unsettled by evidence that caps, but not loss experience, lowers premiums, because caps are intended to limit losses. High premiums are due to the long tail of losses. Although costs may be low for the first few years, recent entrants are later forced out.

Danzon defended the paper's use of firm-specific investment yield in the regressions by explaining that the expected yield in the market is more likely to affect premiums. Moreover, using the Treasury bill rate would cause problems in the regressions, which already have variables to capture year fixed effects. She also admitted that analysis so far has focused on the mean of premiums rather than medians and that perhaps analysis of groups of insurers or case studies would enable researchers to determine how much greater the fluctuations are at the top quartile than in the mean, where a cyclical pattern is fairly believable.

The regression model used by the authors also provoked discussion. Ralph Winter of the University of British Columbia suggested that the small coefficient of the capital-premium ratio may be due to a bias induced by duplication of premiums on the left-hand side and in the denominator of the right-hand side. The greater impact that this same variable has in the exits equation supports this possibility. Instrumental variables may help to deal with this issue.

Thomas Holzheu of the Swiss Economic Research Unit suggested that the U.S. market is seeing the coincident effects of two phenomena: the insurance cycle and claims inflation. Perhaps the data collected are better suited to explaining the latter than the former. Year dummies would interfere with describing cyclicality. Right now the two effects are combining to create very high price increases.

Jeff O'Connell of the University of Virginia Law School objected to caps, citing Richard Zeckhauser's paper as highlighting the ills of excessive insurance for small losses and under-insurance for large losses. He also pointed out that even capping only compensation for pain and suffering compromises a bargaining chip in negotiating the value of economic loss. Danzon pointed to the fact that individuals do not purchase insurance for noneconomic losses, perhaps because the product is simply irreplaceable or because the nature of the product leads to moral hazard. Not limiting economic damages does allow for coverage of catastrophic losses.

Robert Litan of Brookings called for a summary analysis of what led to problems in troubled states, whether reforms have alleviated them, and, based on the past, how the market might look two to three years from now. In evaluating the reforms, Danzon asserted that the deterrence effect on malpractice and optimal compensation should inform the debate on caps. The theory of optimal compensation does seem to present a strong case for limiting awards. Steve Carney suggested that not all tort reform is created equal. Liability caps over $500,000 are largely window dressing because they approach the limit of liability carried by a particular physician, the majority of whom are required by their hospital to carry $1 million in coverage. Additionally a rent-seeking industry working full time to find its market niche in spite of reforms inevitably lessens the impact of reform over time.

More broadly, Carney described a pattern in which a crisis that leads to higher premiums attracts a large number of entrants, including not just traditional insurers but also doctors' cooperatives seeking to fill market gaps. Vaughn noted that most new entrants to Iowa are regional medical malpractice insurers that are expanding into new states rather than new companies. Henry Aaron inquired about cross-state correlation within companies, and Carney gave examples of differences in his company's rate increases across state boundaries. Expanding into new states involves uncertainty of risk and reliance on the data and behavior of the incumbent. Michael O'Malley of Chubb regarded many of the pricing errors by insurers as honest mistakes as a result of the dramatic increases in claims.

References

Bovbjerg, Randall R., and Anna Bartow. 2003. "Understanding Pennsylvania's Medical Malpractice Crisis: Facts about Liability Insurance, the Legal System, and Health Care in Pennsylvania." Harrisburg, Pa.: Project on Medical Liability in Pennsylvania, Pew Charitable Trusts. Available at medliabilitypa.org/research/report0603/UnderstandingReport.pdf [March 15, 2004].

Cummins, J. David, and Patricia M. Danzon. 1997. "Price, Financial Quality, and Capital Flows in Insurance Markets." *Journal of Financial Intermediation* 6 (1, January): 3–38.

Danzon, Patricia M. 1984. "Tort Reform and the Role of Government in Private Insurance Markets." *Journal of Legal Studies* 13 (3): 517–49.

Doherty, Neil A., and Georges Dionne. 1993. "Insurance with Undiversifiable Risk: Contract Structure and Organizational Form of Insurance Firms." *Journal of Risk and Uncertainty* 6 (2): 187–203.

General Accounting Office. 2003a. *Medical Malpractice: Implications of Rising Premiums on Access to Health Care.* GAO-03-836. August.

——. 2003b. *Medical Malpractice Insurance: Multiple Factors Have Contributed to Increased Premium Rates.* GAO-03-702. June.

Grøn, Anne. 1989. *Property-Casualty Insurance Cycles, Capacity Constraints, and Empirical Results.* Ph.D. diss., Massachusetts Institute of Technology, Department of Economics.

——. 1994. "Capacity Constraints and Cycles in Property-Casualty Insurance Markets." *Rand Journal of Economics* 25 (1, Spring): 110–27.

Harrington, Scott, and Patricia Danzon. 1994. "Price Cutting in Liability Insurance Markets." *Journal of Business* 67 (4): 511–38.

Myers, Stewart C., and Richard A. Cohn. 1987. "Insurance Rate Regulation and the Capital Asset Pricing Model." In John David Cummins and Scott A. Harrington, eds., *Fair Rate of Return in Property-Liability Insurance.* Boston: Kluwer-Nijhoff.

Smarr, Lawrence E. 2003. "Statement of the Physician Insurers Association of America Regarding Patient Access Crisis: The Role of Medical Litigation." Statement before a joint hearing of the U.S. Senate Judiciary Committee and the Health, Education, Labor, and Pensions Committee, February. Available at www.thepiaa.org/publications/pdf_files/February_11_Testimony.pdf [March 16, 2004].

Winter, Ralph A. 1994. "The Dynamics of Competitive Insurance Markets." *Journal of Financial Intermediation* 3 (4, September): 379–415.

Zuckerman, Stephen, Randall R. Bovbjerg, and Frank Sloan. 1990. "Effects of Tort Reforms and Other Factors on Medical Malpractice Premiums." *Inquiry* 27 (2): 167–82.

Tort Liability, Insurance Rates, and the Insurance Cycle

SCOTT E. HARRINGTON

MARKETS FOR MANY types of property and casualty insurance exhibit soft-market periods, where premium rates are stable or falling and coverage is readily available, and subsequent hard-market periods, where premium rates and insurers' reported profits significantly increase and less coverage is available. Conventional wisdom among practitioners and other observers is that soft and hard markets occur in a regular "underwriting cycle." Like price fluctuations in equity markets, fluctuations in insurance premium rates and coverage availability are difficult to explain fully by standard economic models that assume rational agents and few market frictions.

The mid-1980s "liability insurance crisis" remains the most infamous hard market in the United States. The dramatic increases in commercial liability insurance premiums and reductions in coverage availability for some sectors received enormous attention, motivating extensive research on those specific problems and on fluctuations in insurance prices and coverage availability more generally. Large losses from natural catastrophes in the United States during the late 1980s and early 1990s spurred further interest in and research on the dynamics of pricing in reinsurance and primary insurance markets following large, industry-wide losses. The hard market for commercial property and casualty insurance that began in late 2000 and accelerated following the destruction of the World Trade Center in September 2001 focused renewed attention on markets for commercial

97

property, medical liability, general liability, and workers' compensation insurance. With respect to general liability and medical liability insurance, substantial debate has arisen concerning the causes of increases in rates and reductions in coverage availability and the attendant implications for policy, such as tort reform, to reduce the expected value and uncertain costs of liability insurance claims or additional regulation of insurers to control allegedly imprudent underwriting and investment.

This paper provides an overview of volatility in premiums, coverage availability, and insurers' reported profits in U.S. commercial general liability insurance and examines its broad relation to the U.S. tort liability system.[1] I begin with a synopsis of the perfect markets model of insurance prices (sometimes called the arbitrage model) and its implications for commercial liability insurance. I next describe fluctuations in U.S. general liability insurance premiums, coverage availability, and reported profits during the past two decades and examine whether the perfect markets model is consistent with that evidence. I then summarize other factors that may affect insurance market volatility and provide new evidence concerning one alternative: that aberrant pricing by some firms aggravates soft markets and, by implication, the severity of subsequent hard markets. I conclude with a brief summary of policy implications and areas for future research.

Competitive Insurance Premiums with Frictionless Capital Markets

With rational insurers and policyholders, competitive insurance markets, and frictionless capital markets, insurance premiums will equal the risk-adjusted discounted value of expected cash outflows for claims, sales expenses, income taxes, and any other costs, including the tax and agency costs of capital. The levels and changes in premium rates will coincide with the levels and changes in discounted expected costs. Because the timing of payouts for claims incurred in a given year, nonclaim expenses, and capital costs should be comparatively stable over time, rate changes will primarily reflect changes in expected (forecast) claim and claim settlement costs and changes in interest rates.

---

1. Parts of this discussion draw from Harrington and Niehaus (2000) and Harrington and Danzon (2001). I address many similar issues in my 1988 Brookings paper on the liability insurance crisis (also see Harrington and Litan 1988).

In this perfect markets framework, long-run levels and short-run changes in premium rates for general liability insurance will reflect levels and changes in the following:

—Expected claim costs (incurred losses) and claim settlement costs,

—The timing of future claim payments for incurred losses,

—Interest rates used to discount expected future claim and claim settlement costs,

—Underwriting expenses (commissions, wages to underwriters, policy issue costs, premium taxes, and so on),

—Uncertainty about the frequency and severity of claims, including uncertainty about the form and parameters of the relevant probability distributions, which in turn affects the amount of capital that insurers need to hold to protect themselves against insolvency, and

—The cost of holding capital, including tax and agency costs and any systematic risk that increases shareholders' required returns.

With competitive supply and frictionless capital markets, intertemporal variation in premium rates will be determined by changes in discounted expected costs, and variation in the margin between premiums and discounted reported claim costs (a common construct for the "price" of coverage) will primarily reflect unexpected changes in claim costs. That margin should not be cyclical. Variation in underwriting profits exclusive of investment income should be related to changes in interest rates and should not be cyclical absent accounting and reporting anomalies. Changes in coverage availability should be caused primarily by adverse selection, which may cause low-risk policyholders to lower their policy limits and cause some coverage to be completely unavailable.

Broad evidence indicates that the modern expansion of tort liability has produced long-run growth in expected claim costs, episodes of rapid short-run cost growth, relatively large claims settlement costs (for example, for defense), and substantial uncertainty about the frequency and severity of claims. The long claims tail for general liability insurance increases the risk of large errors in forecasting claim costs and aggravates adverse selection. It also makes premiums more sensitive to changes in interest rates. Rapid growth in expected claim costs in conjunction with heightened uncertainty

Figure 1. Growth in U.S. Property-Casualty Insurer Surplus and General Liability Insurance Net Premiums Written, 1982–2002

Percent

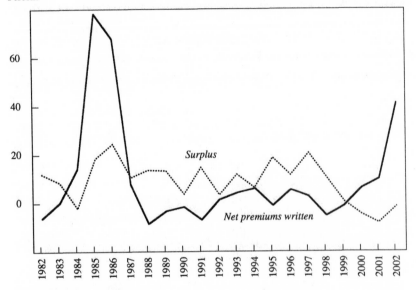

Source: A. M. Best (various years).

about costs and declining interest rates can therefore produce particularly sharp increases in premium rates, and this may be accompanied by increased adverse selection and attendant reductions in policy limits and coverage availability. A key question, however, is whether changes in premium rates and coverage availability are explained largely by these factors, as opposed to other short-run influences that could materially increase insurance market volatility.

Premiums and Underwriting Results in U.S. General Liability Insurance

Figure 1 plots the percentage growth in net (after reinsurance) premiums written for U.S. general liability insurance (including separately reported product liability insurance) during 1982–2002.[2] It also shows the percent-

2. All general liability insurance results reported in this paper include separately reported product liability coverage, unless otherwise indicated.

Figure 2. Increase in General Liability Insurance Premiums, Third Quarter 2001–Third Quarter 2003

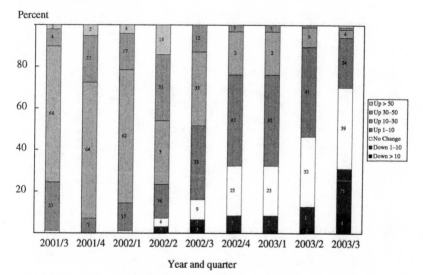

Source: Council of Insurance Agents and Brokers, quarterly surveys.

age growth in reported surplus for consolidated property and casualty insurance (net worth according to regulatory accounting principles) for that period. Dramatic growth in premiums during the mid-1980s was followed by a dozen years of relatively stable premiums. Moderate growth in premiums in 2000 and 2001 was followed by substantial growth in 2002.

Substantial premium growth continued through the first quarter of 2003 but has since shown some signs of abatement. Figure 2 shows the distribution of average increases in premiums by quarter from the third quarter of 2001 through the third quarter of 2003, as reported by large agents and brokers in surveys conducted by the Council of Insurance Agents and Brokers (CIAB). The specific survey questions underlying figure 2 commenced with CIAB's survey for the third quarter of 2001. That quarter included the events of September 11, which are expected to produce at least $10 billion in general liability claims and $40 billion–$50 billion in claims overall. Earlier CIAB surveys (in a different format) indicate that general liability insurance rates began to harden toward the end of 2000.

Declining insurer profits in the early 1980s and a decline in industry surplus during 1984 preceded the sharp increases in general liability premiums

Figure 3. Before-Tax Operating and Underwriting Profit Margins in U.S. General Liability Insurance, 1982–2002

Percent

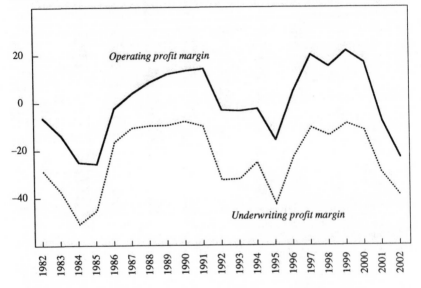

during 1985–87. Substantial growth of surplus, including the effects of substantial flows of new capital, accompanied the increase in premium rates and in reported profits. Growth in surplus continued annually through 1998 but was negligible in 1999. Surplus then declined each year through 2002 in conjunction with deteriorating underwriting profits, shrinking investment income (interest and dividends), and the declining value of insurers' equity holdings. Reported results through the first half of 2003 indicate material growth in surplus, with improved underwriting profits and some inflow of new capital. The growth in surplus shown in figure 1 does not include the effects of billions of dollars of new capital invested in offshore reinsurance entities to back reinsurance on U.S. property and casualty risks in late 2001 and 2002.

Figure 3 plots consolidated before-tax underwriting and operating profit margins for general liability insurance during 1982–2002. The underwriting margins equal earned premiums less underwriting expenses (on an approximate basis of generally accepted accounting principles) less incurred losses

Figure 4. Initially Reported and Developed through 2001 Accident-Year Incurred Losses in U.S. General Liability Insurance, 1982–2002[a]

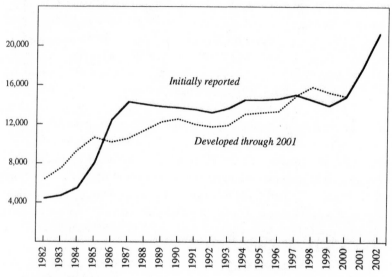

Millions of U.S. dollars

Source: A. M. Best (various years).
a. Data for 2002 is estimated.

(and loss adjustment expenses) as a percentage of earned premiums. Reported incurred losses are on a calendar-year basis: they equal accident-year losses (incurred losses including losses incurred but not reported for events during the year) plus revisions in incurred losses reported for all prior years. The operating margins equal the underwriting margins plus the ratio of net investment income (interest and dividends) plus realized capital gains or losses to earned premiums. The operating and underwriting margins are highly correlated. Operating margins were negative during 1982–86, 1992–95, and 2001–02. As I elaborate later, the negative operating margins during 1992–95 were caused primarily by higher reserves for losses that occurred ten or more years prior to the report-year (for example, from asbestos and environmental claims for old policies). In contrast to the early 1980s and 2001–02, those negative margins were not accompanied by sharp increases in premiums.

Figure 4 plots reported incurred losses for general liability insurance (including "allocated" claim settlement expenses for defense costs and cost containment) on an accident-year basis during 1982–2002. Two series are shown: (1) losses "initially reported" at the end of the year for events during year t and (2) losses "developed" through year $t + 9$ or 2001, if sooner, which reflect subsequent revisions to loss estimates for year t.[3] Large increases in premiums during the mid-1980s were accompanied by sharp increases in initially reported accident-year losses, as I and others have emphasized in post mortems on the crisis.[4] Following those increases, initially reported losses were relatively stable through 2000 and then jumped in 2001 in conjunction with significant increases in premiums. Developed losses significantly exceed initially reported losses for years 1982–85. However, for 1986 through the mid-1990s, developed losses were less than initially reported losses—forecast revisions in accident-year losses were downward—with particularly large downward revisions for 1986–88.

Figure 5 plots three series for 1982–2002: (1) earned premiums less underwriting expenses (including an estimate of nonallocated claim settlement expenses), (2) discounted initially reported accident-year losses, and (3) discounted developed losses. Discounted losses are calculated using the pattern of cumulative claim payments for general liability insurance for accidents in 1992 and spot rates for U.S. treasury securities.[5]

The margin between premiums and underwriting expenses should correspond fairly closely to the policies that produced losses each year. According to the perfect markets model, that margin should equal the discounted costs of expected claims and the tax and agency cost of capital. The large gap during 1987–88 between premium margins and discounted losses would presumably require (1) a significant increase in risk and the amount of capital needed to support the sale of coverage, (2) a significant increase in the tax or agency costs of capital, or (3) unexpectedly favorable claim cost

---

3. Because the data source used—*Best's Aggregates & Averages* (A. M. Best, various issues)—ceased reporting Schedule P information by line of business in the 2003 edition, I did not have access to data on accident-year losses for general liability insurance in 2002 at the time this paper was prepared. The figures that show values for 2002 include estimates assuming that the ratio of accident-year to calendar-year losses was the same in 2002 as in 2001. Best's later issued a supplement including the relevant data. The extrapolation used to create the figures overstated aggregate general liability reported losses for accident year 2002 by 3.4 percent ($21.2 billion extrapolated versus $20.5 billion reported).

4. For example, Harrington (1988); Harrington and Litan (1988).

5. I assume a twelve-year payout period with payments made mid-year and that remaining unpaid losses as a proportion of incurred losses after nine years are paid equally over the next three years. Constant-maturity U.S. Treasury yields are reported for one-, two-, three-, five-, seven-, and ten-year maturities. I use linear interpolation to generate spot rates for years four, six, eight, and nine.

Figure 5. Premium Margins and Estimated Discounted Accident-Year Incurred Losses in U.S. General Liability Insurance, 1982–2002[a]

Millions of U.S. dollars

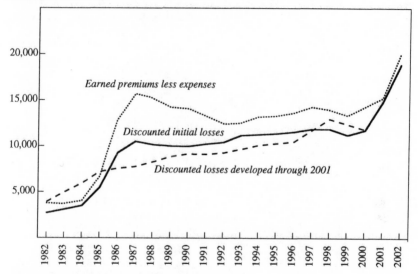

Source: A. M. Best (various years); Federal Reserve. Author's calculations.
a. Data for 2002 is estimated.

realizations for those years following the large increase in discounted initial losses and associated increases in premiums during 1985–86.

Figure 6 highlights the difference between the premium-expense margins and discounted losses over time by plotting operating profit margins based on discounted losses. The discounted operating margin based on initially reported losses declined during the early 1980s, increased significantly during 1985–87, and then declined over the next six years. It ultimately became negative in 2001. The operating margin based on discounted developed losses was substantially negative during 1982–85, with particularly large losses during 1983–84, immediately prior to the mid-1980s' rise in premiums. The operating margins based on discounted developed losses were large and positive in conjunction with those higher premiums, peaking at about 35 percent in 1987 and declining thereafter, except for 2000.

Figures 5 and 6 highlight the question of whether changes in costs can plausibly explain most of the changes in premiums. A number of studies of the experience with general liability insurance in the mid-1980s argue or provide evidence that the growth in premiums and lack of availability of

Figure 6. Estimated Discounted Operating Margins and Initially Reported and Developed through 2001 Accident-Year Incurred Losses in U.S. General Liability Insurance, 1982–2002ᵃ

Percent

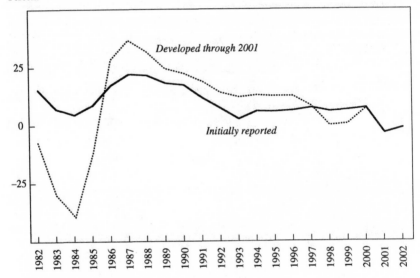

Source: A. M. Best (various years); Federal Reserve; author's calculations.
a. Data for 2002 is estimated.

insurance were caused largely by rapid growth in claim cost forecasts, reductions in interest rates (which increased the present value of predicted claim costs), and increases in the uncertainty of future liability claim costs associated with changes in the tort liability system.[6] The Tax Reform Act of 1986 likely raised premiums further by increasing insurers' expected taxes.[7] A number of studies stress that increased uncertainty associated with tort rules and jury awards increased the amount of capital needed to back coverage and therefore the cost of capital.[8] Cummins and McDonald document greater variance in the distribution of liability insurance claim costs during the early 1980s.[9]

6. For example, Tort Policy Working Group (1986); Clarke and others (1988); Harrington (1988); Harrington and Litan (1988). Also see Abraham (1988); Cummins and Danzon (1997).
7. See Bradford and Logue (1996).
8. For example, Doherty and Garven (1986), Clarke and others (1988); Winter (1988).
9. Cummins and McDonald (1991).

Other research argues that heightened uncertainty is likely to have increased adverse selection, which in turn helps to explain reduced availability of coverage.[10] If the average discounted expected cost per unit of coverage substantially increases, large increases in premium revenues can occur even though the quantity of coverage purchased is shrinking. These studies also suggest that the introduction of claims-made coverage and the exclusion of pollution claims in basic liability coverage were efficient methods of separating low-risk from high-risk buyers and reducing adverse selection.

Is the Evidence Broadly Consistent with the Perfect Markets Model?

The view that changes in the premium rates in general liability insurance are caused primarily by changes in discounted costs has to confront at least two challenges. First, some observers conclude that the large and abrupt increases in premiums in the mid-1980s and the larger growth in premiums compared to discounted losses, especially developed losses, cannot plausibly be explained by competitive product markets with frictionless capital. Second, the perfect markets model is not readily reconciled with evidence that underwriting and operating profits for general liability insurance and other lines of business appear cyclical (exhibit patterns like those shown in figure 3).[11]

Cycles in Reported Underwriting Results

Studies using data prior to the mid-1980s provide statistical evidence that all-lines loss ratios and reported underwriting profit margins (for example, one minus the combined ratio) exhibit second-order autoregression that implies a cyclical period of about six years.[12] Other studies document cyclical underwriting results in a number of other countries.[13] Underwriting

10. Priest (1987); also see Trebilcock (1987).

11. Another challenge, emphasized by Winter (1988, 1994; also see his comment on this paper), is the ability of the perfect markets model to explain coverage availability problems. As noted, increased adverse selection can contribute to availability problems, and, if average expected claim costs are rising rapidly, premium revenues can increase significantly despite shrinking quantity of coverage.

12. See Venezian (1985); Cummins and Outreville (1987); Doherty and Kang (1988).

13. Cummins and Outreville (1987); Lamm-Tennant and Weiss (1997); Chen, Wong, and Lee (1999).

results remain cyclical after controlling for the expected effects of changes in interest rates; that is, operating profits including investment income also exhibit cyclical patterns.[14]

Whether empirical regularities in reported underwriting results could be caused largely or exclusively by financial reporting procedures, reserve reporting bias, or regulation-induced lags in rate changes is uncertain. Cummins and Outreville show how accounting and regulatory lags might generate a cycle in reported underwriting margins without either excessive price cutting during soft markets or sharp reductions in supply during hard markets.[15] They note, however, that regulatory lag and financial reporting procedures are unlikely to explain changes in premiums in commercial liability insurance during the early to mid-1980s.[16] The small number of annual observations available to analyze underwriting results and changes in the mix of business sold and regulatory environment during the past fifty years make it difficult to draw solid conclusions from studies using aggregate data. The results that imply a regular cycle could be spurious or reflect data snooping. Even so, the evidence of second-order autoregression is not readily reconciled with the perfect markets model.

The Forecast Error Problem

The inability to observe insurers' claim cost forecasts at the time policies are priced and the possibility of large but rational forecast errors impede sharp conclusions about the explanatory power of the perfect markets model. Uncertainty concerning the frequency and severity of injuries, tort rules, and jury awards impedes accurate forecasting, especially when many claims for events in the year of coverage may not be paid for a decade or longer. Figure 7 illustrates the length of the claims tails for occurrence and claims-made general liability losses arising from injuries in 1992. For occurrence coverage, a third of estimated ultimate costs (valued as of 2001) had

14. Smith (1989); Harrington and Niehaus (2000). Several studies have considered the short- and long-run relation between underwriting margins, interest rates, and other macroeconomic variables using cointegration analysis and error correction models (for example, Haley 1993; Grace and Hotchkiss 1995). Harrington and Yu (2003) question whether underwriting margins are actually nonstationary (also see Choi, Hardigree, and Thistle 2002).

15. Cummins and Outreville (1987).

16. Analogous to Cummins and Outreville (1987), Doherty and Kang (1988) argue that cyclical patterns in underwriting results reflect slow but presumably rational adjustment of premiums to changes in expected claim costs and interest rates, but they do not consider the causes of adjustment lags.

Figure 7. Cumulative Paid Claims and Bulk and Incurred but Not Reported Reserves for Occurrence and Claims-Made Coverage as a Proportion of Estimated Ultimate Incurred Losses in U.S. General Liability Insurance for Accident-Year 1992

Percent

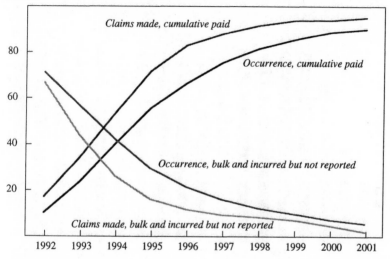

Source: A. M. Best (2002).

not been paid by year-end 1996. For claims-made coverage, less than 20 percent of estimated ultimate costs were unpaid at that time. The shorter claims tail for claims-made coverage reduces the risk of forecast error, which is a major reason for the growth in that form of coverage since the mid-1980s (see figure 8). Figure 7 also shows that a large proportion of initially reported losses represented estimated costs for claims predicted to have occurred but that had not yet been reported to insurers and for bulk reserves (insurers' forecast of how case reserves in the claim files are likely to develop). Incurred but not reported and bulk reserves for occurrence coverage represented more than 40 percent of reported incurred losses as of 1994, two years after the end of the 1992 accident year. Both forms of reserves are subject to large forecast errors.

The possibility of large forecast errors, management of reported losses and thus earnings, and accounting conventions that focus on calendar-year rather than accident-year losses make it difficult to evaluate the relation between growth in premiums and growth in losses. Figure 9 highlights some of the issues for general liability insurance during 1989–2001. It shows (a) initially reported accident-year loss ratios (to earned premiums), (b) calen-

Figure 8. Net Earned Premiums for Occurrence and Claims-Made Coverage in U.S. General Liability Insurance, 1984–2001

Millions of U.S. dollars

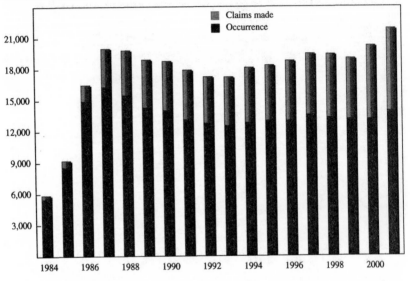

Source: A. M. Best (various years).

dar-year loss ratios, where calendar-year losses equal accident-year losses plus the change during the year in loss estimates for losses in all prior years, and (c) calendar-year loss ratios only including changes in estimated losses for the preceding nine accident years (year $t - 9$ through $t - 1$). The calendar-year loss ratios provide the basis for reported income and earnings per share in insurers' financial statements. They were higher than the accident-year loss ratios in all but one year during 1989–2001. The high calendar-year loss ratios in the early to mid-1990s were caused exclusively by losses for events that occurred ten or more years earlier. When the revisions of those old loss estimates are excluded, the calendar-year loss ratios were below accident-year losses during 1989–2000, indicating favorable reserve development on losses for years $t - 9$ through $t - 1$, which increased reported income. Consistent with the perfect markets model (and perhaps with incentives to strengthen reserves on old policies when current policies are generating reasonable results), the high calendar-year loss ratios during the mid-1990s did not lead to higher premiums.

Figure 9. Accident- and Calendar-Year Incurred Loss Ratios in U.S. General Liability Insurance, 1989–2001

Percent

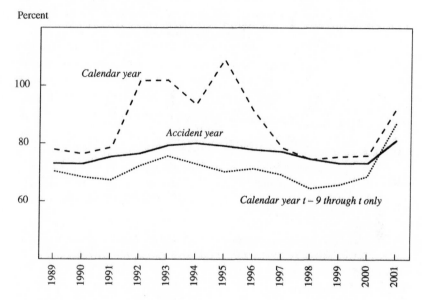

Source: A. M. Best (various years); author's calculations.

Cost Growth and Interest Rate Declines

When evaluating the perfect market model's explanatory power, it is necessary to keep in mind that rapid growth in general liability insurance premiums in the mid-1980s and 2001–02 was accompanied in both instances by substantial reductions in interest rates, which would amplify the effects of expected claim costs on rates of growth in premiums. Figure 10 plots the U.S. treasury term structure (average annual constant maturity rates) for four years: 1984, 1986, 2000, and 2002. Interest rates declined sharply between 1984 and 1986, significantly increasing the present value of insurers' estimated claim costs between 1984 and 1986. Interest rates again fell significantly between 2000 and 2002, raising the present value of estimated claim costs between those two years.

Holding other factors that affect discounted expected costs constant, figure 11 plots two-year growth in premiums implied by the perfect markets model for 1984–86 and 2000–02 versus hypothetical two-year growth in discounted expected claim costs (using the 1992 accident-year payout fac-

Figure 10. Constant Maturity Yields of U.S. Treasuries in Select Years, 1984–2002

U.S. Treasury yield (percent)

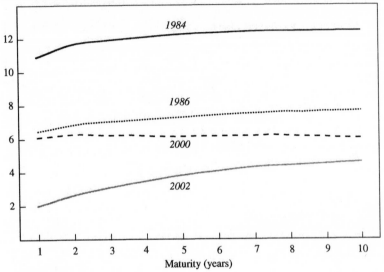

Source: Federal Reserve; author's calculations.

tors employed earlier). The 1984–86 interest rate declines and 40 percent growth in expected claim costs over the two years would produce a 65 percent growth in premiums, other factors held constant. For 2000–02, 40 percent growth in expected claim costs (3 percent less than my crude estimate of initially reported growth in accident-year losses; also see note 3) would produce 53 percent growth in premiums. Actual general liability net earned premiums grew 33 percent during that period; net written premiums grew 55 percent. Unless reported losses are biased substantially upward, these simple calculations imply that growth in costs and declines in interest rates may account for the bulk of growth in premiums during the current hard market.[17]

_____

17. I made the same point in my 1988 paper. Whether subsequent downward revisions in reported losses for the mid-1980s indicate ex ante bias in initially reported loss estimates is an open question.

Figure 11. Impact of Growth in Expected Claim Costs and Changes in Interest Rates on Growth of General Liability Insurance Premiums for Occurrence Coverage

Predicted change in premiums (percent)

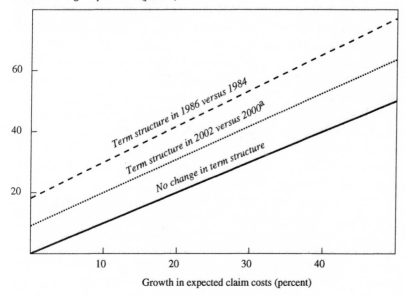

Growth in expected claim costs (percent)

Source: Author's calculations.
a. For 2000–02, net premiums written grew 55 percent, net premiums earned grew 33 percent, and initial accident-year losses grew 43 percent.

Other Explanations

I now turn to other explanations of volatility in premium rates and coverage availability: (a) costly external finance and capacity constraints, (b) asymmetric information, (c) market power, and (d) irrational insurer behavior with possible aberrant players.

Costly External Finance and Capacity Constraints

The 1980s crisis in liability insurance motivated substantial research on the possible effects of shocks to insurer capital on prices and coverage availability. One major development was the capacity constraint model, which posits that (a) industry supply depends on the amount of insurer capital, and (b) industry supply shifts backward and is sharply upward sloping following large negative shocks to capital due to the greater costs of raising external capital compared with internal capital. The main implication, at least of the original models, is that large, negative shocks to capital (for example, from catastrophes or unexpected changes in the costs of liability claims) produce short-run increases in prices and premium rates beyond the levels implied by the perfect markets model, thus materially aggravating hard markets.[18] If insurers could freely restore capital to its pre-shock level (or any new desired level), prices (premium-cost margins) would not increase, and premium rates would increase commensurately with revisions in the discounted expected value of claim costs for new and renewal business. But because the cost of obtaining capital increases following a shock, the post-shock short-run supply curve shifts backward, increasing prices and premium rates. The price increases, in turn, help insurers to replenish capital through retained earnings, which, along with issues of new capital, gradually eliminates the effects of the shock on supply.

Winter and Grøn have developed the basic capacity constraint model, assuming, respectively, that insurers are constrained to have zero insolvency risk or meet a regulatory constraint mandating a low probability of insolvency.[19] Cummins and Danzon, Cagle and Harrington, and Doherty and Garven extend the basic model on several dimensions.[20] The cost differential between internal and external funds is generally attributed to the costs of flotation and the standard "lemons" problem associated with seasoned equity offerings.[21] Cummins and Danzon also stress the overhang problem that arises because new equity issues increase the value of existing policyholders' claims.[22]

Existing capacity constraint models are somewhat opaque about price levels in soft markets. Grøn, for example, implies that soft-market prices are equal to those implied by the perfect markets model.[23] Winter stresses that soft markets persist when shocks are favorable and that soft markets are

18. Similar effects are highlighted in the macro-finance literature (for example, Greenwald and Stiglitz 1993).
19. Winter (1988, 1991a, 1994); Grøn (1994a). Winter (1991b) extends the basic capacity constraint story by examining the possible effect of regulation that restricts an insurer's premium-to-surplus ratio to below a certain level. This regulatory constraint can further exacerbate the reduction in short-run supply following a shock.
20. Cummins and Danzon (1997); Cagle and Harrington (1995); Doherty and Garven (1995).
21. For example, Myers and Majluf (1984).
22. Cummins and Danzon (1997). See also Myers (1977); Grøn and Winton (2001), discussed below.
23. Grøn (1994a).

characterized by excess capital compared with the perfect markets model, because of both the costs of paying out capital and the desire to accumulate capital that will become valuable during a hard market.[24]

The capacity constraint models generally imply that large shocks in the costs of liability insurance claims can produce correspondingly large increases in premium rates above and beyond increases implied by the perfect markets model. When demand is sensitive to insolvency risk, Cagle and Harrington show that any hard-market price increase will be lower than when demand is risk insensitive.[25] Cummins and Danzon stress that prices need not increase and could decrease if demand is sufficiently sensitive to insolvency risk.[26]

Winter emphasizes that uncertainty associated with the tort liability system and the long claims tail for liability insurance can aggravate changes in prices and coverage during hard markets.[27] Using the framework of Froot, Scharfstein, and Stein and of Froot and Stein, Grøn and Winton explain how "overhang" associated with claim liabilities for long-tailed policies sold in prior years can reduce the supply of coverage when capacity (net worth) is low as a result of a likely positive correlation between claim costs on old and new policies.[28] The effect will be worse for long-tailed liability lines given the greater amount of "old" liabilities and a greater correlation between costs of old and new liabilities compared with short-tailed lines.

The capacity constraint model has a number of policy implications. First, because rate increases in hard markets are competitively determined, rate regulation to hold down rate increases would discourage necessary capacity adjustments and aggravate availability problems. Second, any factors that increase the costs of raising new capital or the entry of new firms will make rate changes more volatile. Third, uncertainty associated with claim costs in general and tort liability claims in particular will increase insurers' vulnerability to shocks and increase volatility.

Empirical evidence on the capacity constraint model is inconclusive. Winter calculates a U.S. all-lines "economic loss ratio" for year t as the present value of calendar-year incurred losses in year t divided by premiums in year t.[29] Consistent with the prediction that higher prices (lower expected

24. Winter (1988, 1994).
25. Cagle and Harrington (1995).
26. Cummins and Danzon (1997).
27. Winter (1988, 1994).
28. Froot, Scharfstein, and Stein (1993); Froot and Stein (1998); Grøn and Winton (2001).
29. Winter (1994).

loss ratios) occur when capital is low, he finds that the economic loss ratio was positively related to the lagged value of insurer capital (measured as the deviation from its average value in the previous five years) during the period 1948–80. However, during the 1980s period that motivated development of the capacity constraint model, he finds that the economic loss ratio was negatively related to capital, due in large part to experience during the early 1980s. Winter argues that the 1980s can be explained in part by the omission of international reinsurance capacity in the capital variables.[30]

Grøn finds that 1 minus the loss ratio was negatively related to changes in aggregate capacity of property and casualty insurers for auto liability, auto physical damage, and homeowners' coverage using annual aggregate data for stock insurers during 1952–86.[31] However, the relation was positive for general liability insurance, again in contrast to the principal prediction of the basic capacity constraint model. Using panel data during 1980–88 for forty-five insurers that had at least a 0.5 percent share of the general liability insurance market, Cummins and Danzon find that ratios of the all-lines margin between net premiums and underwriting expenses and dividends to the discounted value of reported accident-year losses (their measures of price) were negatively related to loss shocks, again in contrast to the prediction of the basic capacity constraint model.[32] Cummins and Danzon also conclude that the increases in premiums during the mid-1980s were largely due to changes in expected costs, not capacity constraints.

Grøn finds that the difference between all-lines premiums and underwriting expenses, the ratio of premiums to underwriting expenses, and changes in those measures were negatively related to lagged values of capacity during 1949–90.[33] She also finds that her price measures increased following negative capital growth but that the price measures did not decline significantly following positive capital growth, suggesting a different relation in soft and hard markets. On the one hand, Higgins and Thistle find that all-lines underwriting profit margins during 1934–93 were cyclical only during periods of constrained capacity.[34] They also find that underwriting profit margins were unrelated to capacity during 1973–88, even though they were cyclical during 1968–91. On the other hand, and consistent with the

30. Also see Berger, Cummins, and Tennyson (1992).
31. Grøn (1994b).
32. Cummins and Danzon (1997).
33. Grøn (1994a). See also Niehaus and Terry (1993).
34. Higgins and Thistle (2000).

basic capacity constraint model, Choi, Hardigree, and Thistle find that all-lines economic loss ratios for stock insurers during 1935–97 were positively related to capacity (and negatively related to loss ratio conditional volatility, implying that higher risk led to higher prices).[35]

In related work, Froot and O'Connell analyze the relation over time between catastrophe reinsurance premiums and simulated values of expected claim costs parameterized using historical data on U.S. catastrophe losses to provide evidence of whether costly external finance aggravates changes in reinsurance rates following large catastrophe losses.[36] They argue that changes in expected claim costs ("probability updating") following loss shocks should primarily occur for hazards (for example, hurricanes or earthquakes) and for regions that are closely related to prior loss shocks. They present evidence that rate increases for reinsurance following large catastrophe losses during the early 1990s were broader than implied by revisions in expected claim costs, thus providing indirect evidence that loss shocks reduced capacity with an attendant effect on rates.

Asymmetric Information

Priest argues that asymmetric information about the risks of loss for liability insurance policyholders can aggravate average increases in premiums and declines in coverage during hard markets—as low-risk policyholders reduce their coverage limits and drop coverage—and that coverage may become completely unavailable for some risks as the market for coverage unravels due to adverse selection.[37] He emphasizes that changes in and uncertainty concerning tort liability rules are an underlying cause of these problems.[38]

Doherty and Posey develop a model where a different form of asymmetric information produces rationing of coverage.[39] Their model builds on the notion that the risk of correlated losses generally should be shared between insurers and policyholders.[40] The optimal contract would pay all the idiosyncratic losses of policyholders, but it would divide losses that are economy-wide (such as the effects of unexpected growth in claim costs or

35. Choi, Hardigree, and Thistle (2002).
36. Froot and O'Connell (1997a, 1997b).
37. Priest (1987, 1991).
38. Also see Trebilcock (1987).
39. Doherty and Posey (1997).
40. Marshall (1974); Doherty and Dionne (1993).

catastrophes) ex post among policyholders. Price increases following correlated losses would produce such sharing indirectly. Doherty and Posey argue that stock insurers have an incentive to overstate the magnitude of correlated losses, making the ideal contract infeasible. They suggest that insurers can signal the amount of correlated losses incurred by selling less coverage at a higher price than would otherwise be optimal. Insurers forgo profits through rationing, which credibly signals the magnitude of correlated losses. The main empirical predictions are that premium revenue falls following shocks and that changes in revenue are less for mutual insurers than for stock insurers, given that mutuals have less incentive to overstate correlated losses. Doherty and Posey provide evidence consistent with these predictions for growth in premiums for U.S. general liability insurance using panel data during 1980–89.

Market Power

Some observers have questioned whether insurers may have market power due to the costs of new entry during hard markets and whether prices increase further as a result.[41] Market power is difficult to reconcile with the fragmented structure of commercial general liability insurance markets and the apparent ease of entry for offshore reinsurers. If market power were expected during hard markets, prices would apparently need to be lower than implied by the perfect markets model during soft markets to produce a long-run equilibrium with normal returns on capital.

Some observers have questioned whether insurers' cooperative pricing activities in conjunction with the insurance industry's limited exemption from federal antitrust law might aggravate hard markets. The antitrust exemption in the McCarran-Ferguson Act applies to the extent that these activities are regulated by the states or unless boycott, coercion, and intimidation are involved. Most studies argue that collusive price increases cannot be reconciled with the industry's competitive structure, with the modern operation of advisory organizations, and with pricing discretion exercised by the underwriters of commercial lines.[42] Moreover, cooperative rate-making activities for commercial lines are likely to enhance economic effi-

41. See, for example, Froot and O'Connell (1997b), discussing reinsurance following catastrophe losses in the early 1990s; also see Froot (2001).

42. For example, Clarke and others (1988); Winter (1988); Harrington and Litan (1988); Harrington (1991). Also see Grøn (1995).

ciency rather than amplify cyclical fluctuations.[43] If these activities reduce the likelihood of widespread underpricing in soft markets, they could reduce the volatility in premiums.

Behavioral Influences and Aberrant Players

Capacity shocks should be largely unpredictable. Neither Winter's model nor other capacity constraint stories can readily explain second-order autoregression in profits. The traditional view of underwriting cycles by practitioners and industry analysts emphasizes fluctuations in capacity to write coverage as a result of changes in surplus and insurer expectations of profitability on new business.[44] Supply expands when expectations of profits are favorable, but competition then drives prices down, allegedly until inevitable underwriting losses deplete surplus. Supply contracts in response to unfavorable profit expectations and in an effort to avert financial collapse. Higher prices replenish surplus, leading to another round of price cutting, which ultimately becomes excessive. This explanation of supply contractions is roughly consistent with capacity constraint models, but the explanation of soft markets fails to explain how and why competition would cause rational insurers to cut prices to the point where premiums and anticipated investment income are insufficient to finance optimal forecasts of claim costs (and to ensure a low probability of insurer default).[45]

Why might soft markets culminate in rates that are inadequate ex ante? Winter's model implies that hard markets will be preceded by periods of excess capacity and soft prices, but the folklore about excessive price cutting during soft markets seems to run deeper than that. One conjecture is that a tendency toward price inadequacy could arise from heterogeneous insurer expectations concerning the costs of future losses or from differences in insurers' incentives for safe and sound operation.[46] My 1994 paper with Patricia Danzon develops and tests hypotheses based on this intuition and the literature on optimal bidding and moral hazard in the context of alleged

43. See, for example, Winter (1988, 1994); Harrington (1991).
44. See Stewart (1984); also see Berger (1988).
45. Similarly, popular explanations of "cash flow underwriting" usually imply that insurers are irrational in that they reduce rates too much in response to increases in interest rates.
46. On heterogeneous insurer expectations, see McGee (1986); Harrington (1988). Also see the comments in Stewart (1984); on differences in insurers' incentives, see Harrington (1988). McGee (1986) speculates that insurers with optimistic loss forecasts might cause prices to fall below the level implied by industry average forecasts. Winter (1988, 1991a) mentions the possibility of heterogeneous information and winner's curse effects.

underpricing of general liability insurance during the early 1980s.[47] We posit that some firms may have priced below cost because of moral hazard that results from limited liability and risk-insensitive guaranty programs. Other insurers may have priced below cost due to low forecasts of losses relative to optimal forecasts, giving rise to winners' curse effects. We stress that other firms could cut prices in response to such aberrant firms to preserve market share and avoid loss of quasi-rents from renewal business related to investments in tangible and intangible capital. As a result, relatively few aberrant firms could have a disproportionate impact on the market.

In that study, we use data from the early 1980s to test whether moral hazard or heterogeneous expectations contribute to differences in the price of general liability insurance and the growth of premiums among firms. Loss forecast revisions are used as a proxy for inadequate prices.[48] We find a positive relation between growth in premiums and revised forecasts of losses and some evidence that appears consistent with moral hazard.[49] An implication is that increased market or regulatory discipline against low-priced insurers with high default risk would reduce price volatility. Since the late 1980s, solvency regulation has been strengthened (for example, by the adoption of risk-based capital requirements), insurance rating agencies have increased the sophistication of their analyses, and there appears to have been greater concern among buyers with insurers' financial strength, thus improving market discipline and disincentives for inadequate rates.[50]

---

47. Harrington and Danzon (1994).

48. We have argued that loss forecast revisions will reflect moral hazard–induced low prices assuming that low-price firms understate initially reported loss forecasts to hide inadequate prices from regulators and other interested parties, but that forecasts are revised upward as paid claims accumulate. In addition, if prices vary due to differences in loss forecasts at the time of sale, less-informed firms with low forecasts should revise forecasts upward as information accumulates.

49. Forecast revisions and premium growth were generally related positively and significantly to the amount of liabilities ceded to reinsurers, consistent with the moral hazard hypothesis that reinsurance was used to conceal low prices and excessive growth. We also have found that mutual insurers generally have significantly lower forecast revisions and premium growth than stock insurers, consistent with mutuals being less prone to moral hazard.

50. My paper with Karen Epermanis provides evidence of significant premium declines for property-casualty insurers that experienced financial strength rating downgrades in the 1990s (Epermanis and Harrington, 2003).

Premium Growth and Loss Experience during the
1990s Soft Market

In this section I take another look at the relationship between insurers' growth in premiums and underwriting results during a soft market using data at the insurance-group level for general liability occurrence coverage (excluding separately reported product liability coverage) during 1993–2000. I provide evidence of whether abnormal growth in premiums during an accident year reliably predicts accident-year loss ratios by estimating the following descriptive regression model:

$$(1) \qquad y_{jt} = \beta_0 + \beta_1 \Delta P_{jt} + \beta_2 P_{j(t-1)} + e_{jt},$$

where, for firm j and year t, y_{jt} is either the initially reported accident-year incurred loss ratio (ILR), the developed (through December 2001) accident-year loss ratio (DLR), or the difference between the developed and initially reported loss ratio (DLR – ILR), and ΔP_{jt} equals $P_{jt} - P_{j(t-1)}$, where P_{jt} is log net earned premiums.[51]

Equation 1 can be motivated by the notion that both premium growth and realized loss ratios for a given accident year will depend on a firm's unobservable average price of coverage (that is, on the ratio of its premiums to the discounted value of rational forecasts of claim costs and other costs of providing coverage). If relatively high growth in premiums, on average, indicates a relatively low price, then growth in premiums and realized loss ratios (or loss development) will be positively related ($\beta_1 > 0$).[52] If so, realized loss ratios should also be positively related to lagged (log) premiums ($\beta_2 > 0$) if larger firms, on average, have lower premium growth than smaller firms at a given price because of firm life cycle effects. Greater lagged premiums would then imply a lower price for a given ΔP_{jt}. A positive relation between realized loss ratios and lagged premiums also could arise if larger firms had higher expected loss ratios because, for example, they write large accounts with lower underwriting expense ratios or achieve superior diversification and have commensurately lower capital costs.

51. ΔP_{jt} is thus the log premium (continuously compounded) growth rate during the year. The use of log growth diminishes positive skewness compared with percentage premium growth.

52. If premium growth and loss ratios are each negatively related to unobservable prices, it is easy to show that ΔP_{jt} and the disturbance term in equation 1 will be negatively correlated. The least squares estimate of β_1 will therefore be biased *against* finding a positive relation between loss ratios and premium growth.

A second scenario is that some firms may grow rapidly while exploiting profitable opportunities arising from superior information and risk selection. That scenario would lead to a negative relation between premium growth and loss ratios ($\beta_1 < 0$). A third scenario is that some firms will shrink premiums in response to poor underwriting experience and that poor performance could persist temporarily, which would likewise lead to a negative relation between premium growth and loss ratios. An important implication is that a positive relation between realized loss ratios and premium growth is most likely for growing firms.

I estimate equation 1, including a vector of time dummy variables to allow for fixed-year effects, using panel data for general liability coverage written on an occurrence basis (excluding separately reported product liability coverage) during 1993–2000 and two subperiods: 1993–96 and 1997–2000. The first subperiod was characterized by positive premium growth and (thus far) favorable reserve development (see, for example, figures 5 and 6 and table 1). The soft market deepened during the latter period, prior to the onset of the current hard market, with declining or negligibly growing earned premiums through 1999, heightened concern with allegedly excess capacity and lack of underwriting discipline, and (thus far) unfavorable development of reserves. The sample includes all insurance groups included in the 2001 National Association of Insurance Commissioners (NAIC) database with at least $5 million of net earned premiums in any accident year during 1992–99. The growth in premiums and loss ratio variables are Winsorized at the 0.01 and 0.99 values of the distributions for all insurers that had positive net earned premiums from general liability insurance during that period.

Table 1 presents descriptive statistics for growth in premiums and loss ratios for the overall sample period and the two subperiods. Premium growth and loss ratios varied substantially across insurers in each period. Premiums grew 4 percent, on average, during 1993–96 and declined 1 percent during 1997–2000; developed loss ratios, on average, were lower (higher) than initially reported loss ratios for the former (latter) period. Developed loss ratios were more variable than initially reported loss ratios, as would be expected if initially reported loss ratios were (perhaps even biased) forecasts of ultimate loss ratios.

Table 2 shows least-squares estimates of β_1 and β_2 in equation 1 and associated p values (statistical significance levels) for the coefficients using standard errors that are robust to heteroskedasticity and within-firm corre-

Table 1. Descriptive Statistics for Growth in Premiums of General Liability Insurers and Accident-Year Loss Ratios, 1993–2000[a]

Period and statistic	Mean	Standard deviation	Percentile						
			5th	10th	25th	50th	75th	90th	95th
1993–1996 (N = 442; G = 123)									
ΔP_t	0.037	0.266	−0.389	−0.186	−0.049	0.060	0.155	0.291	0.389
ILR	0.709	0.216	0.370	0.487	0.603	0.696	0.810	0.952	1.031
DLR	0.674	0.254	0.299	0.393	0.513	0.652	0.809	0.995	1.124
DLR − ILR	−0.035	0.243	−0.349	−0.283	−0.152	−0.052	0.068	0.200	0.340
1997–2000 (N = 449; G = 120)									
ΔP_t	−0.014	0.306	−0.462	−0.288	−0.090	0.031	0.104	0.226	0.345
ILR	0.723	0.223	0.411	0.465	0.584	0.701	0.839	0.990	1.140
DLR	0.753	0.310	0.398	0.439	0.553	0.711	0.865	1.080	1.329
DLR − ILR	0.029	0.244	−0.314	−0.190	−0.074	0.002	0.118	0.280	0.428
1993–2000 (N = 891; G = 132)									
DLR	0.714	0.286	0.354	0.421	0.535	0.685	0.844	1.038	1.194
DLR − ILR	−0.003	0.231	−0.342	−0.227	−0.124	−0.018	0.096	0.235	0.409

Source: Author's calculations.

a. The sample includes all insurance groups covered in the 2001 NAIC database with at least $5 million of general liability (including product liability) net earned premiums in any accident-year during 1992–1999. $\Delta P_{jt} = P_{jt} - P_{jt\text{-}1}$ where P_{jt} is log net earned premiums, ILR is the initially reported accident-year incurred loss ratio, and DLR is the developed (through December 2001) accident-year loss ratio. Variables are Winsorized at 0.01 and 0.99 values for all groups with positive net premiums earned in general liability insurance during 1992–2000. N is the sample size (in firm-years); G is the number of firms.

lation in the regression model disturbances. Estimates are shown for each sample period and for subgroups of observations with positive premium growth ($\Delta P_{jt} > 0$) and nonpositive premium growth ($\Delta P_{jt} \leq 0$).[53] The coefficients from the difference in loss ratio (DLR – ILR) equations equal the differences in the coefficients for the DLR and ILR equations. The p-values indicate whether the differences in coefficients are statistically significant.

The results shown in table 2 provide strong evidence of a positive relation between growth in premiums and developed loss ratios and loss ratio development (DLR – ILR) among firms with positive growth in premiums during the 1997–2000 soft-market period. The positive coefficients on ΔP_{jt} are both economically and statistically significant for that period. For the overall 1993–2000 period, developed loss ratios and the differences between developed and initially reported loss ratios are also positively and significantly related to premium growth among firms with positive premium growth. For 1993–96 and observations with positive premium growth, the coefficient on ΔP_{jt} equals –0.12 for the ILR equation and 0.12 for the DLR equation. Although neither coefficient is statistically significant at conventional significance levels, their difference (0.24) is statistically significant. Relatively high growth in premiums is reliably associated with adverse loss development during that period as well.

In contrast to the results for observations where $\Delta P_{jt} > 0$, the coefficients on ΔP_{jt} are not significantly positive during any sample period when observations with nonpositive growth in premiums are included in the samples alone or in combination with the observations with positive growth. A lack of a significant positive relation in these cases is plausibly attributable to shrinking premiums among some insurers in response to poor underwriting performance.

In summary, the results of these descriptive regressions imply that higher growth in premiums among firms with growing premiums is reliably associated with higher developed loss ratios (and loss development). It is not clear whether these results would be predicted by some variant of the capacity constraint model that allows for cross-firm heterogeneity. The results are consistent with the hypothesis that aberrant behavior by some firms could aggravate price cutting during soft markets, with low-priced firms capturing market share and ultimately experiencing relatively high loss ratios. A pol-

53. Selection bias is not a significant issue given that the objective is to estimate parameters for the models conditional on positive or negative premium growth.

Table 2. Least-Squares Estimates of Relation between Loss Ratios and Premium Growth, 1993–96, 1997–2000, and 1993–2000[a]

Period and regressor or statistic	Sample firms						All		
	$\Delta P_t > 0$			$\Delta P_t \le 0$					
	ILR	DLR	DLR – ILR	ILR	DLR	DLR – ILR	ILR	DLR	DLR – ILR
1993–96									
ΔP_t	−0.123	0.120	**0.243**	−0.010	0.024	0.034	−0.123	−0.061	0.063
	(0.16)	(0.23)	**(0.01)**	(0.93)	(0.85)	(0.55)	(0.08)	(0.45)	(0.18)
P_{t-1}	**0.054**	**0.058**	0.004	**0.034**	0.026	−0.008	**0.049**	**0.050**	−0.003
	(0.00)	**(0.00)**	(0.70)	**(0.05)**	(0.23)	(0.57)	**(0.00)**	**(0.00)**	(0.79)
R^2	0.143	0.109	0.049	0.090	0.044	0.040	0.128	0.067	0.026
N	289	289			153		442	442	
G	109	109			89		123	123	
1997–2000									
ΔP_t	**0.163**	**0.424**	**0.260**	−0.153	−0.180	−0.025	−0.095	−0.115	−0.020
	(0.03)	**(0.00)**	**(0.01)**	(0.17)	(0.29)	(0.79)	(0.15)	(0.22)	(0.74)
P_{t-1}	**0.027**	**0.058**	**0.031**	**0.032**	**0.056**	0.023	**0.027**	**0.055**	**0.028**
	(0.03)	**(0.00)**	**(0.01)**	**(0.02)**	**(0.01)**	(0.14)	**(0.01)**	**(0.00)**	**(0.02)**
R^2	0.057	0.147	0.066	0.077	0.062	0.017	0.042	0.065	0.024
N	259	259			190		449	449	
G	101	101			95		120	120	
1993–2000									
ΔP_t	0.013	**0.275**	**0.262**	−0.099	−0.098	0.002	**−0.111**	−0.090	0.022
	(0.83)	**(0.00)**	**(0.00)**	(0.22)	(0.39)	(0.98)	**(0.02)**	(0.17)	(0.61)
P_{t-1}	**0.042**	**0.060**	0.018	**0.033**	**0.040**	0.008	**0.038**	**0.050**	0.012
	(0.00)	**(0.00)**	(0.06)	**(0.01)**	**(0.01)**	(0.54)	**(0.00)**	**(0.00)**	(0.19)
R^2	0.083	0.138	0.061	0.076	0.060	0.050	0.080	0.083	0.034
N	548	548			343		891	891	
G	120	120			120		132	132	

Source: Author's calculations.

a. The regression equation is $y_{jt} = \beta_0 + \beta_1 \Delta P_{jt} + \beta_2 P_{jt-1} + \delta'T + \varepsilon_{jt}$, where, for firm j and year t, y_{jt} is the initially reported accident-year incurred loss ratio (ILR), the developed (through December 2001) accident-year loss ratio (DLR), or the difference between DLR and ILR (DLR – ILR), where P_{jt} is log net earned premiums, and T is a vector of year indicator variables. The sample includes all insurance groups included in the 2001 NAIC database with at least $5 million of net earned premiums in any accident-year during 1992–99. $\Delta P_{jt} = P_{jt} - P_{jt-1}$, where P_{jt} is log net earned premiums, and T is a vector of year indicator variables. The sample includes all insurance groups included in the 2001 NAIC database with at least $5 million of net earned premiums in any accident-year during 1992–99. N is the sample size (number of firm-years); G is the number of firms. One-tailed p values based on robust cluster standard errors are in parentheses beneath the coefficient estimate. Values in bold are significant at the 0.05 percent level for a one-tailed test.

icy implication is that more intensive scrutiny of insurers with abnormally large growth in premiums by regulators and rating agencies might help to deter any "excessive" price cutting in soft markets.

Conclusion

There is little doubt that "much" of the volatility in insurance premium rates—whether for general liability insurance or other types of coverage—is attributable to variation in the discounted value of expected claim costs. Perhaps only a die-hard believer in the perfect markets models would argue that "much" means "all" or "almost all." The capacity constraint model provides an intuitively plausible explanation of possible unexplained volatility, but tests of its predictions have produced mixed results, perhaps due to methodological and data problems. We know relatively little about whether and why insurance prices tend to fall too low during soft markets.

Additional empirical work might provide more evidence on whether costly external capital contributes to hard and soft markets. However, because it is not possible to observe rational forecasts of claim costs when policies are sold, it will likely remain difficult to provide convincing evidence of the extent to which capital costs contribute to volatility in premiums and availability in comparison to changes in discounted expected costs. The relatively small number of usable time-series observations and the potential for data-snooping bias suggest the need for analyses that make creative use of cross-sectional and panel data. Additional theoretical work on capacity constraint models might further elaborate the relationship between costly external capital and capital structure decisions and pricing prior to any shock.

Despite what we do not know and the desire to know more, available theoretical and empirical research is informative with respect to the policy debate. In the long run and—at least to a large extent—in the short run, liability insurance premium rates track the discounted value of expected claim costs and the tax and agency costs of capital needed to back the sale of coverage. An expanding tort liability system that entails substantial uncertainty about the cost of future claims will inevitably lead to increasingly expensive coverage. The cases for the status quo, for further expansion of tort liability, or for contraction through tort "reform" hinge primarily on the deterrent effects and transaction costs of tort liability, not on whether the perfect markets model fully explains prices and availability.

Comment and Discussion

Comment by Ralph A. Winter: Scott Harrington has highlighted the most puzzling aspect of the property-liability insurance market: its sporadic volatility. Premiums are relatively stable, even declining, for long periods (such as 1977–84 or 1988–2001). Then policyholders renewing their policies find that their premiums have skyrocketed. The number of transactions drops dramatically in these hard markets: for many lines, insurance is described as unavailable—meaning unavailable at moderate prices. In 1985–86 and again in 2001, many policyholders renewing their policies saw their premiums double or triple and their coverage drop. Harrington discusses several hypotheses in light of the evidence and then offers some innovative evidence regarding a particular source of instability in the market, which he refers to as "aberrant pricing."

In this discussion of Harrington's paper, I comment on several aspects of the insurance cycle and the evidence he presents:

—The specific empirical features of insurance market dynamics that must be explained by a theory of the insurance cycle,

—Several of the theories that have been offered to explain these features and how they stack up against the evidence, and

—Harrington's evidence of "aberrant pricing" and its role in the insurance cycle. I characterize his results as evidence of information heterogeneity across firms rather than as aberrant pricing, but I agree that his evidence reveals a potentially important source of volatility.

I start with the data. The data on the insurance market are unusual in that we have no direct and reliable time-series evidence on either prices or quantities. We are studying a cycle in a market without reliable data on the two most basic variables. We have, however, time series on revenue: net premiums written. This series is often used as a proxy for prices and sometimes as a proxy for the amount of insurance written. We have to keep in mind that it is neither. The net premiums written time series is revenue: the product of price and quantity.

We can, however, obtain general information on price changes through surveys or—because the changes can be sudden and dramatic—simply through reports in the press. Thus we know that in 1985 and 1986 prices jumped and quantity dropped dramatically. The press was replete with reports of soaring premiums and declining coverage. The March 24, 1986, cover of *Time* magazine stated, "Sorry, America, your insurance has been canceled." We can also combine the strong anecdotal evidence with the available data on revenue. Revenue for liability lines tripled over the 1985–86 period, for example. With the information that the quantity of insurance coverage had dropped—some policies were canceled, some coverage limits were reduced severely, and for many coverage moved from occurrence to a claims-made basis—this jump in revenue meant that prices increased by much more than triple over two years. In short, during hard markets, (1) prices increase sharply, (2) quantity drops, and (3) revenue increases. Hard markets have two additional features as well: (4) the *nonlinearity* of prices increases sharply, in the sense that the marginal price of obtaining high coverage rises even more than the price of basic coverage during tight markets, and (5) hard markets tend to affect particular lines more severely than others, although the recent jump in premiums seems to be more widespread than previous episodes. The task of any economic theory of insurance market dynamics is to explain the unusual dynamics of pricing (stable or declining premiums for some years, interrupted by sharp jumps in premiums) *and* other features of the market, especially the cyclical behavior of quantity and revenue. Quantity is strongly countercyclical to price movements, and revenue is procyclical.

Harrington starts, as he should, with the most fundamental theory of insurance market pricing: the perfect capital markets theory. He puts it succinctly: "With rational insurers and policyholders, competitive insurance markets, and frictionless capital markets, insurance premiums will equal the risk-adjusted discounted value of expected cash outflows for claims, sales expenses, and other costs." It is useful to express this hypothesis more precisely, by noting that "expected" in this statement refers to the expectation conditional on all information available at the time that premiums are established by the market. Thus the premium is the best predictor of the discounted value of future cash flows from the policies; that is, the premium is a sufficient statistic for this value among all available information. The realized error in premiums as predictors is white noise—uncorrelated with any observables at the time that premiums are established. This is simply the efficient markets hypothesis applied to a particular securities market: the market for insurance. Insurance contracts are not traded in secondary markets (setting aside the small trade in viatical contracts), but they are securities.

In less technical language, all fluctuations in premiums must be due to changes in rationally anticipated cash flows or in interest rates in the perfect capital markets model. It is important to note, as Harrington does, that interest rates declined substantially during the mid-1980s and 2001–02 hard markets, which must explain some of the increase in premiums. He shows, in the case of the mid-1980s experience, for example, that the actual decline in interest rates and an assumption of 40 percent growth in anticipated claims over two years would produce a 65 percent growth in premiums over this period. This certainly seems like a large part of the explanation. But is it? In liability lines, premiums increased by much more than 200 percent over this period.

The perfect capital markets hypothesis cannot account for all of the fluctuations in premiums. It can also be rejected on the basis of the second most prominent feature of the insurance cycle: the drop in quantity during hard markets. A drop in interest rates should not affect the demand and supply curves for insurance symmetrically (assuming both sides of the insurance market have access to the same capital markets). And an increase in rationally anticipated claims would increase, not decrease, the gains to trade in insurance if the perfect capital market held.

In an attempt to explain the dramatic changes in quantity, some scholars have added to the perfect capital markets model the well-known feature of adverse selection in insurance markets.[1] If individuals are better informed about their own risks, then even small shocks to the market can lead to large changes in quantity as the market "unravels": an increase in premiums will lead the better risks to drop out of the market, leading premiums to increase further to cover the average of the remaining risks, leading the next best risks to drop out of the market, and so on. Consider the joint

1. Priest (1987, 1991).

hypothesis of perfect capital markets combined with adverse selection, in light of the evidence on prices, quantities, and revenues. Adverse selection can explain the magnification of price and quantity fluctuations to small shocks: prices increase much more than justified by any initial shock, and the theory also predicts that quantities drop during hard markets. But it is rejected by what I have labeled the third feature of the insurance cycle: the procyclicality (with prices) of revenues. As a competitive insurance market unravels, prices rise, quantity falls, and total revenues must *fall*. (This is because the set of transactions shrinks, therefore total cost shrinks, and because the market is competitive, total revenue equals total cost.) In all hard markets, revenues have increased as prices have risen. In sum, the perfect capital market can account for neither the magnitude of the price fluctuations and, even with the addition of adverse selection, can be rejected by evidence on the other features of the cycle.

Harrington reviews the capacity constraint hypothesis as an alternative to the perfect capital market. The capacity constraint, or finance-constrained, approach to insurance markets recognizes that, because there are common factors in the distribution of risks, equity is needed to render insurance contracts credible. (The *pooling* theory of insurance fails because the law of large numbers no longer holds when there are common factors.) In a perfect capital market, this does not matter because corporations can hold any amount of equity, investing the proceeds in financial assets, without transactions or other costs. In reality capitalization requirements, whether imposed by rationality on the demand side of financial markets or by regulation, are not costless. Therefore the stock of corporate equity at any moment can limit the amount of insurance that can be offered rather than be increased without cost. The pivotal assumption in this theory is that the stock of equity cannot be adjusted costlessly at any moment by raising equity or paying out dividends. There is a positive cost, in other words, to the roundtrip of a dollar of equity from a corporation to shareholders and back again. The effect is that, when equity is diminished because of the accumulation of past underwriting losses or (as in the 1970s) because of investment losses, capacity is constrained and, because of this supply-side constraint, premiums rise and quantity falls. Evidence on the capacity constraint hypothesis is provided in my 1993 article and especially in the articles by Anne Grøn as well as more recent literature.[2] Higgins and This-

2. Winter (1994); Grøn (1994a, 1994b, 1995).

tle provide evidence of the capacity constraint model's implication of asymmetry: a given decrease in equity should have a much greater impact when the level of equity is low, relative to demand, than when it is high.[3] Ken Froot's recent papers on the pricing of catastrophe insurance provide additional evidence that insurance markets are financially constrained.[4]

The capacity constraint hypothesis is not a particularly innovative theory: every industry experiences fluctuations in profits and therefore shocks to the stock of low-cost internal capital, which then feed into fluctuations in supply. (Greenwald and Stiglitz explore this effect at a macroeconomic level.[5]) The interesting question is why *insurance* markets are so vulnerable to these shocks. Can shocks to internal capital realistically explain the magnitude of the jumps in premiums and quantity observed? In past articles and in ongoing work, I and others have identified the features of insurance that make this market so sensitive to internal equity shocks. One effect is that the form of solvency regulation (in which substantial weight is placed on the ratio of revenue to equity as a measure of financial solvency) introduces a perverse effect whereby an increase in premiums can, if demand is inelastic, lead to an apparent *lessening* of financial solvency and a further cutback in supply. Even this regulation alone can generate catastrophe dynamics (that is, periodic, discontinuous jumps in market equilibrium).[6] More fundamental aspects of the insurance market also make it more vulnerable to shocks to internal equity than other markets. Not the least of these is the simple fact that, when the internal equity of an insurance market experiences a sudden decrease of, say, 5 percent, the capacity of the market is immediately hit with the 5 percent decrease; this is not true of a conventional product market where the 5 percent shock affects capacity (physical capital) only indirectly by increasing the cost of capital for expansion or replacement.

The financial constraint approach to the insurance cycle is not universally accepted. In fact, Cummins and Danzon offer the opposite theory.[7] Their theory is that high premiums are due to *greater* equity in insurance markets, since greater equity backing insurance policies means both greater value for demanders and a higher expected cost (payout) for suppliers. The Cum-

3. Higgins and Thistle (2000).
4. Froot (2001).
5. Greenwald and Stiglitz (1993).
6. Winter (1991b).
7. Cummins and Danzon (1997).

mins-Danzon view is that the tripling of premiums when buyers renewed policies in 1985 and 1986 was the result of much greater equity, not less equity, than in 1984 and earlier. The mid-1980s experience, in this view, was one of abundant capacity. Both the Cummins-Danzon model and the capacity constraint model can, in theory, explain price increases in the mid-1980s (I set aside the question of whether the magnitude of the jump could be explained by greater assurance of payouts). Price increases in general can be explained by either an increase in demand with an improvement in quality or a drop in supply. The test to distinguish demand versus supply sources of price increases is simple: check the changes in quantity. If the Cummins-Danzon theory of excess capacity were correct, then the enormous price increases of the mid-1980s would have been accompanied by *increases* in the number of insurance transactions. In fact, we observed a massive withdrawal of insurance. Cummins and Danzon claim support for their theory in the positive correlation between capacity and premiums (relative to expected payouts) during the 1980s. But they measure domestic capacity, not the entire capacity available. The latter includes the equity of reinsurers, who were especially hard-hit in the 1980s. As the capacity in the reinsurance market dried up, premiums and domestic equity increased simultaneously through the issuance of shares, just as the capacity constraint hypothesis would predict. The positive correlation between capacity and premiums through the 1980s insurance crisis was spurious.[8] The simplest distinguishing test for the two theories, again, is simply to ask whether transactions increase or decrease in hard markets.

Harrington suggests that the capacity constraint theory cannot explain second-order effects in profits or prices relative to expected payouts and that there is therefore a need to turn to behavioral theories and theories of aberrant players. It is true that the formal models of the capacity constraint theory predict first-order dynamics.[9] Prices follow a first-order Markov process in the theory. But this is merely an artifact of the simplifying assumption of one-period contracts in the model. If the theory is extended to incorporate (a) two-period, overlapping insurance contracts and (b) factors in the distribution of risks that drift stochastically, instead of being stationary, first differences in premiums would persist relative to expected payouts. This would be analogous to the higher-order dynamics of overlapping-generations models of the real business cycle. It is a more

8. Winter (1994).
9. For example, in Winter (1994).

complicated model, with multiple state variables. But it is simply a more realistic version of the finance-constrained approach to insurance markets. Higher-order dynamics alone are not sufficient reason to turn away from rational models toward behavioral models to explain industry dynamics.

Finally, I turn to Harrington's evidence on "aberrant pricing." He finds a strong positive relation across firms between premium growth and loss ratios in the 1990s. A high loss ratio means a low price (relative to expected payouts), so this relation confirms what one might expect: low-priced firms achieve higher revenue growth over a period as demand shifts toward these firms via the entry of new demanders and the switching of some customers to low-priced firms. The more interesting result is his finding that the firms with higher revenue growth (generally the firms with low prices) experience adverse loss over the period. In other words, those firms that set relatively low estimates of future losses (and therefore low premiums) are forced to adjust their loss estimates upward over time. As Harrington indicates, this suggests heterogeneous information in estimates of future losses.

Heterogeneous information can lead to the "winner's curse" effect in insurance markets. Harrington misconstrues this effect, however, in suggesting that it can lead to inadequate prices and to prices below costs.[10] The winner's curse effect refers not to the fact that the lowest prices set in a market with differential information will likely be below cost. (In the standard common-value auction context, the winner's curse effect does not refer to the likelihood of bids exceeding the value.) The effect is in the *anticipation* of this possibility by each bidder or premium setter. Each insurer will adjust its own estimates of losses upward, in a market with information heterogeneity, to account for the fact that, if it is successful in attracting substantial demand, its premium will likely be too low. Heterogeneity of information across insurers leads, through the winner's curse effect, to *high* premiums and, I conjecture, quantity rationing. I am not convinced that it provides a basis for "more-intensive scrutiny of insurers with abnormally large premium growth by regulators" to "help deter any 'excessive' price cutting in soft markets."

Discussion: Scott Harrington began by responding to a question on the difference between figures 3 and 6 in the paper. Figure 6 is based on realized interest rates and dividend income as opposed to prospective bond rates,

10. Harrington and Danzon (1994).

which are used to discount. It is forward looking by incorporating discounted expected future losses in the current book of business. Figure 3, however, uses calendar-year results, which reflect revisions and loss forecasts for claims as long as twenty-five years earlier. While Dave Cummins and Rich Phillips have recently done work suggesting the contrary, the historical consensus is that there is insufficient systemic risk in insurance to compensate investors at S&P 500 levels.

Joan Lamm-Tenent of the General Reinsurance Corporation asked for clarification that the data were "statutory operating margins." The primary financial incentive for the insurance industry is the cheap float generated by premiums, which can be reinvested to generate capital gains, but statutory operating margins do not represent the full incentive to firms because they do not include unrealized capital gains. Mike O'Malley of Chubb seconded this concern with the choice of data. General liability, taken from line 18 of annual statements, represents an amalgamation of many products, from errors and omissions insurance through personal liability assessed over a homeowner's property. The risk in general liability is not at all homogeneous. He also suggested taking into account the common practice of bundling "general liability" with other coverage.

Neil Doherty of the Wharton School suggested that the results may reflect two different phenomena. The first, which the paper seeks to explore, is that, in a soft market, premium growth leads to an inflow of bad experience, and this relationship does appear in the data. A different model, one of adverse selection in which information is gained over time, predicts the same. The insurer and insured have different information, but as time passes the insurance company can purge the worse risks; companies cross-sectionally different from those that are improving their portfolio would be growing more slowly but improving their risk ratio. This adverse selection model should operate in both a hard and a soft market, while the perfect markets model should only work in a soft market. This distinction should allow one to discriminate which of the two models is at work.

Harrington concluded, ceding that the capacity constraints model helps to explain fluctuations in quantity and price but that the magnitude of the effect remains uncertain. For the present, the capacity constraint model has intuitive merit; empirical evidence to support it will probably come with time. The adverse selection issue may become more important with an increase in asymmetric information, causing a drop in the quantity of policies or policy limits, but revenues may continue to grow.

References

Abraham, Kenneth S. 1988. "The Causes of the Insurance Crisis." In Walter Olson, ed., *New Directions in Liability Law*. New York: Academy of Political Science.

Berger, Lawrence A. 1988. "A Model of the Underwriting Cycle in the Property/Liability Insurance Industry." *Journal of Risk and Insurance* 55 (2): 298–306.

Berger, Larry A., J. David Cummins, and Sharon Tennyson. 1992. "Reinsurance and the Liability Insurance Crisis." *Journal of Risk and Uncertainty* 5 (July): 253–72.

A. M. Best. Various issues. *Best's Aggregates and Averages*.

Bradford, David F., and Kyle D. Logue. 1996. "The Effects of Tax-Law Changes on Property-Casualty Insurance Prices." NBER Working Paper 5652. Cambridge, Mass.: National Bureau of Economic Research.

Cagle, Julie, and Scott Harrington. 1995. "Insurance Supply with Capacity Constraints and Endogenous Insolvency Risk." *Journal of Risk and Uncertainty* 11 (3, July): 219–32.

Chen, Renbao, Kie Ann Wong, and Hong Chew Lee. 1999. "Underwriting Cycles in Asia." *Journal of Risk and Insurance* 66 (1, March): 29–47.

Choi, S., Don Hardigree, and Paul Thistle. 2002. "The Property/Liability Insurance Cycle: A Comparison of Alternative Models." *Southern Economic Journal* 68 (January): 530–48.

Clarke, Richard N., Frederick Warren-Boulton, David K. Smith, and Marilyn J. Simon. 1988. "Sources of the Crisis in Liability Insurance: An Economic Analysis." *Yale Journal on Regulation* 5 (Summer): 367–95.

Cummins, J. David, and Patricia M. Danzon. 1997. "Price, Financial Quality, and Capital Flows in Insurance Markets." *Journal of Financial Intermediation* 6 (1, January): 3–38.

Cummins, J. David, and James B. McDonald. 1991. "Risk Probability Distributions and Liability Insurance Pricing." In J. David Cummins, Scott Harrington, and Robert Klein, eds., *Cycles and Crises in Property/Casualty Insurance: Causes and Implications for Public Policy*. Kansas City, Mo.: National Association of Insurance Commissioners.

Cummins, J. David, and François Outreville. 1987. "An International Analysis of Underwriting Cycles in Property-Liability Insurance." *Journal of Risk and Insurance* 54 (2): 246–62.

Doherty, Neil A., and Georges Dionne. 1993. "Insurance with Undiversifiable Risk: Contract Structure and Organizational Form of Insurance Firms." *Journal of Risk and Uncertainty* 6 (2): 187–203.

Doherty, Neil A., and James Garven. 1986. "Price Regulation in Property-Liability Insurance: A Contingent Claims Analysis." *Journal of Finance* 41 (5): 1031–50.

———. 1995. "Insurance Cycles: Interest Rates and the Capacity Constraint Model." *Journal of Business* 68 (3): 383–404.

Doherty, Neil A., and Han Bin Kang. 1988. "Interest Rates and Insurance Price Cycles." *Journal of Banking and Finance* 12 (2): 199–214.

Doherty, Neil A., and Lisa Posey. 1997. "Availability Crises in Insurance Markets: Optimal Contracts with Asymmetric Information and Capacity Constraints." *Journal of Risk and Uncertainty* 15 (1, October): 55–80.

Epermanis, Karen, and Scott E. Harrington. 2003. "Market Discipline in Property/Casualty Insurance: Evidence from Premium Growth Surrounding Policyholder Rating Changes." Unpublished Working Paper. University of Hartford; University of South Carolina.

Froot, Kenneth. 2001. "The Market for Catastrophe Risk: A Clinical Examination." *Journal of Financial Economics* 60 (2-3, May-June): 529–71.

Froot, Kenneth, and Paul O'Connell. 1997a. "On the Pricing of Intermediated Risks: Theory and Application to Catastrophe Reinsurance." NBER Working Paper 6011. Cambridge, Mass.: National Bureau of Economic Research.

———. 1997b. "The Pricing of U.S. Catastrophe Reinsurance." NBER Working Paper 6043. Cambridge, Mass.: National Bureau of Economic Research.

Froot, Kenneth, David Scharfstein, and Jeremy Stein. 1993. "Risk Management: Coordinating Corporate Investment and Financing Policies." *Journal of Finance* 48 (December): 1629–58.

Froot, Kenneth, and Jeremy Stein. 1998. "Risk Management, Capital Budgeting, and Capital Structure Policy for Financial Institutions: An Integrated Approach." *Journal of Financial Economics* 47 (1): 55–82.

Grace, Martin, and Julie Hotchkiss. 1995. "External Impacts on the Property-Liability Insurance Cycle." *Journal of Risk and Insurance* 62 (4): 738–54.

Greenwald, Bruce, and Joseph Stiglitz. 1993. "Financial Market Imperfections and Business Cycles." *Quarterly Journal of Economics* 108 (1, February): 77–114.

Grøn, Anne. 1994a. "Capacity Constraints and Cycles in Property-Casualty Insurance Markets." *Rand Journal of Economics* 25 (1, Spring): 110–27.

———. 1994b. "Evidence of Capacity Constraints in Insurance Markets." *Journal of Law and Economics* 37 (October): 349–77.

———. 1995. "Collusion, Costs, or Capacity? Evaluating Theories of Insurance Cycles." Working Paper. Northwestern University.

Grøn, Anne, and Andrew Winton. 2001. "Risk Overhang and Market Behavior." *Journal of Business* 74 (4): 591–612.

Haley, Joseph. 1993. "A Cointegration Analysis of the Relationship between Underwriting Margins and Interest Rates: 1930–1989." *Journal of Risk and Insurance* 60 (3): 480–93.

Harrington, Scott E. 1988. "Prices and Profits in the Liability Insurance Market." In Robert Litan and Clifford Winston, eds., *Liability: Perspectives and Policy.* Brookings.

———. 1991. "The Liability Insurance Market: Volatility in Prices and in the Availability of Coverage." In Peter Schuck, ed., *Tort Law and the Public Interest: Competition, Innovation, and Consumer Welfare.* W. W. Norton.

Harrington, Scott E., and Patricia Danzon. 1994. "Price Cutting in Liability Insurance Markets." *Journal of Business* 67 (4): 511–38.

———. 2001. "Liability Insurance." In Georges Dionne, ed., *The Handbook of Insurance.* Boston: Kluwer.

Harrington, Scott E., and Robert E. Litan. 1988. "Causes of the Liability Insurance Crisis." *Science* 239 (February 12): 737–41.

Harrington, Scott E., and Greg Niehaus. 2000. "Volatility and Underwriting Cycles." In Georges Dionne, ed., *The Handbook of Insurance.* Boston: Kluwer.

Harrington, Scott E., and Tong Yu. 2003. "Do Property-Casualty Insurance Underwriting Margins Have Unit Roots?" *Journal of Risk and Insurance* 70 (4): 715–33.

Higgins, Matthew, and Paul Thistle. 2000. "Capacity Constraints and the Dynamics of Underwriting Profits." *Economic Inquiry* 38 (3): 442–57.

Lamm-Tennant, Joan, and Mary A. Weiss. 1997. "International Insurance Cycles: Rational Expectations/Institutional Intervention." *Journal of Risk and Insurance* 64 (3): 415–39.

Marshall, John. 1974. "Insurance Theory: Reserves versus Mutuality." *Economic Inquiry* 12 (4): 476–92.

McGee, Robert. 1986. "The Cycle in Property/Casualty Insurance." *Federal Reserve Bank of New York Quarterly Review* 11 (Fall): 22–30.

Myers, Stewart C. 1977. "Determinants of Corporate Borrowing." *Journal of Financial Economics* 5 (2, November): 147–75.

Myers, Stewart, and Nicholas S. Majluf. 1984. "Corporate Financing and Investment Decisions When Firms Have Information That Investors Do Not Have." *Journal of Financial Economics* 13 (2): 187–221.

Niehaus, Greg, and Andy Terry. 1993. "Evidence on the Time-Series Properties of Insurance Premiums and Causes of the Underwriting Cycle: New Support for the Capital Market Imperfection Hypothesis." *Journal of Risk and Insurance* 60 (3): 466–79.

Priest, George L. 1987. "The Current Insurance Crisis and Modern Tort Law." *Yale Law Journal* 96 (June): 1521–90.

———. 1991. "The Modern Expansion of Tort Liability: Its Sources, Its Effects, and Its Reform." *Journal of Economic Perspectives* 5 (3): 31–50.

Smith, Michael. 1989. "Investment Returns and Yields to Holders of Insurance." *Journal of Business* 62 (1): 81–98.

Stewart, Barbara D. 1984. "Profit Cycles in Property-Liability Insurance." In John D. Long, ed., *Issues in Insurance.* Malvern, Pa.: American Institute for Property and Liability Underwriters.

Tort Policy Working Group. 1986. *Report of the Tort Policy Working Group on the Causes, Extent, and Policy Implications of the Current Crisis in Insurance Availability and Affordability.* U.S. Department of Justice.

Trebilcock, Michael J. 1987. "The Social Insurance-Deterrence Dilemma of Modern Tort Law." *San Diego Law Review* 24: 929–1002.

Venezian, Emilio. 1985. "Ratemaking Methods and Profit Cycles in Property and Liability Insurance." *Journal of Risk and Insurance* 52 (3): 477–500.

Winter, Ralph A. 1988. "The Liability Crisis and the Dynamics of Competitive Insurance Markets." *Yale Journal on Regulation* 5 (2): 455–99.

———. 1991a. "The Liability Insurance Market." *Journal of Economic Perspectives* 5 (3): 15–136.

———. 1991b. "Solvency Regulation and the Property-Liability Insurance Cycle." *Economic Inquiry* 29 (3): 458–71.

———. 1994. "The Dynamics of Competitive Insurance Markets." *Journal of Financial Intermediation* 3 (4, September): 379–415.

Insuring against Terrorism: The Policy Challenge

KENT SMETTERS

T HE TERRORIST ATTACKS during the past decade in London, Israel, the United States, and elsewhere have spawned an interest in understanding not only how governments can mitigate terrorism risk but also how governments might help to finance future losses. A burgeoning academic literature—and an intense lobbying effort by various industries—have argued that government assistance is needed due to a host of problems: the large size of potential losses, the difficulty of pricing the losses, the government's existing role as the guarantor of last resort, asymmetric information, the relationship between terrorism losses and government military policies, and other reasons. These arguments served as an important catalyst for the Terrorism Risk Insurance Act (TRIA) that President Bush signed into law in November 2002. Although TRIA's passage was held up in Congress for almost a year over a debate on limiting tort actions, both Democratic and Republican leaders supported the act.

Over the past fifty years, the public has accepted a larger role for the government in insuring *natural* catastrophic losses.[1] The general acceptance of the U.S. government's role in financing *non-natural* terrorist

The author benefited from conversations with David Cummins and Neil Doherty. Jeffrey Brown and the discussant, Howard Kunreuther, provided valuable and detailed comments, as did other conference participants.

1. Moss (1999, 2002).

losses, therefore, is probably not surprising, especially since the losses are partly in the government's control.

This paper takes a contrarian view. I argue that *mostly unfettered* insurance and capital markets are capable of insuring large terrorism losses, even losses ten times larger than the $40 billion loss incurred on September 11, 2001. A $400 billion loss in capital markets is common. U.S. capital markets alone routinely gain or lose $100 billion on a *daily* basis and often several *trillion* dollars on a monthly basis. Moreover, a significant amount of these risks can be traced to new companies that have very little history or few close substitutes from which investors can accurately assess future earnings. Furthermore, a significant amount of the net earnings of most corporations is influenced by the government's nonmilitary policies through a vast sea of tax regulations, oversight regulations, and torts. Despite these numerous problems and government policy risks, investors provide enormous liquidity to U.S. firms, producing one of the most efficient mechanisms for financing risks that has ever existed. Product and environmental liability markets have also remained vibrant despite shifting court standards during the 1970s and 1980s that generated large, correlated losses to insurers. Indeed, shifts in legal standards are probably less predictable than many terrorist acts.

So why do insurers *appear* to have a hard time providing insurance against a large loss that is "chicken scratch" in comparison to daily losses in other capital markets? This paper argues that capital and insurance markets are not to blame. Rather, if there is any "failure," it rests with *government* policies. Government tax, accounting, and regulatory policies make it costly for insurers to hold surplus capital. They also hinder the implementation of instruments that could securitize the underlying risks. In other words, the "market failures" that appear to justify government intervention in the terrorism insurance market are best viewed as "government failures." Correcting these policies would likely enable private insurers to cover both terrorism and war risks.

To be clear, the purpose of this paper is not to provoke. In general, I believe that government policy, including progressive income taxation, can sometimes play an important role in enhancing risk sharing.[2] Indeed, one of the justifications for the government's largest historic intrusion into insurance markets—the creation of the Social Security system—is that people are either too myopic (if they do not anticipate retirement) or too

2. Nishiyama and Smetters (2003).

smart (if they strategically save too little in order to rely on public aid) for their own good or the good of society. But the idea that government tax and regulatory policies can hinder the development of insurance markets and securitization should not be surprising. For example, whereas the commercial mortgage-backed securities market was very small a decade ago, deregulation and tax reforms played an important role in its phenomenal growth over time, reaching a record of almost $100 billion issued in 2001.[3]

Rather than adopting a particular political view, I approach this topic with an eye toward identifying deviations from the first welfare theorem of economics. The first welfare theorem shows that the private market without government is Pareto efficient unless property rights fail (for example, externalities) or trading markets are incomplete—such deviations are generically referred to as "market failures." The following section documents many of the ways in which private insurance markets appear to have "failed" after September 11, which helped to motivate creation of the TRIA legislation, which is discussed in the second section. The market reaction to TRIA is then discussed in the third section. The fourth section critiques several theoretical arguments in favor of government-subsidized terrorism insurance. The most common arguments lack a clear explanation of why the first welfare theorem fails and how the government can cover terrorism losses more efficiently. To rationalize government intervention, it is not enough simply to argue that the private market has a difficult time insuring terrorism losses. Probably the most compelling argument for government intervention stems from incomplete markets between generations. But, even here, general-equilibrium considerations suggest that the government's optimal policy might be radically different—in fact, completely *opposite*—from the subsidized insurance approach taken in TRIA.

Insurance Markets before and after September 11

In theory, the Terrorism Risk Insurance Act of 2002 was responding to the inability of the insurance industry to provide coverage against terrorist acts. Before turning to how the insurance industry reacted to the terrorist acts of September 11, this section discusses the provision of terrorism insurance before the attacks.

---

3. Riddiough and Chiang (2003).

The Insurance Industry Prior to September 11

It has often been argued that that terrorism coverage was essentially provided "for free" before September 11, 2001, because standard commercial property-casualty policies did not contain specific terrorism exclusions.[4] This claim was buttressed by Warren Buffett's admission in a letter to shareholders that he and management did not even price terrorism losses into Berkshire Hathaway's premium structure.[5]

It is not obvious, however, that major insurers, much less Mr. Buffett, failed so miserably. Indeed, Buffett already had some experience with large catastrophic exposures. Just five years earlier, in 1996, he wrote a $1.05 billion contract that provided reinsurance to the Californian Earthquake Authority. It is especially unimaginable that any insurer of the World Trade Center would never have considered the possibility of *another* attack. Just eight and a half years earlier, on February 26, 1993, a 1,200-pound bomb exploded inside a rented Ryder van parked in the World Trade Center's garage, producing about $550 million in insured losses. When the attack mastermind, Ramzi Ahmed Yousef, was eventually captured in February 1995, he announced his only regret: that the 110-story tower did not collapse into its twin tower as planned. The entire World Trade Center complex, therefore, was clearly a marked target for terrorists. The second World Trade Center bombing in 2001 was also the culmination of more than a dozen terrorist attacks on U.S. interests, although mostly in foreign countries, during the previous decade.

One possible explanation for the insurance industry's ex post "plea of ignorance" following September 11 was that it was an integral part of the industry's lobbying strategy to secure a government subsidy to finance future losses. After all, it is hard to argue for a government subsidy for losses that are "hard to predict" if you rationally anticipated the vicious attacks of that day. In light of the earlier bombing, this plea lacks credibility *unless* insurers believed that they were not on the hook for a larger loss.

Another complementary explanation, therefore, is that prior to September 11 insurers believed that a larger and more coordinated attack, like the one that actually occurred on September 11, could only have been a by-product of a larger "act of war" that is expressly excluded under most commercial general-liability policies. Since the Vietnam War, war exclu-

---

4. Real Estate Roundtable (2002a).
5. Buffett (2001).

sions have been written very broadly by including "declared or undeclared" subclauses intended to bar claims even if the U.S. Congress does not formally declare war under article I, section 8, of the U.S. Constitution. Most war exclusions also include subclauses such as "warlike operations" that attempt to exclude the types of acts that would normally be part of a war, such as a large coordinated attack.

The legal applicability of war exclusion clauses appears to hinge on whether the violent action was taken under the direction or knowledge of a sovereign nation.[6] In particular, in *Pan American* v. *Aetna* the U.S. Second Circuit Court found that Aetna's war exclusion clause was not applicable because the hijackers of a single aircraft "were the agents of a radical political group, rather than a sovereign government."[7]

In the case of September 11, insurers could have argued, maybe consistent with their expectations, that such a large and coordinated attack *did*, in fact, require and receive the help of a sovereign nation. The Taliban government of Afghanistan was clearly complicit in the actions of Osama bin Ladin and al Qaeda by providing them with land and the resources to train for terrorist attacks. For example, President Clinton signed an executive order in 1999 prohibiting transactions with the Taliban "for allowing territory under its control in Afghanistan to be used as a safe haven and base of operations for Usama bin Ladin and the Al-Qaida organization who have committed and threaten to continue to commit acts of violence against the United States and its nationals."[8] The Taliban always understood that al Qaeda intended to harm the United States. While in Afghanistan, bin Ladin issued numerous fatwas before 2001 urging attacks on the United States:[9]

> We—with God's help—call on every Muslim who believes in God and wishes to be rewarded to comply with God's order to kill the Americans and plunder their money wherever and whenever they find it. We also call on Muslim *ulema*, leaders, youths, and soldiers to launch the raid on Satan's U.S. troops and the

6. *Pan American World Airways, Inc.* v. *Aetna Casualty & Surety Company*, 505 F.2d 989 (2d circuit 1974), applying New York law; *Holiday Inns, Inc.* v. *Aetna Insurance Company*, 571 F. supp. 1460, 1499–503 (S.D.N.Y. 1983).

7. *Pan American World Airways, Inc.* v. *Aetna Casualty & Surety Company*, at 1015; upheld on appeal.

8. Clinton (1999).

9. In *Al-Quds al-'Arabi*, February 23, 1998.

devil's supporters allying with them and to displace those who are behind them so that they may learn a lesson.

The relationship between the Taliban and bin Ladin was certainly less than arm's-length. Although bin Ladin has never been directly tied to the 1993 World Trade Center bombing, evidence has linked him to the 1997 truck bombing of the U.S. military barracks in Khobar, Saudi Arabia, and some earlier attacks. After a retaliatory attack by the U.S. military on Afghan training camps as well as a Sudanese pharmaceutical plant in 1998, the Taliban leadership demoted bin Ladin's status from an "official guest" to simply a "guest." However, the change in rhetoric rang hollow with the rest of the world: while Mullah Mohammed Omar was the Taliban's spiritual leader, it is widely accepted that bin Ladin was the movement's financier and de facto political leader.[10] After the 2001 attack on the United States, Omar, along with the Supreme Council, continued to accept bin Ladin as a guest even though doing so ensured war with the United States. The Taliban prepared the Afghanistan people: "Stay united and prepare for jihad against U.S. invaders."[11]

For insurance policy purposes, the Taliban appears to have been "a sovereign government" at the time of the 2001 attack. To be sure, the United States has never officially recognized the Taliban as the ruler of Afghanistan. However, thirty years earlier, the U.S. government also did not officially recognize the North Vietnamese government during the Vietnam War, a conflict that motivated much of the broad language in the modern war exclusions. Moreover, Clinton's 1999 executive order gave de facto political status to the Taliban: "The term 'the Taliban' means the political/military entity headquartered in Kandahar, Afghanistan that as of the date of this order exercises de facto control over the territory of Afghanistan."[12]

Indeed, there seems to be little material difference between the Taliban and the "cult-like" Japanese imperial government in power sixty-two years ago during the attack on Pearl Harbor. In both cases, the sitting U.S. president described the attack as an "act of war."[13] Moreover, President

10. See, for example, "Helping Hand: Where Did the Taliban Come from? How Did They Finance the Drive to Impose an Islamic State?" *Newsweek,* October 13, 1997.

11. Reported by the Taliban's Bakhtar News Agency, as quoted by the Associated Press, September 18, 2001.

12. Clinton (1999).

13. See, for example, Sciolino (2001).

Roosevelt and President Bush both received congressional approval for war, authorizations that would not have been required for defending the country against a gang of terrorists without at least de facto legal standing. In fact, the Afghanistan War had more legal standing with Congress than the Vietnam conflict.

If there was any "failure" on the part of insurers, it was probably their lack of understanding of how difficult it would be to enforce war exclusions ex post in the presence of some potential ambiguity regarding their meaning. First, ambiguity tends to be resolved by courts in favor of the insured rather than the insurers, and so insurers were not guaranteed a victory despite the strong connection between the Taliban and al Qaeda. Insurers, therefore, were not willing to risk losing face as a result of a potentially enormous public backlash. Indeed, insurance companies are generally very sensitive to public perception about them. For example, after the Vietnam War ended, most life insurers dropped war exclusions from their policies and they paid death benefits to families of military personnel killed during the Gulf War. After the 2001 World Trade Center attack, insurers had no real choice but to take the "high ground," a decision for which they received only limited fanfare—mostly self-generated in the form of newspaper ads. If I were an insurer, I would unquestionably also have paid the claims. Second, insurers received pressure from the administration along with hope for a subsidized backstop for future losses.

Reaction of the Insurance Market after September 11

After the terrorist attacks on September 11, an extreme "hard market" for terrorism-related losses emerged. By February 2002, forty-five states had approved terrorist loss exclusions in commercial policies; the exceptions were California, Florida, Georgia, New York, and Texas.[14] Fire losses produced by terrorist acts, though, were not excluded. For other lines, such as workers' compensation, and personal lines, such as life insurance, exemptions typically were not allowed. The approved commercial terrorism exclusions formalized what many insurers had probably taken for granted: they were not responsible for losses caused by "warlike" actions.

While major insurers of small and medium-size risks with annual premiums below $1 million, including Travelers, typically did not write terrorism exclusions into property-casualty policies for nonlandmark prop-

14. General Accounting Office (2002a).

erties,[15] exclusions began to be routinely enforced in 2002 for larger and more obvious targets. An anonymous survey by the Real Estate Roundtable, a proponent of a government subsidy, "identified" $15.5 billion in real estate transactions as of September 2002 that were delayed or canceled due to concerns about terrorism insurance: twenty-four office projects, ten retail projects, eight apartment buildings, six hotel and industrial projects, and three mixed-use developments.[16]

To be sure, it is likely that many of the postponed projects were on the verge of being delayed anyway, due to a sharp reduction in commercial fixed investment before September 11:[17] higher insurance costs were probably at most "tip factors" for delay. Moreover, even if this suspended activity was mostly due to terrorism concerns, it constituted only a small fraction of the almost $4 trillion in annual commercial and residential construction combined. Still, commercial construction activity had started to shrink before September 11, 2001, and so the terrorist attacks only seemed to make things worse. The president argued that "300,000 jobs" hung in the balance unless Congress passed a government backstop.[18] Democratic New York senators Chuck Schumer and Hilary Clinton also had a vested interest in government action.

Some new projects were canceled or put on hold, and some existing ones found it hard to obtain terrorism coverage when they renewed their policies in 2002. A 2002 survey by the Risk and Insurance Management Society, which represents larger companies and is a leading proponent of a federal government terrorism insurance backstop, found that two-thirds of its respondents (about 14 percent of those surveyed) had no terrorism coverage. The Miami Dolphins, New York Giants, and some other National Football League teams were unable to insure their stadiums. Amtrak also went without terrorism coverage when its $500 million property insurance policy came up for renewal on December 1, 2001. Amtrak claimed that it was not able to get enough coverage at reasonable rates.

In many other cases, terrorism coverage was eventually obtained, but at much higher premiums and with less coverage. Just days before the Salt Lake City Olympic Games were to begin on February 8, 2002, the U.S.

15. See A. M. Best (2002).
16. Real Estate Roundtable (2002a, 2002b).
17. See Bureau of Economic Analysis (2001, table 1).
18. See, for example, "Agreement Close on Aid to Insurance Industry," *Houston Chronicle*, October 19, 2002, sec. A, p. 24

Olympic Committee, for example, was able to secure terrorism coverage equal to only 5 percent of its expiring general-liability limit. Yet it paid the full price of its former broader coverage, for about a twenty-fold increase in cost per dollar of coverage. It agreed to these terms only because forty different insurance companies previously had refused coverage. The Mall of America was finally able to re-obtain terrorism coverage in March 2002, but with severely restricted limits and at much higher costs (the owner is prohibited from discussing the exact details). Although, as the old legalese cliché goes, "hard cases make bad law," the seemingly uninsurable nature of some of the nation's commercial and noncommercial landmarks provided further motivation for a government subsidy.

Although the prices of commercial property-liability insurance were beginning to rise prior to September 11, the terrorist attacks hardened the general-liability market even more.[19] Golden Gate Park, for example, was unable to obtain terrorism coverage and yet saw its premiums for *nonterrorism* coverage rise from $500,000 in 2001 to $1.1 million in 2002. Moreover, coverage was reduced from $125 million to $25 million. The magnitude of this price increase and coverage reduction, however, was *not* common in most other commercial policies that were less obviously terrorist targets. Insurers likely sharply increased premiums even for nonterrorism losses for potential targets like Golden Gate Park because of the legal ambiguity of loss classification ex post. Insurers are understandably cautious. During the previous two decades, insurers suffered large environment liability losses when courts began limiting the applicability of "sudden and accidental" clauses that were intended to exclude fairly predictable, and hence noninsurable, toxic emissions.[20] Similarly, many insurers were reasonably concerned that they would be forced to pay for a seemingly violent act that they believed was excluded under their policies.

Toward the Creation of a Federal Backstop

Just a few days after September 11, insurance company officials met with U.S. Treasury officials and then with the president at the White House. As one of the few Treasury officials in the first consultative meeting with insurance executives, I saw that the initial mood among policymakers

19. See, for example, American Academy of Actuaries (2002).
20. For example, *City of Albion* v. *Guaranty National Insurance Company*, no. 1:98-XC-676 (W.D. Mich. October 15, 1999).

within Congress and the administration was quite favorable toward providing a government backstop, with only a couple exceptions, including Senator Phil Gramm (R-Texas). The insurance executives also perceived a mostly friendly atmosphere. Since prominent members of both of the major political parties, including then Senate Majority Leader Tom Daschle, a Democrat, and the president, agreed on the need for a backstop, its creation was not really in doubt early on.[21]

This initial optimism was dimmed somewhat by a House-Senate disagreement that emerged on tort liability. The Republican-majority House wanted to limit tort actions, while the Democratic-majority Senate objected. Republicans hoped that prominent Democratic senators from states with large cities would eventually blink. Senate Democrats, however, recognized that the federal backstop was an integral part of the president's job creation program. Since Democrats were not in a hurry to secure an agreement before the 2002 midterm elections, they wanted the Republicans to concede. In the end, Democrats essentially won: the language on tort limitations was eased in conference committee after the midterm elections, even though Republicans knew at that point that they would soon control both chambers. The president signed the Terrorism Risk Insurance Act on November 26, 2002.

But Did Insurance Markets Really Fail So Badly?

A major part of the impetus in Washington toward reaching an agreement in the fall of 2002 was a massive lobbying effort by representatives of construction unions, business executives, realtors, and insurers armed with "evidence" of higher premiums and lower coverage levels. Often their facts were outdated or misleading. For example, an often-cited September 4, 2002, survey by the Real Estate Roundtable claimed that terrorism coverage accounted for *42 percent* of insurance premiums among "survey respondents who reported being able to obtain terrorism coverage."[22] The Real Estate Roundtable, however, failed to disclose in its press release that the "survey" was unscientific (almost anyone can answer its surveys by going to its website) and not even remotely representative of market conditions in September 2002. Other industry groups—the Financial Services Roundtable, the American Insurance Association, and the Coalition to

21. Some exceptions include Senator Phil Gramm of Texas.
22. Real Estate Roundtable (2002a).

Insure Against Terrorism—also presented gloomy statistics, often focusing on isolated "hard cases."[23]

A more objective reading of the facts paints a very different picture. By September 2002, premiums had dropped as much as 75 percent per unit of coverage from the beginning of the year. Limits as high as $1 billion were available and limits were increasing over time.[24] At least ten start-up insurers were formed, and other insurers continued to add capital.[25] Two months before TRIA became law, insurers already had added $30 billion of capital, with another $10 billion in new issues pending. Moreover, even the Building Owners and Managers Association, a proponent of TRIA, acknowledged that three-quarters of larger commercial and residential building owners had secured terrorism coverage.[26] The Shadow Financial Regulatory Committee, an independent group of leading U.S. academic scholars and experts, concluded, "Private insurance, reinsurance, and lending markets have made and are continuing to make substantial progress in adjusting to the post–September 11 world. Given those developments, the case for a federal backstop for terrorism insurance, which was not clear-cut late last year, is certainly less compelling now."[27]

It was not even clear that the supply restrictions in early 2002 provided much evidence of an insurance market failure as opposed to a *government* failure. Quite impressively, insurers raised $21 billion only three months after September 11 in order to replace lost capital.[28] But the appearance of a general agreement to a government backstop in late 2001 likely slowed the entry of *even more* capital into the insurance industry, thereby itself creating "evidence" in support of the need for the backstop—a self-fulfilling prophecy. Taxes on insurers' capital income alone would naturally discourage insurers from raising much capital "just in case" Congress failed to pass a backstop. Moreover, as discussed later, the inability to have previously securitized these risks created added pressure. A similar type of "expectations effect"—anticipation of future incentives reduces investment immediately—had previously been a concern with the investment

---

23. See, for example, Financial Services Roundtable, American Insurance Association, and Coalition to Insure Against Terrorism (2002).

24. Shadow Financial Regulatory Committee (2002).

25. Guy Carpenter (2003).

26. See "Terrorism Insurance Survey Reveals Disturbing Trends," PR Newswire, September 20, 2002.

27. Shadow Financial Regulatory Committee (2002).

28. Morgan Stanley (2001).

tax incentives passed earlier in 2001. The Bush administration dealt with this problem by allowing the tax incentives to cover investments in 2001 made prior to passage of the legislation. No clear mechanism existed, however, for government-backed terrorism reinsurance.

A sharp short-term reduction in insurance supply also followed Hurricane Andrew in August 1992, which caused $15.5 billion in insured losses.[29] Reinsurance rates increased 75 percent between January 1992 and July 1994. Primary insurers and state regulators lobbied Congress and the Clinton administration intensely for a federal backstop.[30] Five congressional bills were introduced over the next several years—which likely slowed the inflow of capital into the market—although none became law. Within five years, though, the capacity available to pay for catastrophes was almost double relative to capacity before Hurricane Andrew.

While landmark targets, in particular, faced higher premiums after September 11, it is not obvious that even these "hard cases" reflected a market failure. Indeed, theoretically, insurance supply restrictions can be an efficient short-run response of insurers operating within a dynamic setting with implicit contracts if moral hazard exists in the loss adjustment phase.[31] Such "ex post moral hazard" could be especially relevant for the almost $10 billion in business interruption claims produced by the World Trade Center attack, which are difficult to verify.[32] Three additional factors are worth considering.

First, soon after September 11, insurers increased their subjective priors of another attack. Even fair premiums would be expected to increase significantly if insurers believed that the world fundamentally changed on September 11, as many Americans did. Insurers were likely especially averse to the short-run *ambiguity* about the underlying loss probability *distribution*, which could produce even higher premiums (although Froot and Posner argue that this secondary effect is probably small for some catastrophic exposures).[33] This aversion is not itself inefficient unless the government can more accurately estimate loss distributions, which I doubt. While large insurers could have quoted higher premiums for landmark properties—the values of the properties themselves being obvious upper

29. Froot and O'Connell (1999).
30. Congressional Budget Office (2001).
31. Doherty, Lamm-Tennant, and Starks (2003); Doherty and Posey (1977).
32. Morgan Stanley (2001).
33. Cummins and Lewis (2003); Froot and Posner (2002); Kunreuther and others (1995).

bounds—insurers would have been accused of "price gouging," which might have triggered a regulatory response. Many states had already started to regulate terrorism premiums in commercial lines; it made little sense to antagonize the regulators even more.[34] Hence, insurers chose to "close the pumps" rather than sell "gas at $10 a gallon." Large insurers could then be victims instead of victimizers. Very few large insurers defected from this strategy in the short run.

Second, after September 11 but before TRIA, the government *might* have bailed out uninsured landmarks if yet *another* attack occurred (although see the caveats discussed later in this paper). This type of moral hazard was first referred to as the "Samaritan's dilemma" by Nobel laureate James Buchanan and has received a large amount of attention in the subsequent public finance and insurance literature.[35] The idea is as follows. The Good Samaritan (here, the government) wants to help after a loss but, in so doing, creates a moral hazard problem by encouraging inefficient risk taking by those who are implicitly insured; hence the "dilemma." The possibility of ex post financing of losses by the government reduces the shadow premiums that property owners are willing to pay to a level below the minimum reservation price across insurers. It therefore makes little sense for insurers to offer policies—even if fairly priced—that property owners likely will reject, especially when the offers themselves potentially could be detrimental to the image of insurers.

Third, and probably most important, some of the evidence of a "supply restriction" based on low take-up rates might be better interpreted as evidence of low demand. Indeed, it is likely that it is not even efficient for many property owners to purchase terrorism insurance. Most landmark and large properties are owned by diversified shareholders whose demand for insurance stems mainly from asymmetric information problems and the costs associated with financial distress. These motives are less important for terrorism risks relative to other risks, and they are likely to be dominated by large underwriting and loss adjustment costs. Indeed, since the TRIA subsidy, the demand for terrorism insurance has not increased much, even though the pricing has been fairly good.

---

34. Florida regulators capped terrorism charges for property insurance at 1 percent of the premium (see, for example, www.radeylaw.com/articles.cfm?Articleid=71 [March 15, 2004]). Many other states de facto capped terrorism rates at the amount filed by rating services. I am grateful to Debra Ballen for this information.

35. Buchanan (1975).

The Creation of a Federal Backstop

This section outlines the TRIA bill that was signed into law in November 2002 as well as alternatives that were also considered.

The Terrorism Risk Insurance Act of 2002

Although TRIA does not impose any pricing requirements on insurance companies, it does require them to provide coverage for "certified" foreign acts of terrorism in property and casualty lines under the same conditions as the underlying policy.[36] For example, if the policy covers business interruption for nonterrorism losses, then it must provide the same coverage for terrorism losses. Although TRIA gave the Treasury secretary discretion to extend this mandatory coverage to group life contracts, the Treasury announced on August 15, 2003, that it did not see a need to do so.[37] Moreover, as recently clarified by the Treasury, the "make available" rule does not require insurers to provide protection for chemical, biological, or radioactive losses if such exemptions are allowed for nonterrorism losses under state law or if the insurer is outside direct state regulatory oversight.[38] The "make available" rule expires at year-end 2004, but the Treasury secretary can extend it for one year, until year-end 2005.

In exchange for this mandate, the federal government agreed to indemnify 90 percent of the insurer's losses above a retention level equal to 7 percent of direct earned premiums in 2002. This retention level is scheduled to increase in 2004 to 10 percent of 2003 direct earned premiums. In 2005 the retention will increase to 15 percent of the 2004 direct earned premiums. Covered losses, however, are limited to $100 billion; Congress can use its discretion in financing losses above that amount.

The TRIA subsidy is financed out of general revenue. But, similar to state-level guarantee funds, the Treasury secretary could recoup some of the government's losses through policyholder surcharges provided that the aggregate value of these charges plus the retention of insurers fell below $10 billion in 2003; this limit was scheduled to increase to $12.5 billion in 2004 and to $15 billion in 2005, when TRIA sunsets.

36. Only violent acts in the interest of foreigners against the United States can be certified by the Treasury secretary in concurrence with the secretary of state and the U.S. attorney general.

37. U.S. Treasury (2003).

38. *Federal Register* (2003).

TRIA contains very few of the restrictions on tort claims that Republicans originally desired. Instead, TRIA establishes an exclusive federal cause of action for claims arising from a certified terrorism attack, and it consolidates all claims under the jurisdiction of the federal district court where the attack occurred. It also bans the federal government from paying punitive damages awarded by courts in actions certified under TRIA.

Key Elements of TRIA

The administration's original terrorism insurance proposal, which provided the framework for the bill passed in the Senate (S. 2600), did not include a mechanism for charging the private sector for any of the government's liability either ex ante or ex post, which drew the ire of academics.[39] This free coverage was motivated largely by the Treasury secretary, who made it very clear in public that he viewed the backstop as a financial obligation of the government stemming from its war on terrorism. In contrast, the Council of Economic Advisers as well as some other members of the administration initially argued for explicit pricing of the coverage. The administration, though, was also interested in a "receding" plan that would sunset; an ex ante pricing mechanism would require forming a new bureaucracy that could later attempt to justify its continued existence before Congress—egged on, of course, by industry. In sharp contrast to the Senate bill, the preconference House bill (H.R. 3210) was mostly a loan program financed by ex post assessments on insurers as well as premium surcharges, which eventually mostly found their way into the legislation but with stricter aggregate caps. While ex post assessments do not control moral hazard or risk-based ex ante premiums, they require less government involvement. State-level guarantee funds (except in New York) also rely on ex post assessments.

The administration's original proposal did, however, cap covered losses at $100 billion. During the predecisional phase, I originally believed that a ceiling on the government's liability was not needed because the government would already be "on the hook" for larger losses. A phone call to David Cummins at the Wharton School, however, quickly changed my mind. Cummins pointed out that this reasoning cuts both ways: if the government is implicitly obligated for large losses anyway, then it makes more

39. For example, see Cummins (2001).

sense to give the government some flexibility. He suggested a cap of $100 billion, a feature that was immediately incorporated into the proposal.

The small deductible in TRIA reflected the Treasury secretary's publicly stated belief that terrorism coverage is the obligation of the government. In sharp contrast, the Council of Economic Advisers initially argued for a much larger deductible.

The overarching principle was that TRIA would only provide help on a temporary basis to the private insurance market. Whether TRIA will disappear as planned in 2005, however, is not clear. Several industry groups hope that that TRIA will be extended after it officially sunsets. If history is any guide, they might get their wish. Indeed, TRIA is not so different from the 1957 Price-Anderson Act (42 U.S.C. 2014) almost a half century earlier, which provided third-party "public liability arising from a nuclear accident." The Price-Anderson Act relied on pro rata ex post assessments on 110 nuclear reactors if damage from a nuclear incident exceeded the $200 million insurance policy that each reactor was required to purchase. The act also capped the ex post assessments (at $10 million per reactor) and contained some tort reforms. This act was originally designed to last only ten years, with the hope that the private sector would eventually provide coverage. But the act was renewed and amended in 1966, 1969, 1975, and 1988, finally expiring on August 1, 2002. The Energy Policy Act of 2003 (H.R. 6) would have extended the Price-Anderson Act until 2012, but it was not passed.

Alternative Designs

Shortly after September 11, insurance executives lobbied the administration and Congress for a reinsurance pool (known as a Pool Re). In theory, insurers would agree to create a $10 billion pool; the government would cover terrorism losses above that amount. The Pool Re approach had some precedence. The British government, for example, established a Pool Re in 1993 to finance terrorism losses after terrorist bombings in London in 1992 and 1993 that produced $1 billion and $500 million in insured damages, respectively. The British Pool Re *appears* to be working fine, although its efficiency has been questioned, and it has never been tested by a major loss.[40] But the Pool Re model advocated by U.S. insurance executives differed from the British model in one startling way: it appeared that

40. Bice (1994).

U.S. insurers never intended to fund the pool! Their plan omitted a schedule of private sector payments into the pool, and they were quite cagey when asked about it. Despite getting some initial traction within the administration and the Senate, the Pool Re structure was quickly dropped from serious consideration. The pool became viewed as a backdoor excess-of-loss policy with *no* deductible or coinsurance—and as a freebie that would likely stick around.

My own preferred "second-best" approach for a government backstop (the "first best" being no backstop) was for the government to sell excess-of-loss contracts similar to the catastrophic call options that previously traded on the Chicago Board of Trade (CBOT). The payoffs in CBOT contracts were linked to aggregate regional or national insured losses as determined by the Property Claims Service. To be sure, the CBOT options, in particular, suffered from "basis risk" due to the imperfect correlation between aggregate losses and an insurer's actual losses.[41] They also suffered from limited capital backing from CBOT, thereby producing credit risk for large trades. The CBOT market also might have suffered from coordination problems (discussed more below). But all of these problems are less applicable to the government, especially if the options were purchased by reinsurers holding a largely diversified portfolio.

A similar type of plan was proposed by the Clinton administration to deal with natural catastrophic losses after Hurricane Andrew and has been analyzed in various works.[42] Like the Property Claims Service options, government payouts would have been linked to an aggregate index of losses rather than to firm-specific losses, thereby reducing ex post moral hazard by eliminating a buyer's incentive to inflate losses. The government could also collect money ex ante for the protection that it provided, instead of passing yet another unfunded liability to future generations in the form of a state-contingent guarantee. This liability is not small. Using loss probability estimates by the Congressional Budget Office, Russell estimates that a bill like TRIA is not cheap. It is *expected* to cost about $6 billion, about $92,000 per job saved![43] The *actual* costs could be much larger.

---

41. Cummins, Lalonde, and Phillips (2004).

42. Cummins, Lewis, and Phillips (1999); Lewis and Murdock (1996, 1999). Cummins and Doherty (2001), though, consider a slight modification that they call "excess of relative loss" contracts, which pay out *relative* to the insurance industry's available surplus.

43. Russell (2002).

Selling excess-of-loss contracts, though, had some practical problems. First, it would have required new regulations for a new auction. Second, the contracts would have generated some basis risk unless they were purchased by reinsurers who were geographically diversified. Most of the larger reinsurers, though, were *foreign*. Since these contracts would likely have been subsidized, this approach would not have sold well with Congress. Third, since the reinsurance market is fairly concentrated, competitive pressures might have been insufficient to ensure that any subsidy would be passed to U.S. ceding insurers and their customers. Fourth, as Cummins and Doherty note, foreign insurers would be hard to audit.[44] Fifth, even if the government collected money ex ante for the backstop, the money would likely have been added to the "unified budget surplus," thereby allowing Congress to spend it as they had other trust funds.[45] TRIA's eventual excess-of-loss design, therefore, was a compromise between this ideal market and the Pool Re that insurers wanted.

Demand for TRIA Terrorism Insurance

TRIA was not exactly the legislative outcome that U.S. insurers desired. Their dissatisfaction with TRIA might explain the startlingly empirical results recently found by Brown, Cummins, Lewis, and Wei.[46] Their paper shows that TRIA appeared to *reduce* the share price of insurers at key points in the legislation's consideration, reflecting the possibility that insurers had hoped for something better than TRIA.

Stylized Facts

On the demand side, large property owners do not seem particularly impressed with TRIA either. According to a March 2003 survey by the Council of Insurance Agents and Brokers, about half of the respondents indicated that fewer than 20 percent of their larger property and casualty clients had purchased terrorism coverage. In June 2002 Allianz, Hannover Re, Scor, Swiss Re, XL Capital, and Zurich Financial Services established a new company to insure property against acts of terrorism. The company,

44. Cummins and Doherty (2001).
45. Smetters (2004).
46. Brown and others (2003).

Special Risk Insurance and Reinsurance Luxembourg, was out of business in just one year due to low demand for terrorism coverage. The low take-up rate of TRIA-subsidized terrorism insurance is sometimes interpreted as a sign of the legislation's failure to provide adequate coverage.[47]

High prices probably do not explain the low demand for TRIA insurance, especially in light of the fairly generous subsidies. To be sure, in late 2002 some insurers had difficulty purchasing reinsurance to cover their retention and copayments. However, even in May 2003, the reinsurance market continued to soften, allowing primary insurers to follow the general pricing guidelines for terrorism coverage established by the Insurance Services Office (ISO), an advisory firm to the industry.[48] ISO ranks cities into three risk tiers. Tier 1 includes cities for which the risk of an attack is 100 times more than average: New York, Washington, Chicago, and San Francisco. Tier 2 includes cities for which the risk of an attack is five times more than average: Los Angeles, Philadelphia, Boston, Seattle, and Houston. Tier 3 includes all other cities. As of May 2003, ISO recommended a premium of 3 cents per $100 worth of terrorism coverage in tier 1 cities. For tier 2 and 3 cities, the recommended premiums were 1.8 cents and 0.1 cent, respectively. An analysis by Marsh in February 2003 of about 1,500 accounts representing a range of risks in terms of type and geography shows that terrorism pricing is between 8 and 10 percent of the all-risk premium. Overall, premiums are viewed as reasonable.[49]

Mechanisms other than price, therefore, likely explain the low take-up following TRIA. One possibility is the Samaritan's dilemma mentioned earlier. But this theory is less believable *after* the government made subsidized catastrophic insurance available. While policymakers may continue to bail out homeowners without flood insurance after a flood, they probably are less likely to bail out a large corporation that gambles and loses, except maybe after a very large *cataclysmic* shock (for example, a thermonuclear blast). Instead, we need to start with a theory of the demand for terrorism insurance.

47. For example, see Hofmann (2003).

48. See, for example, the interview with ISO spokesman Dave Dasgupta (*Knowledge@Wharton* 2003).

49. See Hofmann (2003).

Theory

It is not obvious that many large firms should rationally purchase terrorism coverage. Individuals and firms buy insurance for different reasons. *Individuals* purchase insurance to hedge an asset (for example, their house, body, or car) that is hard to diversify in the capital market due to moral hazard. But large *firms* affected by TRIA are typically owned by diversified shareholders who should place little weight on firm-specific losses. In fact, with *perfect* insurance and capital markets, insurance is "spanned" by the portfolio choices made by investors. So insurance does not increase shareholder value.[50]

The field of corporate risk management concerns itself with deviations from perfect markets that might explain why firms owned by diversified shareholders purchase insurance. The most important motivations (besides tax incentives) for business insurance focus on a firm's desire to reduce the costs of financial distress as well as principal-agent problems.[51]

Financial distress costs include expected bankruptcy costs, which insurance reduces. Another cost of financial distress consists of the premiums that a firm must pay for the risks that it imposes on parties that have a nondiversified relationship with the firm (for example, employees, dedicated suppliers, business customers, and creditors who have incurred large underwriting costs). By reducing the chance of bankruptcy, insurance gives nondiversified parties more confidence in the firm's survival, reducing these premiums.

The most important principal-agent problem that insurance helps to alleviate is the "underpricing effect" that a firm faces if it instead chooses to self-insure and then raise new capital after a loss. Since shareholders (the principals) cannot perfectly observe the actions of managers (the agents), shareholders might misinterpret a short-term loss as a longer-term loss, that is, a loss that is more correlated over time. Shareholders, therefore, · might incorrectly "underprice" the firm's value after a temporary shock. As a result, managers facing a takeover risk tend to insure against losses that are more *temporary* in nature, which helps to resolve this asymmetric information problem.[52]

50. Cummins (1976); Doherty and Tinic (1981).
51. See surveys in Doherty (2000); Meulbroek (2002).
52. Doherty and Sinclair (2003).

High underwriting and loss adjustment costs, however, discourage the purchase of insurance. Again, personal and business lines of insurance differ dramatically here. With *personal* lines of insurance, underwriting and adjustment costs are typically a small share of the premium. The reason is that human beings, cars, and houses are fairly homogeneous entities. With just a few variables, an accurate premium can be given in most personal lines, which is why personal insurance can often be purchased over the Internet. With *business* insurance, though, underwriting for lines like general liability is very expensive because the nature of the risks varies dramatically between firms. For example, General Motors is more worried about product liability than Yahoo!, whereas Yahoo! is more worried about copyright infringement and denial of service attacks. Loss adjustment for business insurance, especially business interruption, is also costly. Underwriting and loss adjustment costs can account for a third or more of the premium.

Combining these competing forces, a firm owned by diversified shareholders rationally purchases insurance only if the benefits from lowering financial distress and principal-agent costs are larger than the underwriting and adjustment costs. Otherwise, forgoing terrorism insurance is efficient and not a sign of a market failure.

Inefficiency of Terrorism Insurance for Many Companies

Although I have not yet found exact figures, the marginal costs of underwriting terrorism insurance and loss adjustments are likely to be larger than the costs of underwriting other losses, even though insurers do not have as much incentive to be aggressive in the presence of TRIA. So buying terrorism insurance is rational only if it significantly reduces a firm's financial distress costs and underpricing risks, which I doubt. I consider each in turn.

The most important financial distress cost for many firms stems from their creditors. Traditionally, creditors demanded "full" general-liability insurance coverage in order to ensure repayment. In early 2002, some property owners were in default of their bank loans because they could not obtain terrorism coverage. Some property owners, including the owners of the Mall of America, appealed for court protection because they believed that the tight market for terrorism insurance was the cause of their lack of compliance.

But within six months after the World Trade Center attacks—well before TRIA—creditors began to yawn at terrorism exclusions that were being written into some commercial insurance contracts—much like the war exclusions in the past. Indeed, the Federal Reserve's Board of Governor's April 2002 Senior Loan Officer Opinion Survey on Bank Lending Practices found that most creditors have diversified away most of their high-risk properties. About 70 percent of domestic lenders indicated that less than 5 percent of the dollar volume of their commercial real estate loans outstanding (on books or securitized) is backed by "high-profile" or "heavy-traffic" commercial real estate properties. Another 20 percent of lenders indicated that such loans comprise between 5 and 10 percent of their portfolio; the remaining 10 percent of lenders listed such loans as accounting for 10 to 20 percent of their portfolios. The same survey showed that almost three-quarters of domestic banks require terrorism insurance on less than 10 percent of loans financing even "high-profile" or "heavy-traffic" commercial real estate properties. Of the few banks that generally require terrorism insurance coverage, the most common response to a lack of coverage is to rewrite the lending contract to require more collateral or to allow for partial coverage. Terrorism insurance is not required for loans of less than $10 million.

The commercial mortgage-backed securities market also seemed to be relatively unfazed by terrorism risk. After the issuance of commercial mortgage-backed securities reached a record high of $97 billion in 2001, issuance fell to only $36 billion during the first half of 2002. While some observers blamed the weak economy and terrorism risk as the main culprits, the ease with which investors could diversify terrorism risks using commercial mortgage-backed securities suggests that most of the blame probably lay with the weak economy.[53] Indeed, in its monetary report to Congress on July 16, 2002, the Federal Reserve notes that the low risk spread observed in the commercial mortgage-backed securities market "suggests that concerns about terrorism insurance have not been widespread in the market for commercial mortgages."[54]

The problem of underpricing is important in general. It alone motivates corporations to purchase insurance as much as if not more than do financial distress costs and tax incentives.[55] But the underpricing effect is less

---

53. For example, Muldavin (2002).
54. Board of Governors of the Federal Reserve System (2002, p. 17).
55. For example, Hoyt and Ho (2000).

important for terrorism losses. A terrorist strike will likely be interpreted by investors precisely as what it is and not be confused with a larger shock that is more correlated over time. Hence, the motivation for purchasing insurance is reduced.

Is There a Rationale for Government Provision of Terrorism Reinsurance?

A recent and growing literature has examined the potential role that the government can play as a reinsurer for large catastrophic and terrorism losses as well as the difficulty that the private sector has in insuring extreme events.[56] Although it is not obvious that private insurance markets failed after September 11, this section argues that any problems probably stemmed from a failure in *government* policies. A mostly unfettered insurance market combined with sensible government policy should be able to provide insurance against terrorism and war losses.

Difficulty of Forecasting Future Losses

The most popular argument in favor of government-subsidized terrorism insurance is that private insurers have a difficult time constructing loss distributions for future terrorist acts due to a lack of *reliable* time-series evidence. The emphasis on "reliable" is important because a time series on losses from past terrorist attacks *does* exist.[57] Unlike most losses, though, terrorists might avoid past techniques in order to increase their likelihood of a costly attack. These strategic choices render the time-series evidence less reliable. In statistical language, the time series of terrorism losses is fraught with "structural breaks."

This argument, however, does not *alone* support a role for the government since it does not explain why the government can do a *better* job than

56. See, for example, American Academy of Actuaries (2002); Brown, Kroszner, and Jenn (2002); Brown and others (2003); Congressional Budget Office (2001); Cummins and Doherty (2001); Cummins and Lewis (2003); Cummins, Lewis, and Phillips (1999); Cutler and Zeckhauser (1999); Doherty, Lamm-Tennant, and Starks (2003); Froot (1999, 2001); Froot and O'Connell (1999); General Accounting Office (2002b); Grøn (1999); Jaffee and Russell (1997); Kleindorfer and Kunreuther (1999); Kunreuther (2002); Kunreuther, Michel-Kerjan, and Porter (2003); Lewis and Murdock (1996, 1999); Moss (2001); Priest (1996); Russell (2002); Woo (2003).

57. As documented in Blomberg, Hess, and Orphanides (2003).

the private sector of financing the losses. The government's main advantages stem from its superior access to information and its ability to tax, both of which I consider in more detail below. But the argument that the private sector market has difficulty insuring losses does not alone rationalize government action.

PREVALENCE OF OTHER RISKY MARKETS. Indeed, many private markets seem to work fine despite the apparent lack of reliable time-series evidence. The market for initial public offerings, for example, has raised *trillions* of dollars in venture capital even though most underwriters have no concomitant time series or close substitutes on which to rely. Furthermore, as with terrorist losses, government policy influences a significant amount of net earnings and losses of most corporations. For example, about 10 percent of the value of U.S. firms can be traced solely to the tax deductibility of corporate interest payments on debt.[58] Yet investors provide enormous liquidity to U.S. firms.

Indeed, capital markets routinely take bets on very novel risks. For example, while models of hurricane losses are becoming better over time, models of *earthquake* losses are still in their infancy. Yet a private market exists for insuring earthquake losses even outside state-level subsidies. In 1996 National Indemnity, the super-catastrophe reinsurance unit of Berkshire Hathaway, underwrote the California Earthquake Authority with a four-year $1.05 billion reinsurance contract.[59] Catastrophe bonds have also been devised to insure against earthquake losses in the U.S. Midwest, Tokyo, and other regions. As another example, commercial aircraft and satellites were insured long before a viable time series on losses became available.[60] The marine insurance market also developed long before accurate weather models became available.[61]

Environment liability insurance also operates in a setting of high uncertainty since courts often change standards, producing large *correlated* losses for insurers.[62] Although estimates before 1991 are less reliable,[63] estimates of total losses for abandoned hazardous waste sites and asbestos

---

58. Kemsley and Nissim (2002).
59. Buffett, however, received a very good return on this particular investment: the premium was equal to 530 percent of the expected loss (Stulz 1999).
60. Borch (1990).
61. Jaffee and Russell (1997).
62. Viscusi and others (1993).
63. Note 24 to the annual statement that insurers submitted to state insurance regulators prior to 1991 did not require reporting information on payments.

through just 1995 are as high as $150 billion.[64] Most of these payments were indemnified under occurrence-based insurance contracts written before 1986 and were not reasonably anticipated by insurers.[65] Yet the commercial general-liability insurance market is still vibrant. To be sure, "absolute" environmental exclusions are now being routinely written into new commercial general-liability policies, but those exclusions were a response to the courts' narrow interpretation of "sudden and accidental" exclusions intended to exclude pollution that was more deterministic in nature. Environmental protection is still available through "environmental impairment liability" policies that cover all emissions, whether "sudden and accidental" or not.

The product liability insurance market also operates in a very unpredictable environment. This market became very unpredictable after the famous 1981 mass tort case, *Grimshaw* v. *Ford Motor Company*, which awarded $128 million ($125 million in punitive damages), the largest jury verdict ever in a personal injury case at that time. The jury found Ford negligent in putting aside cost-benefit safety analysis demonstrating that the cost of a safer gas tank *exceeded* the marginal benefit. Their reasoning was upheld on appeal:[66]

> There was evidence that Ford could have corrected the hazardous design defects at minimal cost but decided to defer correction of the shortcomings by engaging in a cost-benefit analysis balancing human lives and limbs against corporate profits. Ford's institutional mentality was shown to be one of callous indifference to public safety. There was substantial evidence that Ford's conduct constituted "conscious disregard" of the probability of injury to members of the consuming public.

The displacement of clear cost-benefit standards in this and subsequent decisions threw the product liability insurance market into disarray. Yet the market still exists. According to the actuary consulting firm Tillinghast-Towers Perrin, the inflation-adjusted tort cost per U.S. citizen grew more than eight times from 1950 to 2001.[67] According to the same study, *insured* tort claims in 2001 *alone* amounted to $146.3 *billion*, a figure that excludes four big-ticket items: payments for medical malpractice, self-insured

64. Referenced in ISO (1996). ISO estimates that about $40 billion were paid between 1991 and 1995.

65. ISO (1996).

66. *Grimshaw* v. *Ford Motor Company*, 119 Cal. App. 3d 757, at 813 (1981).

67. Tillinghast-Towers Perrin (2002).

losses, "one-time" tobacco settlements, and punitive damages. Punitive damages in the largest ten cases in 1999 totaled $19 billion.[68] Although punitive damage awards are not insurable in all states, appeals courts have created additional uncertainty by often ignoring the guidelines that the Supreme Court set forth in *BMW of North America Inc.* v. *Gore.*[69] This decision, although admittedly somewhat vague, was intended to limit punitive damages. Only recently did the Supreme Court clarify its position in *State Farm Mutual Automobile Insurance Company* v. *Campbell,* which many observers have interpreted as setting a ceiling on punitive damages equal to nine times actual damages.[70]

The continued operation of the environment and product insurance markets should give proponents of a government terrorism backstop considerable pause. New legal precedents produce large and correlated risks for insurers in these markets. My own reading of the historical evidence is that court decisions—acts completely in the government's control—are probably *more novel* and *less predictable* than many terrorist acts, including the 2001 World Trade Center bombing that occurred just eight and a half years after the 1993 attack.

The Ninth Judicial Circuit, the largest circuit court in the nation, with jurisdiction from Arizona to Guam, alone provides ample evidence. Most recently, this court reinstated a lawsuit against gun manufacturer Glock.[71] This suit alleges that Glock committed "distribution negligence" by selling a gun that eventually was used in a murder, even though Glock sold the gun in question to a police department, which later resold it on the open market. The Ninth Judicial Circuit found that this novel theory of negligence could proceed. The plaintiffs could reasonably argue that Glock should have anticipated the resale of their products! Not surprising, the Supreme Court routinely overturns the Ninth Circuit's decisions. But even if Glock successfully defends itself, it will have to incur large litigation costs. According to the Tillinghast-Towers Perrin survey cited earlier, defense costs—not including plaintiff costs—and administrative costs constitute 35 percent of insured liability costs.[72]

68. Thornburgh (2000).
69. *BMW of North America Inc.* v. *Gore,* S Ct. US 1995; five to four decision.
70. *State Farm Mutual Automobile Insurance Company* v. *Campbell,* S Ct. US 2003; six to three decision.
71. *Ileto* v. *Glock Inc.*, Ninth Judicial Circuit No. 02-56197.
72. Tillinghast-Towers Perrin (2002).

THE UTILITY OF TIME-SERIES EVIDENCE. Not only do many nonterrorism capital and insurance markets operate in a very risky environment, it is important to recall why time-series evidence is even important in the insurance industry. Historical evidence is especially relevant if an insurer must fund its losses using ex ante premiums. In this case, the insurer must accurately assess its total losses and the distribution of those losses across insured parties.[73] Ex ante premiums are required, for example, in most *personal* lines of insurance, where the credit risk of the insured party is a major concern. But such projections are less important for the large firms actually affected by TRIA. (As noted, terrorism exclusions are typically not written into contracts with annual premiums below $1 million.) Large firms have better credit, allowing for more flexibility in contract design.

For example, loss-sensitive contracts with either retroactive premiums or reciprocal relationships can be constructed so that insured firms share ex post *aggregate* shocks. The only determination that must be made ex ante is how to distribute the weights of ex post losses among the insured. (One exception is when the contract embeds caps on losses that would pass some risk to the shareholders of the insurance company.) But assigning these weights only requires estimating the *relative* differences in expected losses, which is much easier than estimating the absolute value of expected losses. Indeed, the tiered city-level risk structure estimated by ISO, discussed earlier, provides exactly the information that is required for determining the weights.

Consider, for example, two buildings, B1 and B2. Suppose B1 is located in Washington, while B2 is in Manhattan. It might be challenging to estimate the probability of an attack in either city, making it difficult to rely only on ex ante premiums, although not necessarily more difficult for the private sector than for the government. But it would be reasonable for the market to believe, as does ISO, that the probability of an attack in both cities is *similar*. So B1 and B2 would receive the same loss weights per dollar of coverage. If B2, however, is in Des Moines, Iowa, then B1 might be assigned a weight 100 times larger than that of B2. Weights can also be adjusted to control for moral hazard (for example, building design) that might be relevant for some types of attacks. Retroactive premiums can also be partially sensitive to one's own losses.

73. Kunreuther (2002).

SUMMARY. In sum, capital markets and insurance lines already provide considerable liquidity under conditions when future losses are very difficult to predict based on time-series evidence. Moreover, the historical record is most useful when the credit risk of the insured undermines the potential for ex post risk sharing. Credit risk is a large problem in personal insurance lines, but less of a problem for firms of the size affected by TRIA.

Large Risks

Another common argument for government intervention is that potential terrorist losses can produce large and correlated losses in relation to the insurance industry's capital. Of course, as discussed earlier, changing legal standards also produce large and correlated risks in the environmental and product liability insurance markets; both markets appear to operate vigorously. But I do not belabor this point.

Just how large a loss can the property and casualty insurance industry currently absorb? The U.S. property and casualty surplus stood at $334 billion in 1999 and $290 billion at the end of 2001 (which includes about $10 billion in World Trade Center losses paid by that point).[74] But these estimates alone do not really address insurance *capacity* because they ignore the distribution of capital and limited liability. Cummins, Doherty and Lo, therefore, use a novel options pricing approach to estimate that U.S. insurers would be able to finance about 92.8 percent of a $100 billion catastrophic loss.[75] Although a majority of a $300 billion loss could probably be paid, such a loss would place a substantial strain on the industry at current levels of insurance capitalization.

Of course, the insurance market's capacity is an endogenous variable that responds to market conditions. When at least some losses are funded using ex ante premiums, relevant market conditions also include expectations of future losses based on historical losses. In other words, the supply of insurance capital is not fixed. As discussed earlier, catastrophic insurance capacity doubled within five years after Hurricane Andrew, even though it was probably discouraged by the possibility of a government backstop. Insurers quickly began to replace capital that was lost on Sep-

---

74. See, for example, American Academy of Actuaries (2002).
75. Cummins, Doherty, and Lo (2002).

tember 11, although TRIA presumably discouraged even more capital inflow.

Besides providing insurance, such as TRIA, that directly crowds out the private provision of insurance, other government policies constrain or at least discourage the private market's effort to increase capital after a loss. Many states, for example, cap insurance rates or require insurers to underwrite various lines below cost. Insurers in the United States are hit particularly hard by regulations that require them to insure terrorist-related workers' compensation claims at premiums well below actuarial costs. Rates are often restricted in other property and casualty lines as well. Three additional types of federal and state policies also make it costly for insurers to hold capital or to securitize the underlying risks: taxes, accounting policies and regulations, and their concomitant enhancement of agency problems.[76]

GOVERNMENT TAX POLICY AND INSURANCE CAPITAL ACCUMULATION. The first large capital cost stems from taxes. Shareholders of *noninsurance* companies face a "double tax" in the form of corporate income taxes plus personal taxes (on dividends or capital gains). Shareholders of *insurance* companies also face a "third layer" of taxes on their capital income: the insurer must pay taxes on the capital income that it receives even though it was already taxed as corporate income. Since the deadweight loss from taxes increases with the *square* of the tax rate, the distortion caused by this third layer of taxation is likely larger than the distortion caused by the first two layers *combined*. Although part of this third tax layer can be reduced by holding reserves offshore in places like Bermuda, this solution is very imperfect since offshore locations do not provide the same investment opportunities as onshore locations. For example, an offshore insurer cannot invest its capital back in the United States and escape U.S. taxes. Moreover, if the insurer is not admitted (licensed to do business) in the United States, then premiums are subject to federal excise taxes, and premiums might not be deductible against state income taxes.

GOVERNMENT ACCOUNTING POLICY AND ONSHORE SECURITIZATION. Tax reform alone, however, will *not* likely expand catastrophic protection dramatically. Insurers presumably must also be able to tap into the multi-*trillion*-dollar capital market by securitizing their risks. Securitization gives investors, in the words of Cummins, a "pure play" on the underlying

---

76. See Jaffee and Russell (1997) for a complementary discussion.

insured risk, much like a "tracking stock."[77] These tailored risks allow investors to achieve better portfolio diversification with lower information costs. Also, when the security's payoff is indexed to *aggregate* (not firm) losses or some other trigger outside of the firm's control, securitization can reduce ex post moral hazard that exists between primary insurers and reinsurers, but at a cost of some basis risk reflecting the mismatch between aggregate and individual losses.[78]

The most important factor inhibiting the development of risk-linked securitization is state-level regulation. In 1999 and 2001 the Insurance Securitization Working Group of the National Association of Insurance Commissioners recommended that state insurance regulators encourage alternative sources of capacity by examining the use of risk-linked securities.[79] But only a few states currently allow a U.S. insurer to include a derivative instrument as a claim-amount recoverable asset on its balance sheet. Even then, only securities with no basis risk are allowed, that is, indemnity-based securities. Illinois, for example, gave INEX permission to complete its first securitization in 1999 in which Kemper Insurance Group used a special-purpose vehicle to cover $100 million of top-level New Madrid earthquake exposures in the U.S. Midwest. Payoffs were paid on an excess-of-loss basis and had no basis risk.

The development of a vibrant onshore securitization market in the United States might, though, require the legal acceptance of risk-linked securities that incorporate *basis risk*, that is, nonindemnity securities. These instruments give investors a "super pure play," since the payoffs depend on more easily measured indexes and are not subject to moral hazard. But such a development would require additional regulatory changes in the face of considerable resistance. While the Securitization Working Group is also examining these types of securities, intense lobbying by the Reinsurance Association of America, for example, has raised concerns about

---

77. Cummins (2002).

78. Doherty and Smetters (2002); Froot (1999).

79. The National Association of Insurance Commissioners (NAIC) adopted the Protected Cell Model Act in 1999, and a working group within the NAIC proposed the Onshore Special-Purpose Reinsurance Vehicle (SPRV) Model Act in 2001. Currently, the SPRV entity is illegal in the United States and faces considerable legal uncertainty (General Accounting Office 2002b). One advantage of the SPRV is that it can be used by noninsurers, whereas protected cells are generally available only to insurers. Another advantage is that it legally is more effective at isolating the assets from other potential claims during bankruptcy.

basis risk, which could hamper the approval of trigger-based risk-linked securities by state regulators.[80] Moreover, even the regulatory jurisdiction of instruments with basis risk is not clear. While the 1945 McCarran-Ferguson Act leaves the primary authority for insurance regulation with the states, the federal government plays a much more active role in the securities market. The state jurisdiction over securities with basis risk is not clear since it is not obvious that these instruments satisfy the triplicate standard for insurance set by the Supreme Court in *Union Labor Life Insurance Company* v. *Pireno*.[81] My own reading is that the Court's tests are *probably* satisfied, but there is certainly some room for debate.

CONCERNS OVER EQUITABLE TAX TREATMENT. Reinsurers claim to resist onshore securitization, in part, out of concerns that it could lead to an unequal tax treatment of reinsurance capital and securitized assets, especially if onshore securitization is given the same tax advantages as offshore securitization.[82] To be sure, many of these concerns could be addressed by allowing traditional reinsurers to deduct *expected* catastrophic losses, as in some European nations, rather than just actual losses.[83] In the United States, only reserves allocated to actual (or highly predictable) losses can be deducted.[84]

But a strong case can be made, at least in the short run, for *unequal* tax treatment that gives preference to securitization. The reason is that the current securitization market likely suffers from a coordination failure. In particular, the relationship between a reinsurer and a ceding insurer is an implicit long-term contract that is costly to abandon, maybe due to fixed underwriting costs (see, for example, the paper by Doherty and Muermann in this volume). A rational ceding insurer will desert this long-term relationship for the securitization spot market only if the spot market will likely remain liquid in the future, which, in turn, requires other ceding insurers to make the same choice. In other words, the securitization spot

---

80. See, for example, the presentation by Kading (2000), senior vice president of the Reinsurance Association of America.

81. *Union Labor Life Insurance Company* v. *Pireno* 458 U.S. 119 (1982). The triplicate standard is as follows: (1) Does the instrument transfer or spread a policyholder's risk? (2) Is the instrument an integral part of the relationship between the policyholder and the insurer? (3) Is the practice limited to entities within the insurance industry?

82. Klein, Grace, and Phillips (2000).

83. Jaffee and Russell (1997).

84. Bradford and Logue (1999) outline the impact of tax law on reserve capital.

market is potentially being inhibited by demand externalities that produce multiple equilibriums: there is little incentive to be the first player in the spot market. The government can use preferential tax treatment in the short run to move the insurance market from the "inferior" equilibrium, where insurers primarily cede their risks to traditional reinsurers, toward the "superior" equilibrium with securitization.

AGENCY PROBLEMS. Besides taxes and regulations, insurers also face agency costs when holding capital, produced by asymmetric information between shareholders and managers. Some agency costs (for example, potential theft of assets) are no different than those with a mutual fund. But insurer shareholders must also worry about the insurer's credit risk in the face of potential losses and bankruptcy costs since, unlike a mutual fund, an insurer's losses are not necessarily fully passed through to the insured using retroactive premiums, for example.

Government state regulation is intended to reduce some of these agency costs. But, ironically, the government taxes and regulations *enhance* agency costs by giving insurers incentives to locate offshore, beyond the accounting and legal arm of the U.S. government. As noted earlier, insurers might want to locate offshore in order to avoid some of the "triple tax," but at a cost of portfolio restrictions and other taxes. Offshore insurers also have more latitude to issue risk-linked securities, including those with basis risk.

To be sure, a firm domiciled in a U.S. state usually cannot purchase insurance from an offshore insurer unless the insurer is admitted to do business in that state and is regulated. But an important exception is often granted to foreign insurers that finance the upper layers of large losses if it can be proven that a suitable admitted insurer does not exist in the state— a very relevant exception in the discussion herein. In particular, excess coverage is often provided by foreign insurers outside U.S. jurisdiction. At best, states can attempt to regulate the brokers through whom the insurance is purchased.

SUMMARY. In sum, the capital capacity of insurers is a legitimate concern for financing terrorism losses. But important frictions can be traced to government policy itself. The government could significantly increase insurance capacity through a combination of tax and regulatory reforms that would increase the capacity of traditional insurers and reduce the barriers to broader securitization.

Asymmetric Information

Another potential argument for government provision of terrorism insurance is that the government has more access to sensitive information than the private sector. This superior information might allow the government to assign prices for reinsurance more accurately than a private market reinsurer. Moreover, since the government plays a unique role in mitigating terrorism risks, a government-subsidized backstop gives politicians the incentive to invest in the proper level of loss control. More mitigation reduces the likelihood of having to make politically unpopular decisions like raising taxes, cutting other spending, or producing larger deficits after a terrorism loss.

ABILITY OF THE GOVERNMENT TO CONSTRUCT MORE ACCURATE LOSS DISTRIBUTIONS. This line of reasoning raises several issues. First, the argument's basic premise is suspect. To be sure, the U.S. government can monitor al Qaeda "chatter" more easily than the private sector, although the chatter itself and the costs associated with "code orange" security might be the newest form of terrorism. But it is unlikely that the government will hold closely the information that would allow it systematically to construct superior loss distributions relative to private firms that have money on the line.

Even the U.S. Department of Defense does not believe that it has both a monopoly on information and also the ability to *process* it better than the private sector. In July 2003 the Department of Defense's Defense Advanced Research Project Agency announced an initiative—the Policy Analysis Market—to improve its human intelligence. This market would have allowed participants to bet on futures contracts over various political and civil outcomes, including the assassination of Palestinian leader Yassar Arafat and a missile attack by North Korea. The Department of Defense defended its plan, saying that a market system was highly accurate at predicting such outcomes. The plan was abandoned only after pressure from some members of Congress, including Senator Ron Wyden (D-Ore.) and Senator Byron Dorgan (D-N.D.), who referred to it as "unbelievably stupid."[85]

Since the Department of Defense market was not implemented, it is impossible to determine how well it would have worked in practice. But the "Saddam Hussein Futures Market," created by TradeSports Exchange in

85. Meyer (2003).

Ireland earlier in the year, gives *some* initial clue. As of February 10, 2003, it predicted there was only a 43 percent chance that Hussein would be deposed as the ruler of Iraq by March 31, 2003, but an 82 percent chance that he would be gone by May 30, 2003.[86] These accurate predictions were made by the market (after 42,000 trades) well before ground troops invaded Iraq in March 2003 and well before President Bush declared an end to major military operations in May 2003.

The widespread belief that the U.S. government secretly holds vastly superior information was buttressed by media reports after the September 11 attacks suggesting that the government had access to key information that should have helped it to predict these attacks. To be sure, the Department of Defense's National Security Agency collects more information *every day* than is stored in the Library of Congress. But most of this ex post criticism of the National Security Agency and the Federal Bureau of Investigation—some of it coming from whistle-blowers—appears to be twenty-twenty hindsight, including the observation that some foreigners of Arabian background were training at American flight schools. When viewed objectively, the government likely knew very little more than the private sector about the risks.

Even the idea of simultaneously hijacking multiple aircrafts or using an aircraft as a missile against a U.S. landmark was not novel. Similar missions had been attempted previously but were either of smaller scale or mitigated. In 1994 Islamic terrorists, for example, hijacked an Air France plane in Algiers with the intention of crashing it into the Eiffel Tower. In the same year, a small aircraft operator crashed his plane on the White House grounds. In 1995 the Philippine government uncovered Project Bojinka, in which Islamic terrorists planned to blow up eleven American airlines as well as crash an aircraft with explosives into Central Intelligence Agency headquarters. All of these events were widely reported well before September 11.[87]

Private sector antiterrorism specialists had also discussed the possibility of crashing aircraft into U.S. landmarks, including the World Trade Center, before the actual attacks.[88] A more personal anecdote relates to a case study that I conducted of the 1993 World Trade Center attack as part

86. "Saddam Hussein Futures Offer Bets on His Removal," Bloomberg News, February 10, 2003.

87. Bone and Road (1997).

88. Fainaru (2002).

of an undergraduate course in 1998, three years before the 2001 attack. One student, marveling at the fact that the main tower could withstand a 1,200-pound bomb exploded at its base, asked me what it *would* take to bring down one of the buildings. In response, I conjectured that even flying a jumbo aircraft into the main tower probably would *not* have collapsed it. To be sure, I was clearly wrong. But I am not an expert in structural engineering, and I was only partly familiar with the structural details of the Word Trade Center. (If the Empire State Building had been attacked in a similar fashion, there is a good chance that it would not have collapsed, given its higher concentration of cement relative to metal as well as other differences in design.) Insurance companies, though, often hire structural engineers as part of their underwriting.

THE DIFFICULTY OF EXPLOITING ANY INFORMATIONAL ADVANTAGE. There is a second problem with the asymmetric information justification for government-subsidized terrorism insurance. For the sake of argument, suppose that we accept the premise that the government *does* hold closely superior information that would allow it to construct more accurate terrorism loss distributions. This information advantage, however, would give the government an advantage in *financing* terrorism losses only if the government attempted to charge ex ante for the reinsurance that it provides, which it does not in TRIA, for the practical reasons discussed earlier.

Even if the government *did* attempt to price the terrorism reinsurance it provides, considerable care would be needed. For example, the government could *not* sell this insurance at auction if it really wanted to take advantage of its superior information. An efficient auction solution would not depend on the information set of the government serving as the Walrasian auctioneer of such a market; the auctioneer would simply increase or decrease prices in response to positive or negative excess demand. Achieving a socially efficient auction would require the *buyers* to have valid information, which, by assumption, they do not. For the same reason, if buyers in this market really had inferior information, a secondary market would not produce efficient prices either.

Instead, government bureaucrats would have to construct a system of subsidies or taxes to ensure that the private market is purchasing enough— but not too much!—terrorism coverage. The government's experience running other insurance backstops (for example, the Pension Benefit Guaranty Corporation, the Federal Insurance Savings and Loan Corporation, and the Federal Emergency Management Agency) gives reason for considerable pause about the ability of the government to operate so efficiently.

THE MISALIGNMENT BETWEEN BACKSTOP AND POLICYMAKERS' INCENTIVES. Finally, while the government provision of terrorism insurance might appear to give politicians an incentive to invest in the optimal amount of loss control, it would likely work in the *wrong* direction. Policymakers already have an enormous amount of nondiversifiable "human capital" invested in fighting terrorism vis-à-vis their reelection prospects. Indeed, the rhetoric in Washington after September 11 was that terrorism should be fought at any cost. For example, Congress passed the September 11 Victim's Compensation Fund, which will pay almost $5 billion to victims of this attack, but not previous attacks, after only ninety minutes of debate.[89] Forcing politicians to raise taxes, cut spending, or increase deficits after a terrorist loss would likely move mitigation even further from a proper weighing of the costs against the benefits.

Time-Inconsistent Policies

Another common argument for a subsidized federal backstop is the Samaritan's dilemma, in which many people will rationally forgo insurance since they believe the government will bail them out after a major loss. By assumption, the government cannot *credibly* commit ex ante to *not* bailing out the uninsured ex post. In other words, any such commitment would fail to be subgame perfect. In still other words, a no-bailout policy is not *time consistent*; that is, any "hard knuckles" promise will be broken ex post.

In theory, subsidized government insurance could encourage some "free riders" without insurance to purchase insurance before a loss actually occurs. Many households and firms, though, may continue to assume that the government will bail them out even if they do not buy insurance. Still, subsidized insurance should increase coverage if some participants believe that they can get a better deal relative to the free bailout. Coverage could also increase if politicians themselves believe that the provision of cheap insurance strengthens the popular "moral case" against ex post bailouts. This latter "defensive" position, for example, might have motivated some fiscally conservative policymakers to support TRIA in light of the harden-

---

89. See "September 11 Fund Claims Top 98 Percent," FoxNews.com, January 16, 2004.

ing market for terrorism insurance in 2002. In both cases, however, a fairly generous subsidy is needed in order to sharply increase coverage.

While TRIA *subsidizes* terrorism insurance, the French government *mandates* catastrophic coverage as part of virtually every property-liability policy.[90] In other words, the only way to avoid terrorism coverage in the French system is to forgo coverage altogether, if allowed. This subsection compares both approaches. But, in doing so, it is critical to distinguish between nondiversifiable and diversifiable risks.

NONDIVERSIFIABLE RISKS. The Samaritan's dilemma is an often-cited reason why the U.S. government subsidizes some forms of insurance, including flood, hurricane, and earthquake insurance. But these subsidies are not without problems. For example, as of 2001, the National Flood Insurance Program (NFIP) had 4.3 million policies in force, with more than $570 billion in coverage.[91] NFIP loses about $800 million on average each year by setting premiums below their actuarially fair value; much of this loss comes from "older properties."[92] (Many new properties as well as remodeled existing properties are effectively covered as well.) While the NFIP technically does not have a formal appropriation in the budget to cover this shortfall, the surplus is financed with federal income taxes that distort the labor and saving decisions of households. The insurance also causes adverse selection problems and encourages the inefficient development of vacation homes, rental properties, and small businesses in high-risk locations.

Since most properties, such as houses, covered by NFIP are hard to diversify in the private capital market, the purchase of flood insurance is likely rational, especially since the underwriting costs are pretty low. So a more efficient approach than subsidized pricing would be simply to *mandate coverage* for homeowners' losses stemming from floods. Mandatory coverage would address the Samaritan's dilemma without distorting prices if premiums were actuarially fair. For example, NFIP has resisted charging fair prices out of concern that people would select out of the program.[93] Mandatory coverage would prevent this problem. Moreover, mandatory coverage is more efficient than a subsidy that encourages poor households—as well as wealthy households with vacation homes—to build in

90. Moss (1999).
91. Leikin (2001).
92. Leikin (2001).
93. Leikin (2001).

risky areas; indeed, NFIP is planning to relocate more than 10,000 households to safer locations.

Mandatory coverage is probably the most efficient approach for insuring hurricane and earthquake losses as well. Indeed, the state-sponsored windstorm pools in Florida and Texas, along with the California Earthquake Authority, exist in large part to deal with the Samaritan's dilemma problem. But a more efficient solution would be simply to mandate coverage from private insurers without any government subsidy.

Mandatory coverage is not novel. About 170 countries mandate participation in a social security system.[94] Mandatory coverage in this case prevents people from rationally undersaving for retirement and then relying on the government for provision during retirement. Some U.S. states, such as Pennsylvania, also mandate the purchase of a minimum amount of auto insurance in order to prevent people from exploiting limited-liability protection after causing an automobile accident.

DIVERSIFIABLE RISKS. While mandatory coverage of earthquake, hurricane, and flood losses is probably the most efficient policy since the underlying assets are *nondiversifiable*, firms affected by TRIA tend to be owned by *diversified* shareholders, for whom the loss of property is less severe. It follows that it is not even obvious that a Samaritan's dilemma really exists for diversified risks. Moreover, the terrorism exclusions before TRIA were generally not written into policies with annual premiums below $1 million, except for rather high-risk properties. Hence, unlike the flood, hurricane, and earthquake state subsidies, terrorism exclusions did not affect politically sensitive groups such as farmers and homeowners.

The Samaritan's dilemma justification, therefore, for government intervention in the terrorism insurance market seems fairly weak, especially since, unlike the case of nondiversifiable risks, it is not obvious that the purchase of insurance is actually rational. A subsidized rate could encourage some firms to purchase insurance even though it is more efficient for their shareholders or creditors to diversify terrorism risk in the capital markets. Indeed, the current low demand for the heavily subsidized TRIA coverage could easily reflect an inefficient *excess* demand for terrorism protection and not an insufficient demand.

SUMMARY. Although *subsidized* insurance, as in TRIA, is difficult to justify on efficiency grounds under a wide range of circumstances, *mandatory*

94. Mulligan and Sala-i-Martin (1999).

coverage probably makes sense for certain risks that (a) are hard to diversify in capital markets *and* (b) are borne by interest groups such as homeowners and farmers that are likely to be bailed out after a significant loss. Neither of these conditions is satisfied by firms owned by well-diversified shareholders.

Myopia

Another argument for government intervention is that households and firms might not rationally purchase adequate amounts of terrorism coverage if they suffer from a lack of foresight, that is, myopia. In two works, Kunreuther, in particular, presents compelling evidence that many people apparently need to experience some previous exposures to losses in order to plan properly for similar future risks.[95] Of course, when a government backstop exists, myopia is observationally equivalent to the Samaritan's dilemma unless the "rationality" of the economic agent can be measured by actions independent of the insurance decision itself. Hence, it is sometimes difficult to distinguish between evidence of the Samaritan's dilemma and of myopia. Still, the evidence suggests that many people might indeed be myopic.

The possibility of myopia can rationalize some paternalistic government policies, including, for example, controls over the safety of the workplace. Although, in theory, workers in riskier occupations should be compensated with higher wages, many workers might not have enough foresight to investigate the underlying risks fully. As another example, compulsory social security programs protect myopic households from entering retirement with too few assets. Indeed, it seems reasonable that paternalism can justify government controls over some *personal* decisions such as choice of workplace conditions and retirement saving. Personal choices are not subject to the competitive pressures of the marketplace. Nor can many mistakes be easily corrected in the future. One cannot, for example, learn from one's previous inadequate preparation for retirement and try again. Moreover, personal mistakes can be very costly because the underlying asset, such as a person's life, is difficult to diversify in the capital market. Furthermore, the nondiversifiable nature of the underlying asset implies that a government requirement to insure the asset will likely be optimal.

95. Kunreuther (1996); Kunreuther and others (1978).

Most *business* decisions, however, are subject to competition and repetition. Moreover, the assets of large firms, like those firms mostly affected by TRIA, are owned by a diversified set of shareholders. Even the bankruptcy of a large firm would have a small impact on the total rate of return of a broadly diversified portfolio. The diversifiable nature of those assets also implies that self-insurance might be more optimal than insurance in the presence of large underwriting and adjustment costs. Justifying government intervention, therefore, becomes substantially more difficult. Government bureaucrats would have to (a) be armed with better information than the private sector or (b) be more concerned about the well-being of the private sector than its own managers.

Presence of Landmark Externalities

Certain landmarks, such as the Sears Tower in Chicago and the Golden Gate Bridge in San Francisco, are more obvious targets for terrorists than other structures. Landmarks, therefore, may create positive production externalities for other structures by forming a "focal point buffer" of sorts. These externalities might not be compensated with Coasian side payments due to large transaction costs when there are many property owners. As a result, the production of new buildings could be distorted. For example, a developer might decide to build the second tallest building in a particular area rather than the tallest, in order to avoid becoming the new terrorist focal point.

In theory, the government could attempt to reproduce the efficient market solution by subsidizing the production of landmarks with taxes on nonlandmarks, thereby mimicking the Coasian side payments that would exist if transaction costs were zero. Unlike TRIA, however, it would not be optimal for government to distort the price of terrorism insurance itself: efficient prices would still reflect the underlying risks since the externality is produced by the existence of landmarks and not whether they purchase insurance.

But several problems arise even with a tax-and-transfer program. First, the government's information set would have to be extensive. The government would have to determine the terrorist-related landmark qualities of each property, determine the reservation prices of builders, properly distinguish between new and existing buildings, and much more. Of course, this process would also have to be unhindered by lobbying efforts from the property owners and their legislative representatives. Failing to make correct estimates could cause more economic damage than not estimating at all.

Second, attempting to "fix" this nonmarket externality potentially contradicts the "theory of second best," which states that it is not always optimal to remove distortions in specific sectors of the economy when the distortions cannot be removed in all sectors. Specifically, landmark properties are already better positioned to leverage their status in order to earn economic rents. Since the government does not currently levy taxes on fairly inelastic "landmark status rents," it is not necessarily efficient to subsidize landmarks further. The larger "tax" that is paid by landmarks in the form of higher premiums is likely efficient.

Incomplete Trading Markets

Another potential argument for the government provision of catastrophic coverage is that governments can smooth large shocks intertemporally more easily than can the private sector. This argument for government intervention is really about time diversification and not about the "size of shocks" considered earlier. As a practical matter, however, government actions would still be limited to larger shocks.

Unfortunately, the underlying theoretical model that supports this argument is not clearly specified in the literature. This omission is important. For example, in the standard neoclassical (Ramsey) growth model, the representative household has an infinite planning horizon, and production is constant returns to scale. In this setting, the government has no particular advantage over the private market at smoothing shocks over time. Hence, we must look elsewhere to rationalize government involvement. There must be a source of *incomplete trading markets* either between or within generations. This subsection considers the potential for incomplete *inter*generational markets since that case seems more compelling than the case of incomplete *intra*generational markets.

Incomplete intergenerational markets can be motivated by abandoning the standard neoclassical model in favor of the more realistic overlapping-generations model in which households live a finite length of time. But even here, some care in modeling is needed. For example, if household parents were purely altruistic toward their children, and parents could, hypothetically speaking, legally pass *negative* transfers (inter vivos transfers or bequests) to their children during bad times, then, by the process of recursion, households would have infinite horizons, as in the standard neoclassical model. Intergenerational trading markets would, therefore, be effectively complete, and the government once again would have no particular advantage over the private market. Of course, parents cannot pass negative bequests during bad times. But the intergenerational linkage would still exist if children were also altruistic toward their parents and, hence, were willing to make "gifts" (reverse transfers) to their parents during bad times.

However, the evidence appears to show that households are not so altruistically linked.[96] It follows that incomplete trading markets effectively exist between generations since people alive today cannot write legally binding risk-sharing agreements with the unborn. The government, however, can complete this missing market using its taxation authority.[97]

Still, the exact nature of the terrorist loss is crucial in determining the government's optimal policy. In particular, if the terrorist loss is best viewed mostly as a "depreciation shock" that lowers the return to existing capital owners but does not depress the wages of workers, then the efficient policy *may* involve, depending on different parameter values, having the government subsidize the returns of capital owners with higher taxes on workers. One could view TRIA as an imperfect attempt to do this.

The best available macro evidence, though, suggests that terrorist shocks depress national output beyond just capital income returns.[98] So if the terrorist loss is best viewed as mostly a "total factor productivity shock" that lowers capital returns *and* wages, then the efficient policy is likely just the *opposite* of the type of risk sharing provided by TRIA. In particular, the optimal policy would *additionally* tax the already lower returns of capital owners in order to increase the after-tax wages on future generations of workers by lowering their wage taxes. In other words, capital owners get hit twice: first by the initial terrorist shock and then again by an additional tax. (Policy-induced general-equilibrium effects reinforce this optimal policy.) The intuition for this surprising result is that the shock to future workers is actually costlier than the shock to capital owners, and so the optimal ex ante policy helps workers at the cost of capital owners.

96. Altonji, Hayashi, and Kotlikoff (1997).
97. Smetters (2003).
98. Blomberg, Hess, and Orphanides (2003); Eckstein and Tsiddon (2003).

In general, most terrorist losses can likely be described as a *combination* of a depreciation loss and a reduction in productivity. It follows that there might be some scope for government intervention once general-equilibrium effects are considered. The exact combination of underlying model parameters, though, is critical for determining whether there is a valid role for the government in sharing terrorist losses across generations, and so some caution is required. Indeed, the theoretical results described above suggest that government-subsidized insurance could actually do more harm than good by effectively compensating the wrong generations. This area of research deserves more attention in the future, using calibrated overlapping-generations models.

Conclusions

Private commercial property and casualty insurance markets likely would be able to provide insurance against terrorism and even war losses if government tax, accounting, and regulatory policies were changed in order to reduce the insurer's costs of holding capital and to allow large risks to be more easily securitized in a market with competitive prices. To be sure, the administration and Congress created TRIA within a constrained environment where these changes were not envisioned. But modifying these fiscal policies would likely be much more efficient than the approach taken in TRIA, which has created several potential problems: crowding out the development of private insurance, creating excess demand for subsidized insurance by diversified shareholders, creating ex ante and ex post moral hazard, and imposing unfunded liabilities on future generations. Changing the tax, accounting, and regulatory policies, however, will require considerable coordination between the federal government and the states. The recent movement by the insurance industry toward federalization of insurance regulations would likely speed things along, but at the risk of more lobbying by insurers at the federal level.[99]

The most common arguments in favor of direct government intervention in the terrorism insurance market tend to focus on the difficulties that the private market faces in providing terrorism insurance. Most of these arguments, however, do not explain why the private market solution is actually

99. See, for example, Treaster (2003).

inefficient. Probably the most compelling "market failure" can be traced to incomplete trading markets between generations. In theory, the government can complete this missing market using its taxation authority. But considerable care must be taken since the optimal policy might be exactly the *opposite* of that of subsidized insurance, and so additional research is still required. Furthermore, although this theoretical argument deals with time diversification and not the size of losses, government intervention would, in practice, be limited to very large losses—probably well beyond TRIA's current $100 billion ceiling—due to the other administrative inefficiencies that government intervention could produce.

Discussion

Bill Murray of Chubb and Son discussed reputation as a major motivator in the decision not to invoke the war exclusion after September 11. The decision to cover those losses was voluntary, but the post–September 11 world left insurers vulnerable. While reinsurers have the option of closing shop, the primary business is bound by cancellation and nonrenewal restrictions. Debra Ballen of the American Insurance Association agreed that the Terrorism Risk Insurance Act (TRIA) should be reauthorized for three main reasons. First, a lack of precedent hinders informed projection of future risk. Second, preexisting regulatory constraints do not allow a "free-market" solution. Finally, truly turning risk evaluation over to the free market is politically unacceptable, as seen in the reception of the Pentagon's exploration of a futures market in terrorism.

Thomas Holzheu of the Swiss Economic Research Unit challenged this apparently contradictory faith in financial markets combined with distrust in the free insurance market. The government should play a role if it has better information, as a third-party player in what would otherwise be a symmetric game of noninformation. In some sense, the government may even be a risk maker. On the other hand, the federal government must be very careful about framing an incentive structure that prevents moral hazard. There should be some incentive for individuals to take precautions to reduce the probability or magnitude of damage suffered.

Neil Doherty of the Wharton School called for a corporate view to evaluate insurance. For a firm, an insurance payment provides contingent capital used in some investment; it only makes sense if the net present value is positive. In the event of another attack, the event itself will lower the internal rate of investment, perhaps to the point where there may be no demand.

Even if there is demand for contingent capital, insurance may not be the best means of providing it when a credit risk is associated with the event itself. Mike O'Malley of Chubb challenged Smetters's high-risk examples. Earthquake insurance is heavily subsidized through the California Earthquake Authority in two ways. The amount of the premium tax is allowed to go into the fund annually to accumulate surplus, and the Internal Revenue Service considers it tax exempt, as a political subdivision of the state. In addition, coverage sold by the entity has been cut by about two-thirds. Hurricane insurance in Florida also is heavily subsidized.

Warren Gorlick of the U.S. Commodity Futures and Trading Commission called attention to Basel II. Nominally a set of banking standards, Basel II will ultimately affect securities and futures firms as part of the banking structure. The rules require a reserve against operational risk, which explicitly includes terrorism. Basel rules also prohibit deducting insurance premiums from the amount by which a firm self-insures.

Robert Litan of Brookings lauded the paper for highlighting the lack of real-world evidence arguing for the Terrorism Risk Insurance Act. Agreeing that government tax policies constrain insurers from accumulating capital, he speculated on how recent administrations may have considered the issue. Under the Clinton administration, a pay-as-you-go rule prevented a change in policy to allow tax-deductible reserves for catastrophe insurance. The Bush administration did not support a tax cut for this industry either, presumably for political reasons. Given the limitations of reality—no good tax treatment of the issue exists—arguing for a Panglossian solution may be less useful than working within the regime, providing some backstop insurance where none might otherwise exist. Finally, even without regulatory impediments, there is a limited appetite for catastrophe bonds, which may be explained best by considering that institutional buyers are comprised of individual actors for whom losing on a catastrophe bond would probably end their career.

Smetters concluded by responding to several points. The ambiguity of risk, lacking historical data, should not be so great an impediment. Investors poured money into Amazon.com even though there were no time-series data on the company. While insurance has a lower risk-reward ratio than other industries, this is attributable largely to the difficulty of securitization and the difficulty of diversifying the risk. Smetters discussed the differences between terrorism and natural disasters. Three examples of government involvement in catastrophic events are earthquake, flood, and hurricane insurance. These natural tragedies hit politically sensitive groups, and the single asset risk of homeowners is nondiversifiable. Here the concern is with underinsurance, and there is a role for government in the form of mandates forcing people to buy insurance, but not in subsidies. TRIA, however, primarily affects large firms owned by diversified shareholders, and the concern is more with overinsurance.

References

Altonji, Joseph G., Fumio Hayashi, and Laurence J. Kotlikoff. 1997. "Parental Altruism and Inter Vivos Transfers: Theory and Evidence." *Journal of Political Economy* 105 (6, December): 1121–66.

American Academy of Actuaries. 2002. *Terrorism Insurance Coverage in the Aftermath of September 11.* Public Policy Monograph. Washington, May.

A. M. Best. 2002. "A Year after Terror, Commercial Insurers Look Closer at Concentrations of Risk." BestWire Services, September 12.

Bice, William B. 1994. "British Government Reinsurance and Acts of Terrorism: The Problems of Pool Re, Comment." *University of Pennsylvania Journal of International Business Law* 15 (Fall): 441–68.

Blomberg, S. Brock, Gregory D. Hess, and Athanasios Orphanides. 2003. "The Macroeconomic Consequences of Terrorism." Paper presented at the Carnegie-Rochester conference series on public policy, University of Rochester, Bradley Policy Research Center, and Carnegie-Mellon University, Center for Public Policy, Pittsburgh, November.

Board of Governors of the Federal Reserve System. 2002. "Monetary Policy Report to the Congress." *Federal Reserve Bulletin,* August.

Bone, James, and Alan Road. 1997. "Terror by Degree." *The Times,* October 18, features sec.

Borch, Karl H. 1990. *Economics of Insurance.* Amsterdam: North-Holland.

Bradford, David F., and Kyle D. Logue. 1999. "The Influence of Income Tax Rules on Insurance Reserves." In Kenneth Froot, ed., *The Financing of Catastrophe Risk,* pp. 275–304. University of Chicago Press.

Brown, Jeffrey R., J. David Cummins, Christopher Lewis, and Ran Wei. 2003. "An Empirical Analysis of the Economic Impact of Federal Terrorism Reinsurance." Paper presented at the Carnegie-Rochester conference series on public policy, University of Rochester, Bradley Policy Research Center, and Carnegie-Mellon University, Center for Public Policy, Pittsburgh, November.

Brown, Jeffrey R., Randall S. Kroszner, and Brian H. Jenn. 2002. "Federal Terrorism Risk Insurance." *National Tax Journal* 55 (3, September): 647–57.

Buchanan, James M. 1975. "The Samaritan's Dilemma." In Edmund Phelps, ed., *Altruism, Morality, and Economic Theory,* pp. 71–85. New York: Russell Sage.

Buffett, Warren. 2001. "Letter to Shareholders for Third Quarter Ended September 30, 2001." Omaha, Neb.: Berkshire Hathaway, November 9.

Bureau of Economic Analysis. 2001. *Survey of Current Business.* U.S. Department of Commerce, August.

Clinton, William J. 1999. "Blocking Property and Prohibiting Transactions with the Taliban." Executive order 13129. Washington, July 4.

Congressional Budget Office. 2001. "Federal Reinsurance for Terrorism Risks." CBO Paper. October.

Cummins, J. David. 1976. "Risk Management and the Theory of the Firm." *Journal of Risk and Insurance* 43 (4): 587–609.

———. 2001. "Protecting Policyholders from Terrorism: Private Sector Solutions." Testimony before the Subcommittee on Capital Markets, Insurance, and Government-Sponsored Enterprises, U.S. House of Representatives, October 24.

———. 2002. "Convergence of Financial Services: Opportunities in the Wholesale Market." Paper presented at the International Financial Risk Institute, London, April 11–12.

Cummins, J. David, and Neil Doherty. 2001. "Federal Terrorism Reinsurance: An Analysis of Issues and Program Design Alternatives." Unpublished ms. University of Pennsylvania, Wharton School.

Cummins, J. David, Neil Doherty, and Anita Lo. 2002. "Can Insurers Pay for the 'Big One'? Measuring the Capacity of the Insurance Market to Respond to Catastrophic Losses." *Journal of Banking and Finance* 26 (2–3, March): 557–83.

Cummins, J. David, David Lalonde, and Richard Phillips. 2004. "The Basis Risk of Catastrophic-Loss Index Securities." *Journal of Financial Economics* 71 (1, January): 77–111.

Cummins, J. David, and Christopher Lewis. 2003. "Catastrophic Events, Parameter Uncertainty, and the Breakdown of Implicit Long-Term Contracting: The Case of Terrorism Insurance." *Journal of Risk and Uncertainty* 26 (2–3): 153–78.

Cummins, J. David, Christopher Lewis, and Richard D. Phillips. 1999. "Pricing Excess-of-Loss Reinsurance Contracts against Catastrophic Loss." In Kenneth Froot, ed., *The Financing of Catastrophe Risk*, pp. 233–69. University of Chicago Press.

Cutler, David M., and Richard Zeckhauser. 1999. "Reinsurance for Catastrophes and Cataclysms." In Kenneth Froot, ed., *The Financing of Catastrophe Risk,* pp. 149–91. University of Chicago Press.

Doherty, Neil A. 2000. *Integrated Risk Management: Techniques and Strategies for Reducing Risk.* McGraw-Hill.

Doherty, Neil A., Joan Lamm-Tennant, and Laura T. Starks. 2003. "Insuring September 11th: Market Recovery and Transparency." *Journal of Risk and Uncertainty* 26 (2–3): 179–99.

Doherty, Neil A., and Lisa Posey. 1997. "Availability Crisis in Insurance Markets: Optimal Contracts with Asymmetric Information and Capacity Constraints." *Journal of Risk and Uncertainty* 15 (1): 55–80.

Doherty, Neil A., and Sven Sinclair. 2003. "Risk Management, Transparency, and Executive Compensation." Unpublished ms. University of Pennsylvania, Wharton School.

Doherty, Neil A., and Kent Smetters. 2002. "Moral Hazard in Reinsurance Markets." NBER Working Paper 9050. Cambridge, Mass.: National Bureau of Economic Research. (Forthcoming in *Journal of Risk and Insurance*.)

Doherty, Neil A., and Seha M. Tinic. 1981. "Reinsurance under Conditions of Capital Market Equilibrium: A Note." *Journal of Finance* 36 (4): 949–53.

Eckstein, Zvi, and Daniel Tsiddon. 2003. "Macroeconomics of Terrorism: The Case of Israel." Paper presented at the Carnegie-Rochester conference series on public policy, University of Rochester, Bradley Policy Research Center, and Carnegie-Mellon University, Center for Public Policy, Pittsburgh, November.

Fainaru, Steve. 2002. "Clues Pointed to Changing Terrorist Tactics; Foiled Plots, FBI Data Showed al Qaeda Groups Might Use Airplanes as Missiles." *Washington Post,* May 19.

Federal Register. 2003. "Terrorism Risk Insurance Program; Disclosures and Mandatory Availability Requirements." 31 CFR, pt. 50, RIN 1505–AA98. *Federal Register* 68, no. 201 (October 17).

Financial Services Roundtable, American Insurance Association, and Coalition to Insure Against Terrorism. 2002. "Making the Case for a Federal Backstop for Terrorism Insurance." May 29. Available at www.fsround.org/PDFs/NonFSRquotesExamples.PDF [March 15, 2004].

Froot, Kenneth. 1999. "Introduction." In Kenneth Froot, ed., *The Financing of Catastrophe Risk,* pp. 1–22. University of Chicago Press.

————. 2001. "The Market for Catastrophe Risk: A Clinical Examination." *Journal of Financial Economics* 60 (2–3, May-June): 529–71.

Froot, Kenneth, and Paul G. J. O'Connell. 1999. "The Pricing of U.S. Catastrophe Reinsurance." In Kenneth Froot, ed., *The Financing of Catastrophe Risk,* pp. 195–227. University of Chicago Press.

Froot, Kenneth A., and Steven Posner. 2002. "The Pricing of Event Risks with Parameter Uncertainty." *Geneva Papers on Risk and Insurance Theory* 27 (2, December): 153–65.

General Accounting Office. 2002a. "Catastrophe Insurance Risks: The Role of Risk-Linked Securities and Factors Affecting Their Use." Report GAO-02-941. September.

————. 2002b. "Terrorism Insurance: Rising Uninsured Exposure to Attacks Heightens Potential Economic Vulnerabilities." GAO-02-472T. Testimony before the Subcommittee on Oversight and Investigations, Committee on Financial Services, U.S. House of Representatives, February.

Grøn, Anne. 1999. "Insurer Demand for Catastrophe Reinsurance." In Kenneth Froot, ed., *The Financing of Catastrophe Risk,* pp. 23–43. University of Chicago Press.

Guy Carpenter. 2003. "The World Catastrophe Reinsurance Market: 2003." September.

Hofmann, Mark. 2003. "Few Buying TRIA Cover; Most Buyers Find Offers of Coverage Too Pricey, Too Limited." *Business Insurance,* February 24.

Hoyt, Robert E., and Khang Ho. 2000. "On the Demand for Corporate Property Insurance." *Journal of Risk and Insurance* 67 (1, March): 91–107.

ISO (Insurance Services Office). 1996. "ISO Reports Latest Data on Insurers' Environmental and Asbestos Liabilities." Press release, April 2.

Jaffee, Dwight M., and Thomas Russell. 1997. "Catastrophe Insurance, Capital Markets, and Uninsurable Risks." *Journal of Risk and Insurance* 64 (2, June): 205–30.

Kading, Bradley L. 2000. "Regulatory Issues Regarding the Treatment of Risk Transfer Securitizations." Paper presented to the International Association of Insurance Regulators, Insurance Securitization Panel, October.

Kemsley, Deen, and Doron Nissim. 2002. "Valuation of the Debt Tax Shield." *Journal of Finance* 57 (5, October): 2045–73.

Klein, Robert, Martin Grace, and Richard Phillips. 2000. "Onshore Special-Purpose Reinsurance Vehicles: A Public Policy Evaluation." Unpublished ms. Georgia State University, Center for Risk Management and Insurance Research.

Kleindorfer, Paul R., and Howard C. Kunreuther. 1999. "Challenges Facing the Insurance Industry in Managing Catastrophic Risks." In Kenneth Froot, ed., *The Financing of Catastrophe Risk*, pp. 149–91. University of Chicago Press.

Knowledge@Wharton. 2003. "To Pay or Not to Pay: Business Weighs the Cost of Terrorism Coverage." Interview with Dave Dasgupta, May 7.

Kunreuther, Howard. 1996. "Mitigating Disaster Losses through Insurance." *Journal of Risk and Uncertainty* 12 (2–3): 171–87.

———. 2002. "The Role of Insurance in Managing Extreme Events: Implications for Terrorism Coverage." *Business Economics* 37 (2, April): 6–16.

Kunreuther, Howard, Ralph Ginsberg, L. Miller, P. Sagi, P. Slovic, B. Borkin, and N. Katz. 1978. *Disaster Insurance Protection: Public Policy Lessons*. Wiley.

Kunreuther, Howard, Jacqueline Meszaros, Robin Hogarth, and Mark Spranca. 1995. "Ambiguity and Underwriter Decision Processes." *Journal of Economic Behavior and Organization* 26 (3, May): 337–52.

Kunreuther, Howard, Erwann Michel-Kerjan, and Beverly Porter. 2003. "Assessing, Managing, and Financing Extreme Events: Dealing with Terrorism." NBER Working Paper W10179. Cambridge, Mass.: National Bureau of Economic Research.

Leikin, Howard. 2001. "Remarks." Remarks by the deputy administrator, Mitigation Division, Federal Emergency Management Agency, at the tenth annual Catastrophe Conference, Insurance Management Solutions Group, St. Petersburg, Fla., November 29.

Lewis, Christopher M., and Kevin C. Murdock. 1996. "The Role of Government Contracts in Discretionary Reinsurance Markets for Natural Disasters." *Journal of Risk and Insurance* 63 (4): 567–97.

———. 1999. "Alternative Means of Redistributing Catastrophic Risk in a National Risk-Management System." In Kenneth Froot, ed., *The Financing of Catastrophe Risk*, pp. 51–85. University of Chicago Press.

Meulbroek, Lisa. 2002. "A Senior Manager's Guide to Integrated Risk Management." *Journal of Applied Corporate Finance* 14 (4, Winter): 56–70.

Meyer, Josh. 2003. "Trading on the Future of Terror; A Market System Would Help Pentagon Predict Turmoil. To Critics, It's 'Gambling' on Security." *Los Angeles Times*, July 29, main news sec., pt. 1, p. 1.

Morgan Stanley. 2001. "An Update on WTC-Related Issues." October 10.

Moss, David. 1999. "Courting Disaster? The Transformation of Federal Disaster Policy since 1803." In Kenneth Froot, ed., *The Financing of Catastrophe Risk*, pp. 307–57. University of Chicago Press.

————. 2001. "Testimony before the U.S. Senate Committee on Commerce, Science, and Transportation." October 30.

————. 2002. *When All Else Fails: Government as the Ultimate Risk Manager.* Harvard University Press.

Muldavin, Scott. 2002. "Breaking the Transaction Gridlock." *Real Estate Finance* (August): 23–29.

Mulligan, Casey B., and Xavier Sala-i-Martin. 1999. "Social Security in Theory and Practice (I): Facts and Political Theories." NBER Working Paper 7118. Cambridge, Mass.: National Bureau of Economic Research.

Nishiyama, Shinichi, and Kent Smetters. 2003. "Consumption Taxes and Economic Efficiency in a Stochastic OLG Economy." NBER Working Paper 9492. Cambridge, Mass.: National Bureau of Economic Research, February.

Priest, George L. 1996. "The Government, the Market, and the Problem of Catastrophic Loss." *Journal of Risk and Uncertainty* 12 (2–3): 219–37.

Real Estate Roundtable. 2002a. "Survey Confirms Economic Toll of Terrorism Insurance Gap; Over $10 Billion of Real Estate Projects Affected across the U.S." September 4.

————. 2002b. "Terror Insurance Drag on Real Estate Still Climbing; Over $15.5 Billion of Projects in 17 States Now Affected." September 19.

Riddiough, Timothy, and Risharng Chiang. 2003. "Commercial Mortgage-Backed Securities: An Exploration into Agency, Innovation, Information, and Learning in Financial Markets." Unpublished ms. University of Wisconsin, School of Business.

Russell, Thomas. 2002. "The Costs and Benefits of the Terrorism Risk Insurance Act: A First Look." Unpublished ms. Santa Clara University, Department of Economics.

Sciolino, Elaine. 2001. "After the Attacks: The Overview; Long Battle Seen." *New York Times*, September 16, sec. 1, p. 1.

Shadow Financial Regulatory Committee. 2002. "A Proposed Federal Backstop for Terrorism Insurance and Reinsurance." Statement 182. Washington, September 23.

Smetters, Kent. 2003. "Trading with the Unborn." Unpublished ms. University of Pennsylvania, Wharton School.

————. 2004. "Is the Social Security Trust Fund Worth Anything?" *Papers and Proceedings of the American Economic Review* (May).

Stulz, René M. 1999. "What's Wrong with Modern Capital Budgeting?" Address given at the Eastern Finance Association meeting, Miami Beach, April.

Thornburgh, Dick. 2000. "No End in Sight as Punitive Damages Go Up, Up, Up." *Wall Street Journal*, March 13, p. A47.

Tillinghast-Towers Perrin. 2002. *U.S. Tort Costs: A 2002 Update—Trends and Findings on the Costs of the U.S. Tort System.* New York City.

Treaster, Joseph B. 2003. "Insurers Want One Regulator Instead of 50." *New York Times*, December 26.

U.S. Treasury. 2003. "Treasury Announces Decision on Group Life Coverage under Terrorism Risk Insurance Program." August 15.

Viscusi, W. Kip, Richard J. Zeckhauser, Patricia Born, and Glenn Blackmon. 1993. "The Effect of 1980s Tort Reform Legislation on General-Liability and Medical Malpractice Insurance." *Journal of Risk and Uncertainty* 6 (2): 165–86.

Woo, Gordon. 2003. "Insuring against Al-Qaeda." Unpublished ms. Cambridge, Mass.: National Bureau of Economic Research.

Brokers and the Insurance of Non-Verifiable Losses

NEIL A. DOHERTY
ALEXANDER MUERMANN

C ONSIDER HOW the insurance industry responded to the events of September 11, 2001. It is unclear whether many of the losses at the World Trade Center were really covered under insurance policies. While many policies anticipated some level of terrorist activity and this was covered (or not excluded), most policies excluded acts of war. The events of September 11 and after seem to span terrorism and war. Indeed the U.S. president has continued to refer to the post–September 11 environment as a war situation, and the response has engaged the country in actual wars. Despite some ambiguity in whether the September 11 events were covered, leaders in the insurance industry quickly announced that they would not fight these claims. No doubt reputation and patriotism fed into this decision.

Now, compare this anecdote with the following. Several observers have noticed a recent and, supposedly, disturbing trend in insurance markets. Apparently, insurers are now more likely to dispute large claims, to offer less than 100 cents on the dollar, or to try to get away without paying. Richard and Barbara Stewart have labeled this the "loss of certainty effect," and Kenneth Abraham has talked of the "de facto big claims exclusion."[1] One reason for such disputes is that large claims threaten the solvency of the insurer, and such offers may be seen to resemble workouts in which distressed noninsurance firms negotiate with creditors. But the issue here is

The authors wish to thank Soenje Reiche for valuable discussions.
1. Abraham (2002); Stewart and Stewart (2001).

with the willingness, not the ability, to pay. These writers see the "big claims exclusion" as degradation of the insurance market because risk-averse consumers will place a lower value on such uncertain insurance. Indeed, they see a potential downward spiral of the insurance market if this practice continues.

The loss of certainty may be characterized as ex post bargaining over a settlement rather than a straightforward appeal to the policy conditions. Yet such bargaining should not be a surprise when claims are unusual and it is unclear whether they are really covered. For example, it is a matter of real dispute whether many environmental losses (for example, for cleanup of Superfund sites) are really covered and, if so, how the many policies in force over the long gestation period of such losses should contribute. Indeed, losses of this nature and duration were probably not anticipated when the policies were written, and therefore the policy wording is simply unclear.

Incomplete contract theory provides a very different view of these trends. In a world with rapidly evolving technology and shifting sociopolitical institutions, we might expect to be exposed to new types of losses. As with more traditional losses, there may be a comparative advantage in the transfer of such risk from individuals and firms to insurers and reinsurers whose capital and portfolio structure enables them to absorb such unknown losses at lower cost. But the novelty of these losses presents a problem. If the nature of losses cannot be anticipated with any precision (or if the variety of such potential losses is wide), then it may simply be infeasible to write enforceable contracts to share risk. Can we, then, find a way of arranging the affairs of individuals and potential insurers such that there is sharing of risk, despite the absence of enforceable insurance?

Our model works as follows. Many losses can be anticipated, and enforceable insurance policies can be written against these losses. Let us call such losses *verifiable*. Insurers establish a relationship to cover the verifiable losses, and a contract is written. However, the parties supplement this contract by creating a "forfeit," should the relationship break down. The idea of the forfeit is that because the parties both have something to lose, this will encourage bargaining over the *non-verifiable* loss even though it is not formally covered in the policy. This is the familiar "holdup" problem. The nature and size of the forfeit are set in place ex ante such that the conditions for an ex post bargaining allocation of future non-verifiable losses can be anticipated. In this way, a mechanism is set in place to share the non-verifiable losses.[2]

The size of the holdup is an ex ante decision variable and can take two general forms. First, the parties can make relationship-specific investments. For example, the insurer might make an investment in information about its potential policyholder. This information is specific to the particular policyholder, and if the contract breaks down the insurer loses the benefit of this information. This provides an incentive for the insurer to offer a payment on the non-verifiable loss. Another type of relationship-specific investment is in loss control. The insurer might provide safety-engineering services that enable the policyholder to reduce its expected loss. The insurer continues to reap the benefit into the future as long as the policy continues, again giving an incentive to contribute to non-verifiable losses rather than have the contract canceled.

The second form of the holdup resembles a performance bond. The parties may stake their reputations on the continuation of the contract. In insurance, many commercial contracts are brokered. The brokerage industry is highly concentrated, with three brokers—Aon, Marsh McLennan, and Willis—dominating market. This means that information about contracts and performance is not confined to the parties in question but is effectively disseminated in the market. Thus, to preserve its reputation, the insurer is willing to bargain over a non-verifiable loss even though it is not formally covered. Failure by an insurer to make a reasonable offer to settle may lead the broker to question offering new business to that insurer or may lead the broker to make offsetting demands in the price and conditions of future business. We are not limiting this threat to a withdrawal of the policy in question; the broker can bargain with its whole book of business with the insurer. Of course, both parties might hold hostage their reputations and make relationship-specific investments. If only the reputation of the insurer is at stake, the policyholder can blackmail the insurer to pay for trivial or nonexistent losses. However, the optimal reputation investment from the policyholder might well turn out to be zero.

2. The idea of a forfeit is an example of what has been colorfully referred to as the "ugly princess hostage" (Schelling 1960; Williamson 1985). An example noted by Holmstrom and Roberts (1998) is that Northwestern and KLM chose to rely on single support operations, which increases the costs of a holdup and so gives them an incentive to work together more effectively.

The holdup problem is central to the incomplete contracts literature.[3] This has been applied mainly to explain property rights and the boundaries of a firm. The central concepts in this theory are relationship-specific investments and holdup. If owners, A and B, of different assets plan to engage in joint production and party A makes a non-verifiable relationship-specific investment, this investment will only reap a return if the joint production with B continues. Because the investment is non-verifiable, the parties cannot write a contract conditional on this investment. This creates a dependency that empowers party B, who can now hold up party A (that is, B can force a renegotiation of terms against the threat of withdrawing from the relationship). The anticipation of ex post bargaining over output leads A to make a suboptimal initial investment. The property rights literature proceeds to examine different ownership structures. For example, to minimize the ex ante inefficiencies from holdup, each party may be allocated ownership, and thus control, over those assets most sensitive to its own investments.

In the property rights literature, the parties typically engage in joint production with non-verifiable investments, and holdup is an unfortunate by-product of the production. The ex post bargaining is efficient, but the ex ante investment is not. In our incomplete insurance model, the holdup is created to transfer a risk that is not contractible. Moreover, although there is some transfer of risk through ex post bargaining, the distribution of the verifiable loss is not efficient. The tasks therefore become how to construct the verifiable loss contract and how to determine the relationship-specific investment and the forfeits to maximize the joint efficiency of the sharing of both verifiable and non-verifiable losses.

Our paper is related to a recent pair of papers by Anderlini, Felli, and Postlewaite.[4] They consider an arrangement for delivery of a widget from a buyer to a seller. A contract can be written for foreseen events, but the cost of producing the widget is subject to a noncontractible risk, and the buyer chooses a relationship-specific investment. They show how court rules, which can alternatively uphold or void the contract, can improve the trade-off between efficiency and risk sharing. The main differences with our paper, apart from our specific focus on insurance, is that we select a market institution (brokers rather than a court) to motivate ex post risk sharing and that the parties have some ex ante choice in whether they will face a holdup

3. Grossman and Hart (1986); see Hart (1995) for a summary.
4. Anderlini, Felli, and Postlewaite (2003a, 2003b).

and, if so, in the force of that holdup. Moreover, we bifurcate risk into contractible and noncontractible and are concerned with the impact of the latter on optimal coverage of the former. In one important sense, our analysis falls short of that of Anderlini, Felli, and Postlewaite. Whereas they derive the efficient court rules, we take the broker's role as passive. We salvage this passive role for brokers by allowing heterogeneity and allowing parties to choose the desired level of holdup in their selection of a broker. Nevertheless, an obvious extension of our approach would be to endogenize the strategies of brokers.

Bargaining over Non-Verifiable Losses

In this section, we examine the ex post bargaining process over non-verifiable losses.

The Effect of Profitability and Reputation on Ex Post Bargaining

Imagine the following circumstances. Some unanticipated loss has just occurred. The circumstances of the loss are quite unusual and, although there is a policy covering other anticipated losses, this event simply was not anticipated and does not appear to be specifically covered (nor may it be specifically excluded). Is it reasonable to expect that the insurer will negotiate to make a payment to the policyholder? In the case of the World Trade Center, insurers generally did not appeal to the war exclusion and held that losses were covered. The extraordinary visibility of the loss, and the public declaration that losses would be covered, had clear implications for the reputations of insurers.

Although we have suggested that holdup of insurers can be fueled by relationship-specific investments and by the prospect of reputation losses, we focus on the role of reputation throughout the rest of the paper. In the September 11 incident, the reputation boost for insurers in publicly announcing coverage was probably significant. Insurers were able to join in the expression of solidarity and patriotism that swept the country. Moreover, in a situation where there was likely to be a governmental response to distribute the costs, insurers were able to purchase goodwill. This might have deflected alternative public policy that insurers considered to be less desirable. For example, the loss might have been recovered by an expansion of the tort system or by direct taxation of insurers.

In less visible losses, reputation might also play an important role. The insurer that generates a reputation for generosity in settling claims might be able to attract business on more favorable terms. This benefit will be magnified in the highly concentrated brokered market. Claims settlements will be known to the broker and can be influential in the broker's placement of new business. Thus, in offering to pay a claim that is not clearly covered, the insurer might consider the profitability of the whole account with the broker, not just that from the policy. But this is a two-way street. Brokers also value their reputation with insurers. The pricing and terms of policies can reflect the broker's record for bringing good business. A policyholder that is aggressive in seeking payment for trivial, undeserving, and uncovered losses, or in building up losses, will also gain a reputation with the broker. The broker might be reluctant to jeopardize its reputation with insurers for such troublesome clients.

When contracts are brokered, information about settlements is disseminated widely, and the reputation impact of claims practices is amplified. However, we argue that reputation can be a decision variable. The parties can choose whether brokers are involved and, if so, which brokers. In the absence of brokers, the reputation boost, or penalty, for claims settlements will be small. With small regional brokers, the reputation consequences will be concentrated but limited. With large national and international brokers, the leverage of reputation can be enormous.

Nash Bargaining

We consider losses to be verifiable (non-verifiable) if an enforceable contract can (cannot) be written on such events. The potential range of losses to which we are exposed is enormous, and it may be costly, impractical, or even impossible to specify such types of loss in a legally enforceable document.[5] The fact that losses cannot be specified in advance does not necessarily exclude the possibility that the insurer might have a comparative advantage in bearing these losses. If such losses are diversifiable, they might

5. Some policies specify the perils and losses that are covered. If a loss occurs that is not specified, then it is not covered. Other policies work in the opposite direction, covering everything that is not included. The latter provides a structure for including the unanticipated, but does so at a cost—it is open ended and becomes very difficult to price. Moreover, having such open policies complicates the insurer's financial and risk management.

still be transferable. The problem is with writing the enforceable contract. We assume that even though such losses are non-verifiable, they can be observed after the fact by relevant parties (that is, by the insurer, the insured, and the broker).

Insurance policies are written that cover verifiable losses, denoted v. We assume a simple form in which a portion α of the loss is insured. Proportional insurance is not necessarily optimal,[6] but it is simple to model and does not affect the main insights about the disposition of non-verifiable losses. However, the policies do not cover, or are sufficiently vague about, non-verifiable losses, denoted n. Insurance contracts are written for a single period for a premium, P, but are potentially renewable into the future. If the contract is renewed, the insurer will receive an expected profit, Π, from future business, and the policyholders will receive an expected benefit, $h(\Pi)$, from the continued business.[7] Losses n and v are independently distributed according to density functions $g(n)$ and $f(v)$, and realizations occur at the end of the period. According to policy conditions, the insurer pays type v losses. But if a type n loss occurs, the insurer and policyholder engage in Nash bargaining to reach a settlement. In the absence of a settlement, the policy is terminated, and the parties suffer reputation losses measured as R_i for the insurer and R_p for the policyholder.

In the Nash bargain over non-verifiable losses, the settlement maximizes the product of the gains to the parties from continuing the relationship. This results in an equal division of the total gains from continuation. If the bargaining is successful and the relationship persists, the insurer makes future profit Π, avoids a reputation loss of R_i, but has to make a settlement of b. For the policyholder, continuation secures a bargained settlement of b and avoids a reputation loss of R_p. To motivate a comparative advantage in bearing risk, we assume that the insurer is risk neutral and the policyholder is risk averse with utility function $u(.)$. The initial wealth of the policyholder is w_0.

The Nash bargain for non-verifiable losses thus solves:

(1) $\qquad MAX_b Z(b) = (\Pi + R_i - b) [u(w + b) - u(w - R_p)],$

where $w = w_0 - P - v - n + \alpha n$.

The optimality conditions are as follows:

---

6. Raviv (1979) shows that deductible policies are optimal if contracts are complete, the transaction cost is linear in the amount of insurance coverage, and there is no background risk.

7. The benefit to the insured is specified relative to the next best alternative, which is canceling the policy and taking a new policy with a rival insurer.

(2) $Z'(b) = (\Pi + R_i - b) [u'(w + b)] - [u(w + b) - u(w - R_p)] = 0,$

and

(3) $Z''(b) = (\Pi + R_i - b) [u''(w + b)] - 2u'(w + b) < 0.$

In the following results we suppress the influence of future profit. Unless it is related to the realization of n, its effect on b^* is similar to that of R_i. We underestimate b^* by a constant.

Case 1

In case 1, we assume that R_p is constant, R_i is constant, and the policyholder is risk neutral. This case is not too interesting in itself, but it is helpful for understanding how bargaining works. The Nash bargaining solution is $b^* = \frac{1}{2}(R_i - R_p) = constant$. This result shows clearly that the payout depends on the balance of bargaining power between the parties. The insurer can hold up the policyholder based on the latter's potential loss of reputation, R_p. And the policyholder can hold up the insurer based on the insurer's reputation stake, R_i. Only if $R_i > R_p$ will the insurer make a positive payment to the policyholder. The bargained payout can be quite perverse. If $R_i < R_p$, the payout is negative because the policyholder has more to lose than the insurer and the insurer has greater holdup power. From a risk-sharing point of view, this does not matter in this case because the policyholder is risk neutral. Also notice that if R_i and R_p are not functions of n, the settlement, b^*, will also be independent of n. Thus ex post bargaining will not reduce risk to the policyholder. Clearly, if ex post bargaining is to have any useful hedge properties, then b^* must increase with n.

Notice also that if R_p is constant, the policyholder can hold up the insurer even if no non-verifiable loss has occurred. This is simply a blackmail situation: "Pay me or I will cancel the contract, the broker will know, and your reputation will suffer." If the broker only observes the contract breakdown, this "blackmail" may be plausible. However, if the broker observes the non-verifiable loss, then it is unlikely to blackball the insurer that refuses to pay for a nonexistent loss. In this case, R_p can be an increasing function of b: either a step function or more continuously increasing in b. The increasing function is dealt with in case 3.

Figure 1. Utility Loss from Contract Termination: Risk-Neutral and Risk-Averse Cases

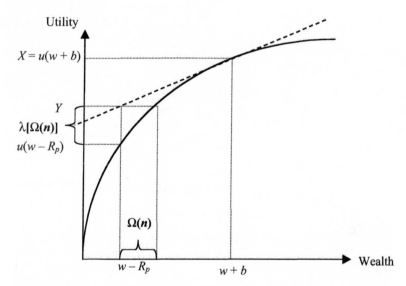

Case 2

In case 2, we assume that R_p is constant, R_i is constant, and the policyholder is risk averse. The solution for the optimal bargain is implicit in equation (2). The change from case 1 lies in the risk aversion of the policyholder. To see how this affects bargaining, consider figure 1.

With policyholder risk neutrality, the utility curve is shown as the dashed line. Thus the utility loss from a breakdown of bargaining and contract termination is $X - Y = u(w + b) - Y$. The slope does not matter since utility is determined up to linear transformation. Now consider that the policyholder is risk averse, as shown by the concave utility function. The total utility loss is now as follows: $u(w + b) - u(w - R_p) = (X - Y) + \lambda[\Omega(n)]$.

We can think of the Nash bargain as a sharing of the total losses from termination, including $\Omega(n)$. So the Nash bargaining solution can be stated as

$$(4) \qquad\qquad b^* = \tfrac{1}{2}[R_i - R_p - \Omega(n)].$$

Thus the policyholder's risk aversion reduces her bargaining power and reduces the bargained settlement by $\tfrac{1}{2}\Omega(n)$. This result is rather unfortunate because one would expect that the efficient ex post transfer from a risk-neutral insurer would *increase* with the policyholder's risk aversion.

Figure 2. Increasing Absolute Risk Aversion (IARA)[a]

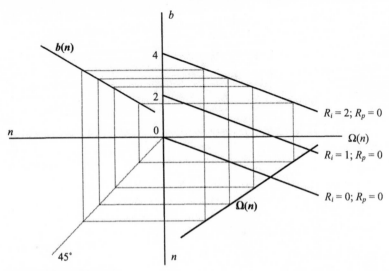

a. $b^*(n)$ increases with n if $\Omega'(n) < 0$.

Notice that this increase in the policyholder's loss by $\frac{1}{2}\Omega(n)$ (and the insurer's holdup) is expressed as a function of n. The properties of this holdup depend on the properties of the utility function. For example, with constant absolute risk aversion (CARA), $\Omega(n)$ is a constant and b^* is also a constant.

Consider another possibility: the policyholder exhibits increasing absolute risk aversion (IARA). In the bottom right quadrant of figure 2, the value of $\Omega(n)$ is shown to be decreasing with n. The top right quadrant shows values of b^* derived from equation 2, with $R_p = 0$, and $R_i = 0, 2, 4$. Notice that these all slope downward, reflecting that the insurer can hold up the policyholder to the tune of $\frac{1}{2}\Omega(n)$. In contrast, the policyholder can hold up the insurer for $\frac{1}{2}R_i$. If we take $R_i = 4$, then b^* will follow the solid downward-sloping line in the top right quadrant. For any level of non-verifiable loss on the lower vertical axis, we can trace in a counterclockwise direction (following the dotted lines) to derive a function $b(n)$ in the top left quadrant. In figure 2, the downward slope of $\Omega(n)$ produces a hedging loss function; that is, $b(n)$ is increasing with n.

If Nash bargaining is to result in a useful hedge, clearly b^* must increase with n (in the limit, of course, if the non-verifiable loss is to be fully hedged, $b^*(m) = n$). Unfortunately, this result may not prevail with plausible policyholder risk preferences. If the policyholder's utility function exhibits

Figure 3. Decreasing Absolute Risk Aversion (DARA)[a]

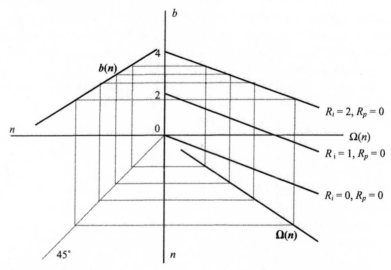

a. $b^*(n)$ decreases with n if $\Omega'(n) < 0$.

decreasing absolute risk aversion (DARA), then anticipated ex post bargaining may compound the policyholder's risk. Figure 3 shows that, with an upward slope of $\Omega(n)$, the Nash bargain produces a gambling loss function; that is, $b(n)$ decreases with n.

It seems clear that we cannot rely on risk preferences alone to produce a bargained risk transfer from the risk-averse policyholder to the risk-neutral insurer. In the general case considered now, we allow the reputation stakes of the parties to be functionally related to n.

Case 3

From these two specific cases, we can interpret the general case. We simply state the main results. The intuition should be apparent from the previous reasoning. First, in order to ensure a hedging bargain function, that is, $b'(n) > 0$, for all risk-averse utility functions, it is necessary either for the insurer's reputation loss to increase with n or for the policyholder's reputation loss to decrease with n. Returning to equation 4, we can isolate the conditions for $b'(n) > 0$. That is,

(5) $$R_i'(n) > R_p'(n) + \Omega'(n).$$

However, we can isolate a special case where, in principle, full insurance of the non-verifiable loss is possible. We state this as Proposition 1: if the reputation loss to the insurer is a function of the size of both types of losses, then there exists a reputation loss function to the insurer such that Nash bargaining generates full coverage of the non-verifiable loss to the policyholder.

The proof is as follows. Set the reputation loss function as

$$R_i(v,n) = n + \frac{u(w_0 - P - v + \alpha v) - u(w_0 - P - v + \alpha v - n - R_p)}{u'(w_0 - P - v + \alpha v)}.$$

The unique solution to the first-order condition $Z'(b) = (R_i - b) \cdot u'(w_0 - P - v + \alpha v - n + b) - [u(w_0 - P - v + \alpha v - n + b) - u(w_0 - P - v + \alpha v - n - R_p)] = 0$ is then $b^* = n$.

Summary

Before considering the optimal ex ante contract, it is of interest to know whether the *anticipated* bargained settlements, $b(n)$, are increasing in the non-verifiable loss. Only in this case will the anticipated bargains hedge the risk-averse policyholder's loss. The bargained payout, b, reflects the balance of both parties' reputation investments and the properties of the policyholder's utility function. Risk aversion alone is not sufficient to produce a hedge, $b'(n) > 0$. For example, with CARA and constant reputation values, $b(n)$ is constant and results in no risk transfer. And with DARA, $b'(n) < 0$, and ex post bargaining thus increases the policyholder's risk. The general problem is that risk aversion weakens the policyholder's bargaining power and, ceteris paribus, lowers the settlements. Alternatively, a hedge of non-verifiable losses can be generated if the reputation loss of the insurer increases in n or the reputation of the policyholder decreases in n. For example, if $R_i'(n) > 0$, the policyholder's bargaining power increases with n, enabling her to hold up for larger settlements, the larger the non-verifiable loss.

Optimal Insurance Contracts

Before looking at optimal ex ante contracts, we examine the information assumptions and the role of brokers.

Brokers, Reputation, and Blackballing

A policyholder can approach an insurance broker to help formulate an insurance strategy and place insurance with appropriate carriers. As an agent for the policyholder, the broker is concerned with issues such as the terms and conditions of the policy, the price, the insurer's financial condition, and its reputation for fair treatment, especially in paying claims. The issue of legal agency is clouded somewhat by the fact that the broker's commission often is paid by the insurer as a percentage of the premium income. Moreover, insurers often supplement this commission by a profit-sharing arrangement that aligns the broker's interests with those of the insurer. This profit sharing encourages the broker to bring business that is profitable to the insurer. Brokers have relationships with several (many) insurance companies, and each insurer has a portfolio of business with each broker. Indeed, insurers compete for the best business in the design of these profit-sharing plans.

The intermediation role of the broker highlights the importance of reputation. If insurers gain a reputation for being difficult in settling claims, then brokers will tend to divert business to other insurers or will seek compensating variations in price or policy conditions. Thus a negative reputation can be costly. In our model, we specifically consider that the termination of a contract due to the breakdown of ex post Nash bargaining will lead to a reputation penalty.

In imposing a penalty on an insurer, the broker must use its information, its judgment, and its bargaining power. Brokers can only sanction insurers by threatening to withhold future business for misbehavior if they observe the misdeeds. Naturally, they know whether a policy has been terminated. Proposition 1 showed that there exists a reputation function such that bargaining over non-verifiable losses will result in a perfect hedge. However, for this function to be operational, brokers would have to observe n (as well as v). We can imagine weaker information assumptions. The broker may know that a loss has occurred but may not be able to quantify it. For example, the event can affect the policyholder's future profits, and estimation of these profits requires considerable judgment.

Judgment also plays another important role. The point of this paper is to examine whether efficient risk sharing can occur by means of ex post bargaining. The important issue is whether the non-verifiable loss is one that would have been insurable had it been verifiable. The events of September 11 were to some extent unanticipated, but they may be quite insurable in the future. However, though not specifically modeled here, some types of risk probably should not be transferred through insurance. For example, the transfer of core business risk creates an obvious moral hazard problem. We would not expect the broker to be unhappy with an insurer that refuses to make a settlement on a property insurance policy for business losses arising from the policyholder's poor marketing, bad management, or poor sales through bad product design. Thus the imposition of a reputation penalty should indeed depend on the type of non-verifiable loss, and this requires judgment by the broker.

The size of the reputation penalty also reflects the broker's bargaining power. Brokers are not homogeneous; some have small books and some large. Making a national broker unhappy by mishandling a claim may have more severe consequences for an insurer than making a regional broker unhappy. This heterogeneity implies that consumers have some degree of ex ante choice over the potential holdup of insurers. Policyholders have some ability to influence the reputation commitments made by themselves and by insurers and thereby have some control over the bargaining function, $b(n)$.

In discussing the role of reputation penalties, it is important to bear in mind that if the information assumptions are very strong (all losses are observed by all parties) and the judgments to be made are trivial (all parties can verify ex post which losses should have been insurable had they been anticipated), then there is no real problem to address; the insurer and policyholder can contract ex ante on all losses. We are stopping short of this in two dimensions. First, judgments on the insurability of losses are not trivial. Second, while we examine the effects of conditioning reputation on fully observed non-verifiable losses, we also examine reputation functions based on weaker information. We show that for interesting results, information available to the broker has to be sufficient to make the reputation an increasing function of n.

Insurance Contracts with Ex Post Bargaining on Non-Verifiable Losses

In the previous section, reputation and other relationship-specific investments led to a holdup in which the parties could bargain over non-verifiable losses. The investment was necessary to the sharing of non-verifiable losses. The questions to be addressed now are: Would the parties, particularly the insurer, make such investments? How will this affect the optimal level of insurance on verifiable losses?

The timing of our model is this. The parties decide whether to use a broker and, if so, which broker to use. The choice of broker indirectly makes the degree of reputation at stake a choice variable. In the simplest case, with one broker or identical brokers, we can think of this as a binary choice over reputation. If no broker is chosen, no reputation is offered for holdup; if a broker is chosen, then exogenous reputation functions, $R_i(n)$ and $R_p(n)$, are in effect chosen. At the other extreme, consider a continuum of brokers all having differing client bases, differing sizes, and differing reputations for using claim settlement to influence the placement of future business. Unbounded variation in these dimensions implies that reputation can be a continuous choice variable.

First, the policyholder chooses a broker, and the broker selects an insurer in a competitive insurance market. The risk-neutral insurer demands a price to sell insurance and to stake its reputation to induce payment against non-verifiable losses. We assume that this combined premium is actuarially fair, that is, $P = E(\alpha v) + E(b^*)$, where α is the level of coinsurance chosen by the policyholder. Losses are realized and payments made either by enforcement of the contract (type v losses) or by bargaining (type n losses). But if the bargaining breaks down, brokers implicitly impose penalties by means of their future selection of clients (policyholders) and the placement of business across insurers.

Notice that assuming a fair price implies that the costs of brokering are zero. This is clearly unrealistic, but it allows us to cut through the complexity and identify the mechanisms by which non-verifiable risk can be transferred. Throughout, we assume that v and n are independently distributed. Finally, it will be clear that the more interesting source of holdup stems from the insurer's reputation, which allows the policyholder to make a recovery in the face of non-verifiable losses. The policyholder's own reputation will limit the size and structure of the recovery. In what follows, we show that many interesting results can be derived using only insurer reputation. Thus, for simplicity, we assume $R_p = 0$.

Before looking at incomplete insurance contracts, it is helpful to look at how traditional models of optimal insurance might address the issue of non-verifiable losses. This serves to set benchmarks against which to measure the incomplete contract results.

Complete Insurance

If both losses—v and n—are contractible, the parties can write an insurance contract contingent on the realizations of each type of loss. The optimal coinsurance rates, α_{CI}^* and β_{CI}^*, with respect to loss v and n are then determined by

$$MAX_{0 \leq \alpha, \beta \leq 1} \, E\{u[w_0 - \alpha E(v) - \beta E(n) - v + \alpha v - n + \beta n]\}.$$

Because all losses are verifiable and contractible, there is no distinction between types v and n losses. Consequently, an insurance contract between a risk-averse policyholder and a risk-neutral insurer creates value. With a fair insurance premium, the efficient contract fully insures all losses, that is, $\alpha_{CI}^* = \beta_{CI}^* = 1$. If premiums include a loading (which increases with coverage), the optimal contract is partial insurance.

Without Nash Bargaining: Background Risk

The second case is where n is non-verifiable and noncontractible and no transfer is generated (by bargaining, litigation, arbitration, or other mechanisms) between the insurer and policyholder relative to this loss. Thus type n losses become a background risk against which the parties can contract to insure the type v losses. The optimal coinsurance rate, α_{BR}^*, with respect to loss v is determined by

$$MAX_{0 \leq \alpha \leq 1} \, E\{u[w_0 - \alpha E(v) - v + \alpha v - n]\}.$$

This situation is equivalent to the demand for insurance in the presence of an independent background risk (uninsurable risk). The result is that, either under DARA and decreasing absolute prudence or under DARA and convex absolute risk aversion, the policyholder demands higher coverage than he would if he did not face background risk.[8] With no loading, the optimal contract on v with independent background risk is full insurance: $\alpha_{BR}^* = 1$.

With Nash Bargaining: Fixed Reputational Losses

The results of this section follow simply and intuitively from the results of Nash bargaining. Recall that when the insurer's reputation loss is unrelated

---

8. See, for example, Gollier (2001, ch. 9).

to n, the potential for a bargained settlement to act as a hedge against non-verifiable losses depends on the properties of the policyholder's utility function. With CARA, $b(n)$ is constant and, since it is prepriced, there is no risk, or wealth, transfer. With DARA, $b(n)$ is decreasing in n (as shown in figure 3). This actually increases the risk to the policyholder. Clearly, the policyholder would not like this. Thus the policyholder would choose not to go through a broker, and there would be no reputation investment by the insurer. This case would now degenerate to the background risk case with no Nash bargaining, and the policyholder would fully insure the verifiable loss.

Finally, with IARA, the Nash bargaining can increase with n, as shown in figure 2. Thus establishing a reputation investment by brokering the contract will provide some hedging capacity for non-verifiable losses. However, this case is unlikely, as IARA has little empirical support.

With Nash Bargaining: Proportional Reputation Losses

The results so far suggest that with plausible risk preferences, CARA or DARA, and constant reputation value, ex post Nash bargaining will not arise and there is no mechanism with which to hedge the non-verifiable losses. Thus the most interesting case arises when the insurer's reputation loss increases with n. We can imagine various versions of this. The simplest would be a step function: reputation loss is zero if the contract is terminated, with $n = 0$; the reputation loss is a positive constant if the contract breaks down, with $n > 0$. With more fine-tuning, b^* might be a continuously increasing function of n. We address the latter case.

Suppose that all brokers can observe v and will choose to blackball insurers who fail to reach bargained settlements on non-verifiable losses. For any broker, we assume that reputation loss of the insurer is proportional to the size of the non-verifiable loss, that is, $R_i(n) = \beta n$. Moreover, suppose that brokers differ in the size of their accounts with different insurers. For example, a national or international broker is likely to have a large portfolio of business with any given insurer. Thus the broker wields considerable power over that insurer, and the reputation loss from contract breakdown can be considerable; that is, β will be large. For a small or regional broker, the account will be smaller and the potential reputation loss also smaller; that is, β will be small. Given a continuum of brokers, the policyholder can now exercise a choice over β as well as over the level of coinsurance, β_{NB}. The optimal coinsurance rate, $\beta_{NB}{}^*$, and sensitivity, β^*, are determined by

$$MAX_{0 \le \alpha, \beta \le 1} E\{u[w_0 - \alpha E(v) - E(b^*) - v + \alpha v - n + b^*]\}, \text{ and}$$

s.t. $Z'(b^*) = 0 \leftrightarrow (\beta n - b^*) \cdot u'[w(\alpha) + b^*] - \{u[w(\alpha) + b^*] - u[w(\alpha)]\} = 0,$

where $w(\alpha) = w_0 - \alpha E(v) - E(b^*) - v + \alpha v - n.$

Proposition 2 is as follows: when the insurer's reputation loss is proportional to n, it is optimal for the policyholder to go through a brokered market; that is, $\beta^* > 0$ and $\alpha = \alpha_{NB}^*$.

We do not present the proof here, but the intuition should follow from the previous discussion. The important issue is that because reputation loss increases with n, the policyholder can bargain for larger settlements, the larger is the non-verifiable loss. Thus ex post bargaining can provide an appropriate hedge against such losses.

There are some special cases and qualifications. We have examined the proportional reputation function here. Other possibilities arise. Recall from proposition 1 that, if the reputation function has a certain form, the Nash bargaining solution will equal the non-verifiable loss, $b^* = n$. While this form is complex, the implications for the contract design are straightforward. Because the non-verifiable loss is effectively fully insured and the premium is assumed to be fair, full insurance is optimal. Thus if this function is available from a broker, the policyholder will select this broker, the expected cost of the bargain will be factored into the premium, and the policyholder will fully insure the verifiable loss.

These two cases (proportional reputation and full insurance) are not exhaustive.[9] We cannot make a general assertion that an increasing reputation function, $R_i'(n) > 0,$ will lead to the selection of a brokered relationship. The problem is that DARA and $R_i'(n) > 0$ have opposing effects on the sign of b' (n). It does, however, follow that with CARA or DARA, $R_i'(n) > 0$ is a necessary condition for $b'(n) > 0$. Thus assuming CARA or DARA, it follows that a necessary condition for the policyholder to select the broker is $R_i'(n) > 0.$

Conclusion

We define a particular role for brokers in potentially completing insurance markets with noncontractible risk. Brokers are the repositories of the

9. Other cases have not been examined. For example, we mention that reputation might be a step function of n; $R_i(0) = 0$; $R_i(n > 0) > 0.$

reputation of insurers and policyholders. If non-verifiable losses occur that are, in principle, insurable (that is, had they been foreseeable, they would have been insurable), the parties can bargain over a settlement. By its subsequent behavior, the broker can influence the outcome of this bargaining. For example, if an insurer fails to reach a satisfactory bargain with its policyholder, the broker might be less inclined to place future business with that insurer. Thus the policyholder can hold up the insurer against this reputation cost. Ex ante, policyholders have some degree of choice in whether they do business in the brokerage market and in their selection of a broker. This, in turn, permits them some degree of control over their prospective bargaining position with their insurer and thus some control over the transfer of non-verifiable risk.

The extent to which ex post Nash bargaining permits effective hedging rests on the information available, the utility function of the policyholder, and the structure of the reputation cost function. In principle, there exists a reputation function that would induce a full transfer of non-verifiable risk though Nash bargaining. But this function is complex and requires the broker to have sufficient market clout and full knowledge of realized losses and of the policyholder's risk preferences. Of course, by making the assumptions too strong, we can always argue that the losses are contractible. With weaker assumptions, there can still be risk transfer. However, this requires that the reputation function be positively related to the size of the non-verifiable loss.

We are also able to determine the limits on such risk sharing of non-verifiable losses. If the broker is unable to condition the reputation of the insurer on the occurrence or size of the non-verifiable loss, then Nash bargaining will *increase* the policyholder's risk. However, it would seem an unlikely set of circumstances. The stylized model with increasing reputation costs does seem to correspond to the functioning of the insurance marketplace. Brokers usually have some access to loss estimates, they do indeed shop around risks, and no doubt policyholders do take refuge behind the bargaining clout of their brokers when it comes to negotiating unusual claims. And brokers do place business, not only according to price, policy conditions, and solvency but also according to the claim settlement records of insurers.[10]

---

10. See Harrington and Niehaus (2003, p. 504).

Discussion

Bill Murray of Chubb suggested a closer examination of the role of the broker. In reality brokers, rather than acting disinterestedly, generally act on different motivations. In many cases, they receive compensation from the insurers to whom they present business and with whom they sometimes have profit-sharing arrangements. The status of a broker's compensation may partly influence where the broker chooses to place business. The paper seems to suggest that the insured should always act through a large national broker, who can provide greater clout in the market and have a greater effect on the insurer's reputational interest; in reality, however, regional brokers thrive. Moderate or midsize companies may receive greater attention from regional brokers. Murray was impressed to see a mathematical justification for reputation, something his corporation values but has difficulty quantifying in self-evaluations.

Richard Zeckhauser of Harvard University highlighted the role of the broker as an arbitrator and reputation spreader. Market participants probably want an outcome that they would consider "fair" or "anticipated," rather than the Nash equilibrium solution, which disadvantages the risk averse. He suggested modifying the model to give the insured analytic ability to distinguish by reputation the "fair" insurer from the hard bargainer. The Better Business Bureau and eBay are two examples of the demand for reputation spreading. Mike O'Malley of Chubb agreed, adding that a broker concerned with reputation constitutes a three-party game. In reality brokers do not always act as impartial arbiters. Thanking Zeckhauser for his suggestion, Neil Doherty expressed interest in modifying the model to allow firms to develop reputation by volunteering a settlement beyond the Nash bargaining solution. Developing the model into a three-way bargaining game seems necessary to develop the study further. Although legally it maybe difficult to establish that brokers act as agents for the insurer, receiving compensation from the insurer certainly points to an agency relationship with the insurance corporation.

Richard Darrig of the Automobile Insurers' Bureau suggested that fairly priced future contracts ought to have future profits set to zero. The loss then should not be forgone profits, but sunk costs in capital or expenses. He also suggested that reputation can be thought of as franchise value, which would allow a firm to command higher prices in the market. Finally, rather than setting $\beta_n = 0$ in failed bargaining, some negative value representing an unpleasant outcome for one side or the other should be reflected in the equation. Doherty responded that zero profit makes sense in a competitive market without an intertemporal aspect to product pricing. Making relationship-specific investments that are recouped in the future distributes profit over time and provides some leverage in bargaining.

Howard Kunreuther of the Wharton School pointed out that insurance firms rely on deductibles to screen out unverifiable claims that may be the result of moral hazard. The importance of the deductible warrants further investigation, and verifiability must be defined more clearly. The challenge of verification may be in the severity of the loss or in whether the cause of the loss was an event covered by the policy. Also a client may evaluate the decision between firms of differing reputation depending on the client's own opportunity cost of litigation. Doherty clarified that "verifiable" in the context of this paper indicates not that loss actually occurred and is quantifiable, but that the event causing the loss is specified in the contract. An event unspecified in the contract constitutes a non-verifiable claim.

Robert Litan of Brookings expressed his belief in the paper's relevance to large commercial insurance. Although individuals may have recourse to a regulator, they hardly have bargaining power. Knowing what percentage of claims are litigated or arbitrated rather than just unilaterally declared would give a greater sense of the magnitude of the issue. There may be more to the choice of broker than the reputation staked: the degree of choice, for example. Finally, considering that most settlements are the result of negotiation rather than arbitration, Nash modeling probably provides the best real-world approximation.

Responding to comments, Doherty continued. Having an expectation of future bargaining would certainly increase premiums, but beyond that it may provide a means of completing a market that could not be covered by normal contracting mechanisms. Recent papers by Richard and Barbara Stewart and Ken Abraham suggest that the insurance industry may implode due to the ex post opportunism of insurers. Making consumers uncertain of a payout to which they feel entitled will reduce demand-increasing financial pressure on the industry and susceptibility to ex post opportunism. The paper seeks to cast bargaining in a more positive light.

References

Abraham, Kenneth S. 2002. "The Insurance Effects of Regulation by Litigation." In W. Kip Viscusi, ed., *Regulation through Litigation,* pp. 212–33. Brookings.

Anderlini, Luca, Leonardo Felli, and Andrew Postlewaite. 2003a. "Courts of Law and Unforeseen Contingencies." Working paper. University of Pennsylvania, Department of Economics.

————. 2003b. "Should Courts Always Enforce What Contracting Parties Write?" Working paper. University of Pennsylvania, Department of Economics.

Gollier, Christian. 2001. *The Economics of Risk and Time.* MIT Press.

Grossman, Sanford J., and Oliver Hart. 1986. "The Costs and Benefits of Ownership: A Theory of Vertical and Lateral Integration." *Journal of Political Economy* 94 (4): 691–719.

Harrington, Scott, and Greg Niehaus. 2003. *Risk Management and Insurance,* 2d ed. McGraw-Hill/Irwin.

Hart, Oliver. 1995. *Firms, Contracts, and Financial Structure.* Oxford University Press.

Holmstrom, Bengt, and John Roberts. 1998. "The Boundaries of the Firm Revisited." *Journal of Economic Perspectives* 12 (4): 73–94.

Raviv, Artur. 1979. "The Design of an Optimal Insurance Policy." *American Economic Review* 69 (1, March): 84–96.

Schelling, Thomas. 1960. *The Strategy of Conflict.* Harvard University Press.

Stewart, Richard E., and Barbara D. Stewart. 2001. "The Loss of Certainty Effect." *Risk Management and Insurance Review* 4 (2, Fall): 29–49.

Williamson, Oliver. 1985. *The Economic Institutions of Capitalism.* Free Press.

Consolidation in the European Insurance Industry

Do Mergers and Acquisitions Create Value for Shareholders?

J. DAVID CUMMINS
MARY A. WEISS

P ERHAPS THE MOST important development in the financial services market of the past two decades has been the integration of the financial services sector. Deregulation, advances in communications and information technology, and economic forces have led to the breakdown of the "firewalls" that traditionally separated financial intermediaries such as commercial banks, thrift institutions, investment banks, mutual fund companies, and insurance companies. The European Union gradually deregulated the financial services sector through a series of banking and insurance directives, culminating in the virtual deregulation of financial services (except for solvency) in the Second Banking Coordination Directive, implemented in the early 1990s, and the Third-Generation Insurance Directives, implemented in 1994.[1] The objective of the banking and insurance directives was to create a single European market in financial services. The introduction of the euro in 1999 also profoundly changed the economic landscape for financial services firms in the European market. European deregulation in insurance was particularly important, because insurers traditionally had been limited to operating within specific European countries, with little or no price competition and cross-border transactions limited mainly to reinsurance and some commercial coverages. The Third-Generation Insurance Directives introduced true price and product compe-

---

1. Group of Ten (2001).

217

tition in European retail insurance markets for the first time in both life and non-life insurance.

The result of deregulation and other economic drivers of financial sector integration has been an unprecedented wave of mergers and acquisitions (M&As) of European financial institutions. There were 2,549 reported consolidation transactions involving European financial firms valued at $504 billion from 1990 through 1999.[2] This total included 507 insurance transactions, valued at $127 billion. Significant consolidation occurred both cross-border and within-border as financial services firms sought to consolidate their position within national markets and to take advantage of deregulation and the monetary union to open up or expand their markets in neighboring countries. The consolidation dramatically changed the structure of insurance markets in most European countries and led to lower prices in most European national insurance markets.[3]

In spite of the dramatic changes in European financial markets, there has been little research to date on the economic impact of these developments. This is particularly true for the insurance market, where some of the more dynamic changes in market structure have been taking place. The purpose of this paper is to remedy this limitation in the existing literature by analyzing the market value effects of mergers and acquisitions in the European insurance industry. We analyze M&A transactions over the period 1990–2002, as reported in Thomson Financial Securities Data's Worldwide Merger and Acquisitions (SDC) database. The sample is defined as including all transactions where either the acquiring firm or the target firm was a European insurance company. Included in the analysis are all transactions reported in SDC that involved significant acquisition of value as well as the subset of these transactions that involved a change in control, defined as an acquisition that increased the stake of the acquiring institution from less than 50 percent to 50 percent or more of the ownership shares of the target institution.

We conduct an event-study analysis to determine the market value effects of the transactions included in our sample. Specifically, we obtained stock price data from the Datastream database and studied the market reaction to the M&A transactions for both target and acquirer firms in a series of event windows surrounding the transaction dates. The use of market value data is more powerful than other approaches in studying the effects of events such as mergers and acquisitions because market prices immediately reflect the

2. Group of Ten (2001).
3. Swiss Re (2000).

market's assessment of new information on the target and acquiring firms.[4] In effect, conducting an event study enables us to capture the market's expectation of the net effect of an M&A transaction on the present value of the expected future cash flow of firms involved in the transaction and thus to determine whether M&As tend to create value for shareholders. Although M&As clearly can have other effects, such as the impact on prices, service quality, and product offerings to customers, studying the effect of the transactions on stock prices provides one important metric of the degree of value creation or destruction resulting from the trends in European mergers.

Studying the market value effects of European insurance mergers is important for a number of reasons. Analyzing whether M&As create value has implications for future regulatory policy in Europe. The objective of the regulatory changes in Europe was to move away from a restrictive regulatory system that focused primarily on solvency toward a system that enhanced economic efficiency and provided better value for consumers by harnessing market forces. Because M&A activity is costly, serious questions would be raised about the efficiency effects of regulatory policy if the resulting M&As failed to create value or actually destroyed value for firms involved in the transactions.

Studying M&A transactions also has implications for antitrust policy. Value creation can have both positive and negative effects from an antitrust perspective. On the one hand, if merged firms gain value because they create market power that allows them to charge supercompetitive prices, then positive gains in market value from mergers might be adverse from an antitrust perspective. On the other hand, if firms gain value because they become more efficient and competitive and take market share away from less efficient rivals, then M&As would not be a serious concern for antitrust regulators. Although determining whether any gains in market value from M&As are due to market power or to more economically desirable effects is beyond the scope of this study, our research provides evidence on whether gains in market value are occurring and on what types of transactions are most likely to produce them.

Finally, studying European insurance mergers has important implications for managers of financial services firms. If mergers tend to be value creating, then it may be worthwhile for managers to devote scarce time and resources to further consolidation activities. If, however, mergers have lit-

4. Schwert (1981).

tle or no impact on value or possibly destroy value, then managerial efforts might be directed more profitably toward other activities such as improving efficiency and productivity. Also information on whether some types of transactions are more likely to create value than others should help managers in formulating M&A strategies.

This study is the first to analyze the market value effects of European insurance mergers.[5] There have been few market value studies of European financial sector M&As of any kind. The leading study of European bank mergers, by Cybo-Ottone and Murgia, analyzes merger transactions in thirteen European countries over the period 1988–97.[6] In their sample, either the target or the acquiring firm had to be a bank. Based on fifty-four deals that involved a change in control, they find significant gains in market value for within-country, bank-to-bank acquisitions and for transactions where banks acquired insurance companies. However, they do not find gains in market value for cross-border transactions or for transactions involving banks and securities firms.[7] A recent study of U.S. bank mergers finds that bank mergers that were activity and geographically focused created value but that diversifying mergers did not create value.[8]

A recent market value study of U.S. insurance mergers finds value creation for both acquirers and targets, although the creation of value was significantly larger for targets than for acquirers.[9] There have been a few studies on the book value effects of insurance M&As, primarily focusing on the United States and Europe. Cummins, Tennyson, and Weiss analyze consolidation in the U.S. life insurance industry using book value data to measure technical, cost, and profit efficiency.[10] They find that the efficiency of M&A target firms improved significantly following an acquisition. Cummins and Rubio-Mises find that consolidation in the Spanish insurance

5. Campbell, Goldberg, and Rai (2003) conduct an event study to gauge the market value impact of the passage of the European Union's Second- and Third-Generation Insurance Directives on the stock prices of European insurers. They find that the non-life insurance directives led to some wealth reduction in the European insurance industry, whereas the life insurance directives led to wealth creation. The Third-Generation directives had a greater impact than the Second-Generation directives.

6. Cybo-Ottone and Murgia (2000).

7. Lepetit, Patry, and Rous (2002) study the market value effects of European bank mergers over the period 1991–2001 and find gains in market value for geographically focusing and activity diversifying mergers.

8. DeLong (2002).

9. Akhigbe and Madura (2001).

10. Cummins, Tennyson, and Weiss (1999).

industry over the period 1989–98 led to significant improvements in efficiency and to price reductions in both life and non-life insurance.[11]

The remainder of the paper is structured as follows. In the next section, we discuss the likely economic effects of mergers and acquisitions, identify ways in which M&As can create and destroy value, and specify our hypotheses. In the second section, we explain our sample selection procedure and event-study methodology. We present the results in the third section and discuss conclusions in the final section.

Mergers and Acquisitions: Hypotheses

Mergers can be somewhat difficult to rationalize in terms of financial theory. According to financial theory, the value of any asset is equal to the present value of its cash flows. Thus a publicly held firm can be considered as a bundle of cash flows expected to be received in the future. Investors are assumed to hold broadly diversified portfolios including value-weighted shares of all firms in the economy (the "market portfolio"). In this construct, M&As do not necessarily add value because they merely combine the rights to cash flows that are already held by diversified investors. Hence, investors should be indifferent between receiving future cash flow streams from two separate firms rather than from one merged firm formed by combining the two separate firms. To the extent that M&As are costly, investors may actually be worse off following an M&A transaction.

Of course, perfect markets finance theory rests on a number of assumptions that hold only as approximations in practice. Among these are the absence of transaction costs, agency costs, other types of friction costs, informational asymmetries between investors and managers, taxation, and regulation. The existence of these and other market imperfections can lead to situations where M&As have the potential to create value. In addition, economic production theory offers other explanations for firm combinations such as economies of scale and scope that can provide economic justifications for M&As that are not inconsistent with financial theory. However, it is important to keep in mind the fundamental insight of finance—that cash flows determine value—when considering the arguments regarding the economic rationale for M&As discussed below. In other words, for an

11. Cummins and Rubio-Misas (2004).

M&A transaction to create value, it must have a favorable impact on the amount, timing, or risk of the cash flow streams of the combined institution in comparison with those of the acquiring and target firms involved in the transaction.

In terms of economic production theory, firms operate with cost, revenue, and profit functions, all of which could be affected by mergers and acquisitions. One rationale often given for M&As is economies of scale, usually associated with the cost function. The usual argument is that firms operating at suboptimal scale may be able to achieve scale gains more quickly through M&As than through organic growth, and, in fact, scale economies are almost always given as a rationale for M&As in the insurance industry and most other industries, usually without any supporting empirical evidence. Although scale economies are potentially important, most prior research has failed to demonstrate that they provide a compelling rationale for financial sector mergers. For example, Cummins and Xie find that M&As in the U.S. property-liability insurance industry during the late 1990s failed to generate significant gains in scale economies, and Cummins and Santomero show that scale economies disappear at relatively small scale in the U.S. life insurance industry.[12] In addition, the pure production theory argument fails to recognize that friction costs arising from post-merger integration problems can more than offset any scale economy gains that may be realized. In many cases, organic growth may be superior to M&As as a method of achieving optimal scale, and other types of inefficiency, such as technical and allocative inefficiency, often are much more significant than scale inefficiency.

Economies of scope provide another production theory rationale for mergers and acquisitions. Scope economies can be present for costs, for revenues, and (on net) for profits.[13] If cost (revenue) economies of scope are present, the costs (revenues) of producing two outputs jointly in a single firm will be lower (higher) than if the outputs are produced by two separate firms. Cost economies of scope generally arise from the joint use of inputs such as managerial expertise, customer lists, computer technologies, and brand names; revenue economies of scope are often said to arise due to reductions in consumer search costs and improvements in service quality from the joint provision of related products such as life insurance and automobile insurance. This is the "one-stop shopping" argument often used to

12. Cummins and Santomero (1999); Cummins and Xie (2003).
13. Berger and others (2000).

justify financial sector mergers. There is some empirical evidence for the existence of economies of scope in insurance, although such economies seem to exist only for specific types of producers and specific subproducts within the insurance industry.[14] In addition, production theory arguments for scope economies generally do not recognize that achieving such economies through M&As can often be defeated by the frictions arising from integrating the corporate cultures of two previously separate firms offering different products, perhaps using different distribution systems and information technologies.

Potential gains in X-efficiency provide another production-based rationale for M&As. X-inefficiency arises when firms fail to operate on the cost, revenue, or profit frontier but rather incur higher costs or earn lower revenues because of various types of suboptimal performance. The principal types of inefficiency include technical inefficiency (failing to operate on the cost-minimizing isoquant), allocative inefficiency (failing to choose cost-minimizing combinations of inputs), and scale inefficiency (failing to operate with constant returns to scale). Similar efficiency concepts can be defined with respect to the revenue frontier. A potentially important justification for a merger or acquisition transaction is to improve the efficiency of the merger target, for example, by replacing inefficient managers or introducing superior technology possessed by the acquiring firm. There is some evidence that insurance M&A transactions have led to efficiency gains in the U.S. life insurance industry and the Spanish insurance industry.[15] The efficiency rationale for M&As may be somewhat stronger for focusing rather than diversifying M&As, however. If the objective is to improve technical or allocative efficiency of the target, it seems reasonable to expect that such improvements are more likely to be realized if the managers of the acquiring firm already have considerable expertise in the types of operations conducted by the target.

One important source of potential efficiency gains from mergers is the possibility of eliminating duplicate or overlapping production, delivery, or back-office systems. For example, the merger of banks operating in the same geographic area may permit a reduction in the number of branches and branch-office employees without a corresponding degradation of customer service. The same rationale may apply in insurance to the extent that the

14. Berger and others (2000).
15. Cummins, Tennyson, and Weiss (1999) and Cummins and Rubio-Misas (2004), respectively.

duplication of agencies, claims adjustment offices, and data-processing facilities can be reduced. This rationale would seem to apply most strongly to intra-country and intra-industry mergers, although diversifying mergers that permit the sale of insurance through bank branches have the potential to realize economies of scope.

Another industrial organization hypothesis about M&As is that consolidation allows firms to acquire varying degrees of monopoly power, permitting them to increase cash flows by raising prices. This rationale would seem to apply most strongly to mergers that increase concentration within specific geographic or product markets. Empirical evidence based on U.S. banking provides some support for the market power hypothesis, especially for large banks, but the quantitative effect on bank profits tends to be small.[16] Empirical evidence also has been presented that consolidation in the Spanish insurance market during the 1990s led to price reductions.[17]

Relaxing the assumptions of perfect markets finance theory provides some additional rationalizations for M&As. One important assumption is the absence of costs of financial distress. In real-world markets, especially in those such as financial services where stringent solvency regulation is the norm, firms face significant financial distress costs. Insurers that are excessively leveraged or in a weak financial condition for other reasons incur higher regulatory costs and potential operating restrictions. Moreover, because buyers of insurance are especially sensitive to insolvency risk, insurers in deteriorating financial health are likely to lose their best customers to rivals. Deteriorating financial condition is also likely to trigger financial ratings downgrades, with accompanying higher costs of capital. Finally, firms with relatively high insolvency risk also face the loss of relationships with key employees and suppliers. Because larger insurers are known to have lower probabilities of insolvency, mergers can be beneficial to the extent that increases in scale are accompanied by reductions in income volatility due to enhanced diversification.[18] This reasoning applies to within-industry mergers but also to cross-industry mergers between institutions such as insurers and banks, providing a possible rationale for both focusing and diversifying M&A activity. The potentially favorable effect of M&As

16. Berger (1995).
17. Cummins and Rubio-Misas (2004).
18. Cummins, Grace, and Phillips (1999) show that larger insurers have a lower probability of defaults.

on expected bankruptcy costs is generally called the *earnings diversification hypothesis*.[19]

The existence of corporate income taxation also provides a rationale for M&As as a possible mechanism for increasing net cash flows. Firms can reduce expected taxes by reducing earnings volatility to the extent that corporate tax schedules are convex or to the extent that they can exploit inter-country tax arbitrage or utilize tax loss carryovers. The extent to which opportunities to reduce taxes through consolidation exist in Europe is not clear.

Another rationale sometimes given for M&As based on relaxing the assumptions of perfect markets financial theory is the creation of *internal capital markets*. The argument is that informational asymmetries between managers and capital markets tend to make capital markets somewhat inefficient in allocating capital among alternative uses and also may lead to higher costs of capital. Managers are said to be able to use their superior knowledge of the firm's investment opportunities to allocate capital efficiently among projects, thereby maximizing firm value. However, the extensive literature on the diversification discount—that is, the tendency of diversified firms to have lower values than their subsidiaries taken independently—as well as theoretical research cast considerable doubt on the internal capital markets hypothesis.[20] This hypothesis may have a somewhat stronger justification in Europe than in the United States because European firms have traditionally relied relatively more on bank financing and less on capital market financing than firms in the United States, suggesting that capital markets may be somewhat less efficient in Europe. However, based on existing empirical and theoretical evidence, we do not find the internal capital markets hypothesis to be convincing.

There are also non-value-maximizing motives for consolidation. Contrary to perfect markets finance theory, considerable evidence exists that real-world managers do not always act in the best interests of shareholders but rather tend to pursue their own interests to varying degrees. Instead of taking actions to maximize firm value, managers may act to maximize their own net worth and income, to consume excessive perquisites, and to take

19. Simulation analyses have shown that there is significant potential for reducing earnings volatility through bank-insurance combinations (for example, Estrella 2001).

20. The existence of a diversification discount has been widely documented in the literature. See, for example, Berger and Ofek (1995); Comment and Jarrell (1995). Theoretical research on internal capital markets has been conducted by Scharfstein and Stein (2000).

other actions not consistent with value maximization. These agency conflicts may lead managers to forgo profitable but risky projects that may threaten their job security. Moreover, and of special relevance for M&As, managers may engage in projects of questionable value that increase the scale of the firm to inflate their compensation and prestige. Managers may also engage in defensive acquisitions designed to head off hostile takeovers that would threaten their jobs. To the extent that managers engage in non-value-maximizing acquisitions, M&As can be expected to have adverse effects on market value.

M&As also may reduce value to the extent that firms are not very successful in conducting post-merger integration. Postmerger integration is likely to be especially difficult for cross-country and cross-industry mergers due to larger national and corporate cultural differences that must be overcome.[21]

The net result of this analysis is that the theoretical prediction with regard to the impact of M&As on market values is ambiguous. A large number of factors come into play that could affect the success of any given M&A transaction, making generalized predictions very difficult. One general result that does seem to emerge from the discussion as well as from past empirical work, however, is that focusing mergers are somewhat more likely to create efficiency gains than diversifying mergers. Focusing can be defined either in terms of activities such as banking, life and non-life insurance, or securities operations as well as in terms of geography. Thus we predict that within-industry and within-country mergers are more likely to create value than activity or geographically diversifying mergers.

Sample Selection and Methodology

This study focuses on European mergers and acquisitions over the period 1990 through 2002. The beginning of the sample period was selected to provide a few years of observations prior to introduction of the European Union's Third-Generation Insurance Directives in 1994, because many European countries introduced deregulatory measures prior to the Third-Generation Insurance Directives to provide time for their domestic insurers to prepare for the overall European deregulation.

21. Evidence that difficulties in integrating data-processing systems are an impediment to efficiency gains in some financial sector mergers is provided in Rhoades (1998).

The data on M&A transactions were obtained from the Thomson Financial SDC database. To focus on insurance M&As, we identified all transactions in SDC in which a European insurance company was either the acquirer or the target. Insurance companies were defined as all firms with two-digit Standard Industrial Classification (SIC) code 63. Thus transactions were included in the sample where non-insurance firms, such as banks, other financial firms, and industrials, acquired insurers, where insurance firms acquired non-insurers, as well as where transactions occurred within the insurance industry. The study focuses primarily on transactions in member countries of the European Union in Western Europe, resulting in the exclusion of a small number of Eastern European transactions.

Following the procedure adopted by the Group of Ten, we captured data on all transactions in SDC involving the acquisition of a value-stake where the target or the acquirer was an insurance company.[22] This included a substantial number of transactions involving minority stakes. We decided that it was useful to include these transactions in order to parallel our results with those of the G-10 and because we thought it would be interesting to look at the entire portfolio of transactions. However, we also conducted the analysis using a subsample of transactions that represented a change in control, which we define as a transaction where the acquirer's stake changed from less than 50 percent to 50 percent or more of the target firm's shares after the merger. We consider the change-in-control transactions to be more important than the other transactions in gauging the impact of M&As on firm value.

The data on stock prices for the event study were obtained from the Datastream database. Using the SDC sample as the transactions database, we then identified all transactions where either the acquirer or the target firm also was present in Datastream and obtained Datastream stock price data for the periods needed to conduct the event study. The event dates used in the analysis were screened to eliminate cases where more than one transaction took place within a window extending from thirty days prior to the event to thirty days after the event.

Event-Study Methodology

We adopt a standard market model event-study methodology, where the returns of the underlying securities are assumed to be jointly multivariate

22. Group of Ten (2001).

normal and independently and identically distributed through time.[23] The analysis involves computing the returns for each of the transactions in our sample using data from the Datastream database. Using this approach, the expected return for any given insurer security can be defined as follows:

$$(1) \qquad R_{jt} = \alpha_j + \beta_j R_{mt} + \varepsilon_{jt},$$

where R_{jt} is the actual dividend-adjusted return on security j on day $t = [\log(\text{Price}_t + \text{Dividend}_t)/\text{Price}_{t-1}]$, R_{mt} is the rate of return on the Datastream General Market Index for the country of the target or acquiring firm, α_j is the idiosyncratic return on security j, β_j is the beta coefficient of security j, and ε_{jt} is the error term of the regression. Under the assumption of joint normality and independently and identically distributed returns, the error of the regression is well behaved, that is, $E(\varepsilon_{jt}) = 0$, $\text{Var}(\varepsilon_{jt}) = \sigma^2_{\varepsilon_j}$.

Using this model, we estimate the market parameters for each of our companies based on the returns to securities over the 250 days ending thirty days prior to the date of the event. Using the parameters estimated from this market model and the movement of the market index during the event period, we then compute the daily unexpected or abnormal return (AR) for each security during the event period. We use several event windows for the study, extending a maximum of fifteen days before and after the event date. The notation for an event window extending m days prior to the event date and p days following the event date is $(-m,+p)$, with the event date as day 0.

The abnormal return on day t in the event window for security j can be expressed as the estimated disturbance term of the market model calculated out-of-sample:

$$(2) \qquad AR_{jt} = R_{jt} - \hat{\alpha}_j - \hat{\beta}_j R_{mt}.$$

The distribution of the abnormal return, conditional on the market return, is jointly normal, with a zero conditional mean and a conditional variance equal to the following:

$$(3) \qquad \sigma^2(AR_{jt}) = \hat{\sigma}^2_{\varepsilon_j} + \frac{1}{L_1}\left[1 + \frac{(R_{mt} - \bar{R}_m)^2}{\hat{\sigma}^2_m}\right],$$

where $\hat{\sigma}^2_{\varepsilon_j}$ represents the sum of the squared residuals (that is, abnormal returns) from the market model estimation divided by $(L_1 - 2)$, and L_1 represents the number of non-missing daily periods over which the market

23. For further discussion of the methodology, see MacKinlay (1997).

model is estimated for firm j. Note that in equation 3 the variance in daily abnormal returns has two components—a disturbance term estimated from the market model residuals and a sampling-error term. Thus, provided that the number of days in the estimation period is sufficiently large (for example, greater than thirty), the variance in abnormal returns converges to $\sigma^2_{\varepsilon_j}$, and $AR_{jt} \sim N(0, \sigma^2_{\varepsilon_j})$.

Because the conditional abnormal returns for all N securities are assumed to be independent and normally distributed, we can aggregate the abnormal returns across securities within any given time period. The average abnormal return and the variance in average abnormal returns across all N securities in a given time period are computed as follows:

$$(4) \qquad \overline{AR}_t = \frac{1}{N} \sum_{j=1}^{N} AR_{jt}, \text{ and}$$

$$(5) \qquad \hat{\sigma}^2(\overline{AR}_t) = \frac{1}{N^2} \sum_{j=1}^{N} \hat{\sigma}^2_{\varepsilon_j}.$$

As expected, the average abnormal return within a given period is also normally distributed, with a zero conditional mean and a conditional variance given by equation 5. Thus, under the null hypothesis of no market impact, we can draw inferences about the impact on the average abnormal returns across the securities in the portfolio by using a standard Z score statistic, computed as the ratio of the average abnormal return divided by the standard deviation of average abnormal returns.

We compute the cumulative average abnormal returns (CAAR) for the N securities across two time periods (τ_1 and τ_2), as well as the variance in the CAAR, as follows.

$$(6) \qquad \overline{CAR}(\tau_1, \tau_2) = \frac{1}{N} \sum_{j=1}^{N} \overline{AR}(\tau_1, \tau_2), \text{ and}$$

$$(7) \qquad Var[\overline{CAR}(\tau_1, \tau_2)] = \frac{1}{N^2} \sum_{j=1}^{N} \hat{\sigma}^2_j(\tau_1, \tau_2).$$

We make several additional adjustments in measuring abnormal returns. First, following Patel, we standardize the abnormal return for each security by dividing by the security's own estimate of variance.[24] This standardiza-

24. See Patel (1976).

tion process helps to ensure that no single firm in the sample dominates the results of the analysis and helps to improve the power of the test statistics. For any given security, we can compute the standardized abnormal return (SAR) within a given period by dividing the abnormal return by our estimate of the security's sample return standard deviation from the market model regression:

$$(8) \qquad SAR_{jt} = \frac{AR_{jt}}{\hat{\sigma}_{\varepsilon_j}} \sim t_{L_1 - 2},$$

where $t_{L_1 - 2}$ represents the t distribution with $(L_1 - 2)$ degrees of freedom. To construct a test statistic of abnormal returns across the N firms in period t, we aggregate the standardized abnormal returns (SAR_{jt}) across all N securities to obtain the total standardized abnormal return ($TSAR_t$).

Many prior studies have documented substantial increases in event-induced variance around event-days.[25] Failure to adjust the event-induced variance will lead to too frequent rejection of the null hypothesis. Many studies show that substantial bias is introduced if event-induced variance is not corrected.[26] Accordingly, we adjust the estimated variance in returns by the contemporaneous cross-sectional variance of the sample by applying the *standardized cross-sectional* (SCS) procedure developed by Boehmer, Musumeci, and Poulsen.[27] We incorporate the Boehmer, Musumeci, and Poulsen variance adjustment by developing a new Z statistic as follows:

$$(9) \qquad Z_t = \frac{TSAR_t}{\sigma_{sar,t} \sqrt{N}},$$

where the adjusted variance is given as follows:

$$(10) \qquad \hat{\sigma}^2_{sar,t} = \frac{1}{N-1} \sum_{j=1}^{N} [SAR_{jt} - \frac{1}{n} SAR_{jt}]^2.$$

---

25. These studies include the examination of earnings announcements by Beaver (1968) and Christie (1982), the work on stock splits by Ohlson and Penman (1985) and Dravid (1987), an event-study analysis of takeover rumors by Pound and Zeckhauser (1990), and an event study by Cummins and Lewis (2003) on the impact of the terrorist attacks of September 11, 2001.

26. See, for example, Boehmer, Musumeci, and Poulsen (1991); Brown and Warner (1985).

27. Boehmer, Musumeci, and Poulsen (1991).

To construct a measure of the standardized cumulative abnormal returns across the portfolio, we start by defining the *standardized cumulative abnormal return* (*SCAR*) for any one security over the period (τ_1, τ_2) as its cumulative abnormal return divided by its corresponding asymptotic variance (for large L_1) as follows:

$$(11) \qquad SCAR(\tau_1, \tau_2) = \frac{CAR_j}{\sigma_j^2(\tau_1, \tau_2)} = \frac{\sum\limits_{t=\tau_1}^{\tau_2} AR_{jt}}{(\tau_2 - \tau_1 + 1)\sigma_{\varepsilon_j}^2}.$$

Finally, we average these standardized cumulative abnormal returns across all N securities and divide by an estimate of the standard deviation of standardized cumulative abnormal returns to obtain a test statistic for the standardized cumulative average abnormal returns for the portfolio. This modified Z statistic is presented in equation 12:

$$(12) \qquad Z_t = \frac{\sum\limits_{j=1}^{N} SCAR_j(\tau_1, \tau_2)}{\sigma_{scar}\sqrt{N}},$$

where

$$\hat{\sigma}_{scar}^2(\tau_1, \tau_2) = \frac{1}{N-1} \sum_{j=1}^{N} [SCAR(\tau_1, \tau_2) - \frac{1}{N} SCAR(\tau_1, \tau_2)]^2.$$

Using equation 12, we can construct tests of the significance of the M&A events on the stock returns of the acquiring target firms in our sample.

A nonparametric test is usually used in conjunction with the parametric test in event studies to verify that the results of parametric tests are not driven by outliers. In this study, we employ Cowan's generalized sign test.[28] It compares the proportion of positive abnormal returns around an event-day to the proportion from the estimation period. This test is also well specified when the variance of stock returns increases around the event-day.

Empirical Results

This section presents the empirical results of the study. We first provide descriptive statistics on the insurance M&As in our sample, based on the

28. See Cowan (1992).

Figure 1. Number of M&A Deals Involving an Insurance Acquirer or Target, by Year, 1990–2002

Number of deals

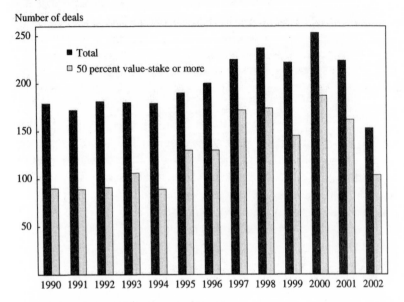

Source: Authors' calculations based on the Thomson SDC database.

Thomson SDC database. We then discuss the selection of the event-study sample of firms by matching the Thomson SDC M&A transactions with the Datastream database as well as the characteristics of the resulting Datastream sample. Finally, we present and analyze the event-study results.

Insurance M&As: Descriptive Statistics

The number of M&A events in our sample, where either the target or the acquirer was a European insurer, is shown in figure 1. There were 2,595 total events involving the acquisition of a value-stake, 1,669 of which resulted in a change in control. The total number of both types of events peaked in 2000, perhaps due to introduction of the euro. Figure 2 shows the value of the total number of deals and the change-in-control deals by year. In interpreting this figure, it is important to keep in mind that SDC does not report the value for the majority of deals. Hence, the number shown in figure 2 is actually interpreted as the total deal value reported by SDC rather than the total value of all deals shown in figure 1. The total value of deals reported

Figure 2. Value of M&A Deals Involving an Insurance Acquirer or Target, by Year, 1990–2002

Millions of U.S. dollars

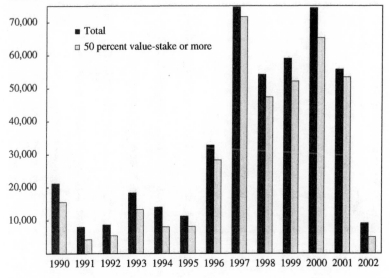

Source: Authors' calculations based on the Thomson SDC database.

by SDC for our sample period was $441 billion, and the total involving a change in control was $378 billion. The value of deals was substantially larger in the 1996–2001 period than in other years. However, this may be attributable partly to more complete reporting of deal values in the more recent years of the sample period. Notwithstanding the data limitations regarding deal value, it is clear that a large number of M&A transactions took place during the sample period, which involved substantial amounts of market capitalization. This suggests that the previous regulatory regime in Europe constituted a binding constraint on the structure of the insurance industry.

Figures 3 and 4 show the number of deals and the value of deals for cases where the target of the transaction was an insurance company. There were 1,440 total transactions with insurance company targets, of which 954 resulted in a change in control. As with the overall sample, the number of deals for the sample of insurance targets peaked in 2000, although there were nearly as many change-in-control deals in 1997. The total reported value of transactions involving insurance targets was $295 billion, and the

Figure 3. Number of M&A Deals Involving an Insurance Target, by Year, 1990–2002

Number of deals

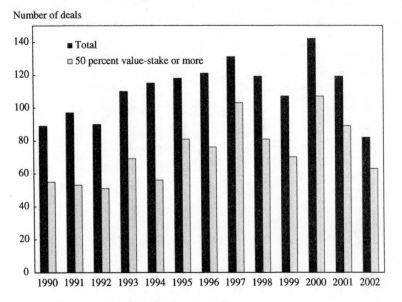

Source: Authors' calculations based on the Thomson SDC database.

total for change-in-control transactions was $252 billion. Comparing figures 1 and 2 with figures 3 and 4 clearly suggests a substantial amount of both cross-industry as well as within-industry transactions involving insurers.

The number of M&A deals by country of the target firm is shown in figure 5. By far the largest number of transactions involved targets in the United Kingdom, where nearly 600 change-in-control transactions occurred. The next largest number of transactions was for targets in France (145 change-in-control deals), Germany (126 deals), Spain (114 deals), and Italy (111 deals). The SDC's reported deal values, included in figure 6, also show that the United Kingdom was the leader in insurance M&A transactions, with a change-in-control deal value of $141 billion. The United Kingdom was followed by Germany ($44 billion), France ($41 billion), and the Netherlands ($40 billion). The transactions value was relatively lower than the number of transactions in Spain and Italy because those countries had unusually large numbers of very small insurers prior to deregulation.

Further information on the number of transactions by country is presented in table 1, which shows the number and value of deals by the country

Figure 4.Value of M&A Deals Involving an Insurance Target, by Year, 1990–2002

Millions of U.S. dollars

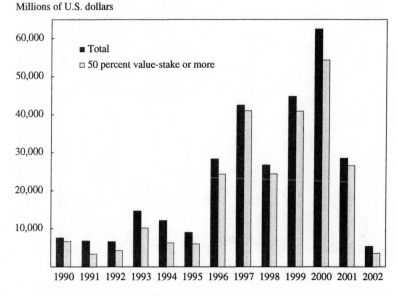

Source: Authors' calculations based on the Thomson SDC database.

of the target and of the acquirer. The table shows only those deals resulting in a change in control. About 65 percent of the transactions were intra-country deals (1,078 out of 1,669). The lowest proportions of intra-country deals were in Belgium (51 percent), Spain (55 percent), and Portugal (55 percent); the highest proportions were in Finland (89 percent), Denmark (83 percent), Norway (79 percent), Germany (79 percent), and the United Kingdom (78 percent). Table 1 also shows that about 60 percent of reported deal value was for intra-country transactions. The lowest intra-country deal volume as a proportion of the total deal volume was in Spain (25 percent) and the Netherlands (49 percent), and the highest was in Denmark (97 percent) and Norway (93 percent).

Table 2 shows the number of deals and the value of deals involving a change in control tabulated by the industry of the target and acquiring firms. In interpreting this table, one should keep in mind that either the target or the acquirer had to be an insurance company in order for the transaction to be included in the sample. Thus cells involving deals between non-insurance firms and other non-insurance firms are blank rather than equaling zero. By

Figure 5. Number of M&A Deals Involving an Insurance Target or Acquirer, by Country of the Target Firm

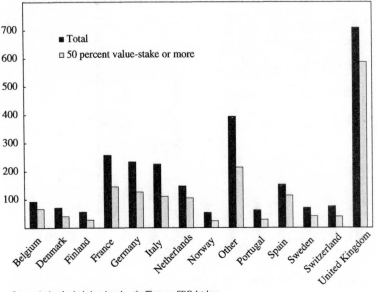

Source: Authors' calculations based on the Thomson SDC database.

far the largest number of deals and the highest deal volume were for life insurance companies acquiring other life insurance companies. Life insurer–to–life insurer deals accounted for 33 percent of all transactions and 46 percent of deal volume. Overall, transactions involving life insurance targets accounted for 57 percent of all deals and 67 percent of reported deal volume.

The dominance of life insurance transactions in the sample deserves some comment. The primary reason for the importance of life insurance transactions is that the life insurance market has evolved very differently in comparison with the non-life insurance market. The non-life market, which is dominated by lines of insurance such as private passenger automobile, homeowners, and commercial property-liability insurance, remains primarily a traditional insurance market where relatively little innovation has occurred in terms of underwriting, claims settlement, administration, and product offerings. Although life insurance once was a sheltered market insulated from competition with other types of financial firms, life insurance

Figure 6. Value of M&A Deals Involving an Insurance Target or Acquirer, by Country of the Target Firm

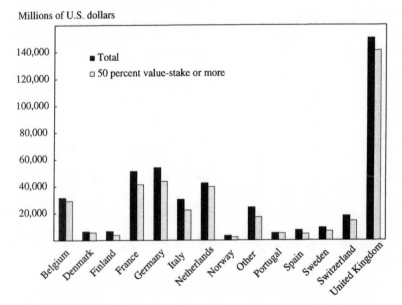

Millions of U.S. dollars

Source: Authors' calculations based on the Thomson SDC database.

has become very much a part of the financial services market. Life insurers increasingly compete with banks, mutual fund companies, and investment advisory firms for the asset-accumulation products in the consumer market and the money management business in the corporate market. Life insurance product offerings have also changed dramatically in recent decades to include "universal" and variable life insurance and annuity contracts where buyers are able to allocate funds among types of investments, much as they do when investing in a family of mutual funds. The increased competition from nontraditional competitors and the introduction of new products has also placed pressure on insurers to cut costs, while at the same time investing in sophisticated technologies to provide competitive services to customers. Because development of new technologies has high fixed costs, the evolution of the market has placed a premium on firm size, such that the relatively small firms that once populated the market are unlikely to remain competitive. Such developments help to explain the dominance of life insurance transactions in our sample.

Table 1. Number and Value of M&A Deals Involving an Insurance Acquirer or Target and a Change in Control, by Country

Indicator and target country	Belgium	Denmark	Finland	France	Germany	Italy	Netherlands	Norway	Other	Portugal	Spain	Sweden	Switzerland	United Kingdom	Total
Number of deals															
Belgium	34	0	0	8	1	0	11	0	4	0	1	3	4	1	67
Denmark	0	33	0	0	3	0	2	0	0	0	0	1	0	1	40
Finland	0	0	25	0	0	0	0	0	1	0	0	1	0	1	28
France	3	0	0	104	8	5	2	0	11	0	0	0	3	9	145
Germany	1	0	0	3	99	2	4	0	6	0	0	0	7	4	126
Italy	0	0	0	0	5	78	3	0	8	1	0	1	7	8	111
Netherlands	10	3	0	5	3	0	76	0	3	1	0	0	3	1	105
Norway	0	1	0	0	0	0	0	19	2	0	0	0	1	1	24
Other	6	6	6	19	36	6	23	1	21	0	15	2	17	56	214
Portugal	0	0	0	4	0	0	0	0	5	16	1	1	1	1	29
Spain	1	0	0	10	3	4	5	0	7	1	63	2	7	11	114
Sweden	0	3	1	0	2	0	1	0	2	0	0	29	2	1	41
Switzerland	0	0	0	1	4	6	0	0	4	0	0	0	23	1	39
United Kingdom	0	1	0	5	3	0	9	1	97	0	0	3	9	458	586
Total	55	47	32	159	167	101	136	21	171	19	80	43	84	554	1,669
Value of deals (millions of U.S. dollars)															
Belgium	15,438	0	0	3,691	0	0	9,748	0	74	0	0	40	175	8	29,175
Denmark	0	5,560	0	0	35	0	117	0	0	0	0	0	0	0	5,712
Finland	0	0	2,847	0	0	0	0	0	0	0	0	793	0	0	3,640
France	125	0	0	26,968	5,536	1,123	0	0	4,212	0	0	0	1,284	2,140	41,389
Germany	0	0	0	0	33,792	5,483	2,338	0	718	0	0	0	1,158	407	43,895
Italy	0	0	0	0	1,201	17,364	30	0	3,157	26	0	0	397	112	22,331
Netherlands	14,810	20	0	4,613	0	0	19,636	0	486	0	0	0	284	0	39,849
Norway	0	0	0	0	0	0	0	2,208	88	0	0	0	85	0	2,381
Other	68	80	212	5,800	893	69	5,572	0	0	3,132	488	0	415	3,443	17,040
Portugal	0	0	0	1	0	0	0	0	431	0	1,556	3	0	0	5,123
Spain	34	0	0	695	133	1	787	0	276	0	1,158	81	462	1,042	4,671
Sweden	0	1,242	0	0	137	0	262	0	560	0	0	5,064	3	0	6,708
Switzerland	0	0	0	236	108	2,517	1,189	0	11,943	0	0	0	11,072	0	14,385
United Kingdom	0	0	0	3,277	0	0	1,189	4	11,943	0	0	869	40,355	83,463	141,208
Total	30,476	6,902	3,059	45,281	41,836	26,557	39,681	2,212	21,945	3,158	3,202	6,895	55,690	90,615	377,508

Source: Authors' calculations based on the Thomson Financial SDC database.

Table 2. Number and Value of M&A Deals Involving an Insurance Acquirer or Target and a Change in Control, by Industry[a]

Target industry	Acquirer industry								
	Commercial bank	Other financial	Life insurance	Property-liability insurance	Other insurance	Insurance agency	Other industries	Unknown	Total
Number of deals									
Commercial bank	...	...	65	1	...	...	...	...	66
Other financial	...	...	68	10	...	...	...	...	78
Life insurance	73	87	550	33	29	92	83	7	954
Property-liability insurance	2	8	28	12	3	17	10	...	80
Other insurance	...	...	83	6	...	1	...	...	90
Insurance agency	...	...	116	18	...	...	...	...	134
Other industries	...	...	253	13	...	...	...	...	266
Unknown	...	...	1	...	...	...	...	...	1
Total	75	95	1,164	93	32	110	93	7	1,669
Value of deals (millions of U.S. dollars)									
Commercial bank	...	...	59,594	...	...	...	...	...	59,594
Other financial	...	...	4,418	251	...	...	...	...	4,669
Life insurance	39,375	23,403	174,450	4,059	2,632	1,936	5,822	1	251,678
Property-liability insurance	867	489	2,169	481	187	141	156	...	4,490
Other insurance	...	...	4,850	1,035	...	...	...	...	5,885
Insurance agency	...	...	22,617	1,050	...	...	...	...	23,667
Other industries	...	...	25,459	2,065	...	...	...	...	27,524
Unknown	...	...	...	...	...	...	...	...	0
Total	40,242	23,892	293,557	8,941	2,819	2,077	5,978	1	377,507

Source: Authors' calculations based on the Thomson Financial SDC database.

a. Industries are categorized according to North American Industrial Classification System (NAICS) codes. Commercial bank = 522110; other financial = investment banking and securities dealers (523110) + portfolio management (523920) + miscellaneous financial investment (523999) + open-end investment funds (525910); life insurance = life direct (524113); property-liability insurance = property and casualty direct (524126); other insurance = other direct insurance (524128) + other insurance funds (525190); other industries = any categories not included elsewhere. Cells involving deals between non-insurance firms and other non-insurance firms are blank rather than equaling zero.

Figure 7. Number of M&A Deals Involving an Insurance Acquirer Included in the Event Study, by Year, 1990–2002

Number of deals

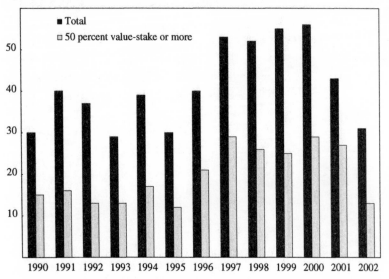

Source: Authors' calculations based on the Thomson SDC database and the Datastream database.

Some firms from other industries were also active in acquiring insurers during our sample period. There were seventy-five transactions where commercial banks and ninety-five where other financial firms, such as investment advisers, acquired insurance companies. There were also 133 transactions where life insurers purchased other financial services firms, including sixty-five commercial banks. Life insurers were also active in purchasing 253 firms in other industries, including financial firms not classified elsewhere (for example, real estate investment trusts) and nonfinancial firms. However, the overall picture that emerges from table 2 is that the majority of transactions were conducted within the insurance industry. Transactions within the insurance industry accounted for 59 percent of deals and 57 percent of deal volume.[29]

29. Deals within the insurance industry are defined as including deals where both the acquirer and the target were in one of the following categories (see table 2): life insurance company, property-liability insurance company, other insurance company, or insurance agency. For example, a life insurance company acquiring an insurance agency is considered a transaction within the insurance industry.

Figure 8. Number of M&A Deals Involving an Insurance Target Included in the Event Study, by Year, 1990–2002

Number of deals

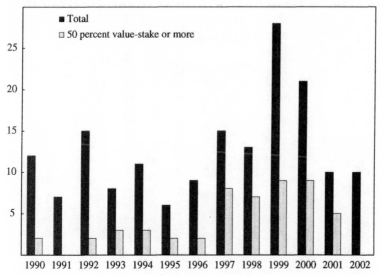

Source: Authors' calculations based on the Thomson SDC database and the Datastream database.

The Datastream (Event-Study) Sample

The next step in the study was to identify transactions included in the SDC database for which adequate stock price data were available to conduct the event study. This was a difficult process, which involved looking up transactions reported by SDC in the Datastream database by name and identification number, such as that of the Committee on Uniform Securities Identification Procedures (CUSIP). It turned out that only a small fraction of the total transactions reported by SDC could be included in the event study. The primary reason is that many of the firms involved in the transactions, especially as target firms, apparently were not publicly traded prior to the transaction. Such firms could be mutuals or closely held companies. However, a substantial proportion of the nontraded targets were subsidiaries of insurance groups. Large insurance groups such as Allianz, AXA, and ING tend to have numerous subsidiaries, and less prominent insurance groups and other financial holding companies also tend to have significant numbers of subsidiaries. Since such subsidiaries are not listed on exchanges,

Figure 9. Value of M&A Deals Involving an Insurance Acquirer Included in the Datastream Sample, by Year, 1990–2002

Millions of U.S. dollars

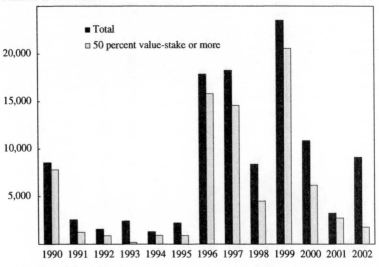

Source: Authors' calculations based on the Thomson SDC database and the Datastream database.

the data on stock prices needed to do the event analysis for these firms were not available. Because the acquirers tended to be parent corporations rather than subsidiaries, a larger number of acquirers survived the SDC-Datastream transaction search than the targets.

The number of M&A acquirer transactions for which stock price data were available is shown in figure 7. There were 535 acquirer transactions for which Datastream data could be located; of this group, 256 were transactions that involved a change in control. The number of targets for which Datastream data could be located is shown in figure 8. The total number of target transactions was 165, but the number resulting in a change in control equaled only fifty-two. This is smaller than would be desirable, but this sample size is comparable with other M&A event studies; for example, Cybo-Ottone and Murgia analyze a total of fifty-four matched target-acquirer deals, and Akhigbe and Madura analyze sixty-one acquirers and twenty-two targets.[30]

The deal values for the M&A transactions included in the Datastream sample are shown in figures 9 and 10. These are deal values as reported by

30. See Cybo-Ottone and Murgia (2000) and Akhigbe and Madura (2001), respectively.

Figure 10. Value of M&A Deals Involving an Insurance Target Included in the Datastream Sample, by Year, 1990–2002

Millions of U.S. dollars

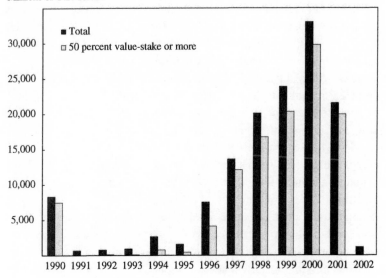

Source: Authors' calculations based on the Thomson SDC database and the Datastream database.

SDC rather than market capitalization prior to the transaction date. Figure 9 shows the deal value for the targets of the transactions for which acquiring firms are included in Datastream. The total deal value was $110 billion, and the deal value for transactions resulting in a change in control was $78 billion. Figure 10 shows the comparable data for the targets in the Datastream sample. Here the total deal value was $135 billion, and the deal value for change-in-control transactions was $112 billion. Hence, even though the number of transactions was fairly small, the value of the deals included in the event-study sample was considerable. The deal value in the target sample was larger than the value in the acquirer sample because publicly traded targets tend to be larger than nontraded targets.

Event-Study Results

The event-study results for all transactions in the Datastream sample are shown in table 3. The table includes results for transactions that did not result in a change in control as well as those that did.[31] The acquirer transactions analyzed in this study tended to have a negative effect on market value for the acquiring firms. The negative effect is small on average (less than 1 percent) but is statistically significant at either the 5 or the 10 percent level for the (-2,+2), (0,+1), and (0,+2) windows, based on both the Patel and SCS Z statistics. The finding of a negative reaction for acquirer stocks is not unusual in the event-study M&A literature.

In contrast to the acquirers, the target transactions summarized in table 3 created significant value. The CAARs are statistically significant at the 1 percent level or better for all windows studied. Based on the (-1,+1) window, stocks of acquisition targets gained 3.88 percent on average; based on the (-15,+15) window, the average market value gain is 8.85 percent. Again, the findings are generally consistent with the prior M&A event-study literature—that is, acquirers tend to lose value and targets tend to gain value in an acquisition.

The target transactions in table 3 are subdivided into cross-border and domestic (within-country) transactions in table 4. The value gains were larger for domestic transactions generally than for cross-border transactions, consistent with the view that focusing mergers are more likely to be beneficial than diversifying mergers. For example, the average abnormal return in the (-1,+1) window for cross-border transactions is 2.97 percent, while the average abnormal return for the domestic transactions in this window is 4.35 percent. However, *t* tests reveal that the differences between the cross-border and domestic average abnormal returns are not statistically significant for any of the windows included in the table, except at the 10 percent level in the (0,+10) window. Hence any conclusions about the superiority of within-country transactions based on these results must be considered tentative.

The acquirer transactions in table 3 are broken into cross-border and domestic transactions in table 5. On the one hand, the domestic transactions generally show negative average abnormal returns, which are statistically significant in several of the event windows. The cross-border transactions, on the other hand, have average abnormal returns that are generally closer to zero than the domestic transactions and are statistically significant in

31. The number of transactions included in the table is less than the total number of cases located in Datastream because the number of observations was too small in some instances to permit estimation of the market model.

Table 3. Cumulative Average Abnormal Returns across Event Windows, All Transactions for All Years, 1990–2002

Market model, equally weighted index

Type of firm and event window (days)	Number	Mean CAAR (percent)[a]	Precision-weighted CAAR (percent)[a]	Positive: negative	Patel Z	SCS Z[b]	Generalized sign Z[c]
Acquirers							
(-1,+1)	499	-0.14	-0.05	226:263	-0.662	-0.545	-0.568
(-2,+2)	499	-0.35	-0.20	222:267	-1.775*	-1.465$	-0.927
(-5,+5)	499	-0.35	-0.13	228:261	-0.973	-0.897	-0.388
(-10,+10)	499	-0.29	-0.06	231:258	-0.632	-0.587	-0.119
(-15,+15)	499	-0.38	-0.19	229:260	-1.279	-1.074	-0.299
(-1,0)	499	0.02	0.12	242:247	1.268	0.989	0.868
(-2,0)	499	-0.05	0.06	236:253	0.374	0.296	0.33
(-5,0)	499	-0.06	0.05	242:247	0.016	0.015	0.868
(-10,0)	499	-0.05	0.08	245:244	0	0	1.137
(-15,0)	499	-0.18	-0.09	233:256	-1.459$	-1.08	0.061
(0,+1)	499	-0.17	-0.13	219:270	-1.653*	-1.395$	-1.196
(0,+2)	499	-0.31	-0.22	220:269	-2.314*	-2.050*	-1.106
(0,+5)	499	-0.30	-0.13	234:255	-1.086	-1.022	0.15
(0,+10)	499	-0.25	-0.09	241:248	-0.66	-0.614	0.779
(0,+15)	499	-0.20	-0.05	232:257	-0.379	-0.318	-0.029
Targets							
(-1,+1)	164	3.88	3.75	94:70	18.348***	4.149***	2.658**
(-2,+2)	164	4.09	3.88	92:72	14.573***	4.070***	2.345**
(-5,+5)	164	4.58	4.05	90:74	10.148***	3.700***	2.032*
(-10,+10)	164	6.87	5.95	97:67	10.343***	4.465***	3.128***
(-15,+15)	164	8.85	7.37	96:68	10.128***	4.771***	2.971**
(-1,0)	164	3.60	3.53	92:72	21.213***	4.053***	2.345**
(-2,0)	164	3.97	3.82	93:71	18.580***	4.307***	2.502**
(-5,0)	164	4.78	4.28	90:74	14.541***	4.362***	2.032*
(-10,0)	164	6.31	5.40	90:74	13.149***	4.994***	2.032*
(-15,0)	164	7.58	6.43	91:73	12.725***	5.380***	2.189*
(0,+1)	164	2.96	3.24	92:71	18.032***	3.775***	2.345**
(0,+2)	164	2.80	3.08	88:75	13.928***	3.439***	1.719*
(0,+5)	164	2.48	2.79	79:84	8.903***	2.905**	0.311
(0,+10)	164	3.24	3.57	86:77	8.417***	3.119***	1.406$
(0,+15)	164	3.94	3.96	86:77	7.518***	3.085**	1.406$

Source: Results reported for all transactions reported in the Thomson Financial SDC database for which corresponding Datastream stock returns data exist, regardless of the percentage of the target firm acquired in any given transaction. Results are for the entire sample period, 1990–2002.

*** Significant at 0.1 percent level.

** Significant at 1 percent level.

* Significant at 5 percent level.

$ Significant at 10 percent level.

a. CAAR = cumulative average abnormal return.

b. SCS Z = standardized cross-sectional Z score.

c. Generalized sign Z = non-parametric test statistic.

Table 4. Cumulative Average Abnormal Returns across Event Windows, All Target Cross-Border and Domestic Transactions for All Years, 1990–2002
Market model, equally weighted index

Type of transaction and event window (days)	Number	Mean CAAR (percent)[a]	Precision-weighted CAAR (percent)[a]	Positive: negative	Patel Z	SCS Z[b]	Generalized sign Z[c]	t test[d]
Cross-border transactions								
(-1,+1)	56	2.97	2.16	30:26	5.398***	2.000*	0.916	
(-2,+2)	56	2.86	2.13	28:28	4.120***	1.946*	0.381	
(-5,+5)	56	3.95	2.46	29:27	3.167***	1.844*	0.649	
(-10,+10)	56	4.56	3.50	33:23	3.184***	2.151*	1.719*	
(-15,+15)	56	7.33	5.26	34:22	3.861***	2.455**	1.987*	
(-1,0)	56	2.08	1.68	33:23	5.142***	1.639$	1.719*	
(-2,0)	56	2.47	2.00	35:21	4.991***	1.927*	2.254*	
(-5,0)	56	3.79	2.84	33:23	4.980***	2.486**	1.719*	
(-10,0)	56	5.07	4.34	34:22	5.575***	3.089***	1.987*	
(-15,0)	56	5.80	4.79	34:22	5.041***	3.283***	1.987*	
(0,+1)	56	2.34	1.77	28:28	5.444***	1.761*	0.381	
(0,+2)	56	1.84	1.42	27:29	3.561***	1.402$	0.114	
(0,+5)	56	1.62	0.91	23:33	1.615$	0.797	-0.957	
(0,+10)	56	0.94	0.44	23:33	0.564	0.342	-0.957	$
(0,+15)	56	2.99	1.76	22:34	1.855*	0.951	-1.225	
Domestic transactions								
(-1,+1)	108	4.35	4.50	64:44	18.722***	3.697***	2.616**	
(-2,+2)	108	4.72	4.71	64:44	14.991***	3.641***	2.616**	
(-5,+5)	108	4.91	4.80	61:47	10.225***	3.260***	2.037*	
(-10,+10)	108	8.07	7.12	64:44	10.453***	3.970***	2.616**	
(-15,+15)	108	9.63	8.38	62:46	9.701***	4.124***	2.230*	
(-1,0)	108	4.38	4.40	59:49	22.438***	3.744***	1.651*	
(-2,0)	108	4.74	4.68	58:50	19.302***	3.907***	1.459$	
(-5,0)	108	5.30	4.96	57:51	14.333***	3.740***	1.266	
(-10,0)	108	6.96	5.90	56:52	12.189***	4.103***	1.073	
(-15,0)	108	8.51	7.21	57:51	12.051***	4.482***	1.266	
(0,+1)	108	3.29	3.94	64:43	18.300***	3.370***	2.616**	
(0,+2)	108	3.30	3.87	61:46	14.599***	3.157***	2.037*	
(0,+5)	108	2.93	3.68	56:51	9.808***	2.830**	1.073	
(0,+10)	108	4.43	5.06	63:44	9.966***	3.247***	2.423**	
(0,+15)	108	4.44	5.01	64:43	7.928***	2.997**	2.616**	

Source: Reports results for all transactions reported in the Thomson Financial SDC database for which corresponding Datastream stock returns data exist, regardless of the percentage of the target firm acquired in any given transaction. Results are for the entire sample period, 1990–2002.
***Significant at 0.1 percent level.
**Significant at 1 percent level.
* Significant at 5 percent level.
$ Significant at 10 percent level.
a. CAAR = cumulative average abnormal return.
b. SCS Z = standardized cross-sectional Z score.
c. Generalized sign Z = non-parametric test statistic.
d. The t test is for the difference between domestic and cross-border mean CAARs.

Table 5. Cumulative Average Abnormal Returns across Event Windows, All Acquirer Cross-Border and Domestic Transactions for All Years, 1990–2002
Market model, equally weighted index

Type of transaction and event window (days)	Number	Mean CAAR (percent)[a]	Precision-weighted CAAR (percent)[a]	Positive: negative	Patel Z	SCS Z[b]	Generalized sign Z[c]	t test[d]
Cross-border transactions								
(-1,+1)	291	0.07	0.10	140:143	0.681	0.589	0.432	$
(-2,+2)	291	-0.13	-0.07	135:148	-0.526	-0.466	-0.156	
(-5,+5)	291	-0.19	0.01	139:144	-0.133	-0.128	0.314	
(-10,+10)	291	-0.16	-0.03	139:144	-0.238	-0.238	0.314	
(-15,+15)	291	-0.27	-0.21	137:146	-0.623	-0.59	0.079	
(-1,0)	291	0.18	0.22	150:133	1.996*	1.618$	1.606$	
(-2,0)	291	0.06	0.09	140:143	0.561	0.477	0.432	
(-5,0)	291	0.15	0.18	143:140	0.74	0.726	0.784	
(-10,0)	291	0.04	0.03	148:135	-0.134	-0.127	1.371$	
(-15,0)	291	-0.09	-0.16	139:144	-0.732	-0.71	0.314	
(0,+1)	291	-0.01	0.01	135:148	0.004	0.004	-0.156	$
(0,+2)	291	-0.08	-0.03	131:152	-0.288	-0.283	-0.626	$
(0,+5)	291	-0.24	-0.04	141:142	-0.25	-0.24	0.549	
(0,+10)	291	-0.10	0.07	149:134	0.304	0.297	1.489$	
(0,+15)	291	-0.07	0.07	142:141	0.248	0.22	0.667	
Domestic transactions								
(-1,+1)	208	-0.44	-0.27	86:120	-1.830*	-1.421$	-1.391$	
(-2,+2)	208	-0.66	-0.40	87:119	-2.128*	-1.613$	-1.252	
(-5,+5)	208	-0.57	-0.32	89:117	-1.349$	-1.179	-0.974	
(-10,+10)	208	-0.46	-0.10	92:114	-0.698	-0.592	-0.557	
(-15,+15)	208	-0.52	-0.16	92:114	-1.244	-0.915	-0.557	
(-1,0)	208	-0.21	-0.03	92:114	-0.397	-0.295	-0.557	
(-2,0)	208	-0.20	0.01	96:110	-0.085	-0.062	-0.001	
(-5,0)	208	-0.35	-0.13	99:107	-0.851	-0.709	0.417	
(-10,0)	208	-0.17	0.15	97:109	0.158	0.126	0.139	
(-15,0)	208	-0.30	0.00	94:112	-1.393$	-0.819	-0.279	
(0,+1)	208	-0.40	-0.32	84:122	-2.564**	-1.926*	-1.670*	
(0,+2)	208	-0.63	-0.49	89:117	-3.243***	-2.571**	-0.974	
(0,+5)	208	-0.38	-0.27	93:113	-1.387$	-1.273	-0.418	
(0,+10)	208	-0.46	-0.33	92:114	-1.381$	-1.206	-0.557	
(0,+15)	208	-0.39	-0.24	90:116	-0.88	-0.69	-0.835	

Source: Reports results for all transactions reported in the Thomson Financial SDC database for which corresponding Datastream stock returns data exist, regardless of the percentage of the target firm acquired in any given transaction. Results are for the entire sample period, 1990–2002.
***Significant at 0.1 percent level.
**Significant at 1 percent level.
*Significant at 5 percent level.
$ Significant at 10 percent level.
a. CAAR = cumulative average abnormal return.
b. SCS Z = standardized cross-sectional Z score.
c. Generalized sign Z = non-parametric test statistic.
d. The *t* test is for the difference between domestic and cross-border mean CAARs.

only a few windows. The cross-border returns are statistically significant and positive in one window (-1,0). For three of the windows, (-1,+1), (0,+1), and (0,+2), *t* tests reveal that the average abnormal returns for the domestic transactions are statistically smaller than for the cross-border transactions. Hence there is some evidence based on the acquirer transactions that geographically diversifying transactions are value-neutral, whereas geographically focusing transactions are value destroying.

Table 6 presents the event-study results for all target and acquirer transactions that resulted in a change in control. The average abnormal returns for the acquirers tend to be small negative numbers, which are statistically significant in several of the windows. For example, the return in the (-2,+2) window is -0.80 percent, statistically significant at the 1 percent level. Targets show substantial value gains, ranging from 7.5 to 16.6 percent, depending on the window, and the results for all windows are statistically significant at the 0.1 percent level based on both the Patel and SCS *Z* tests. Thus, for transactions involving a change in control, there is a small negative effect on acquirers and a substantial positive impact on the value of targets.

The target transactions in table 6 are subdivided into cross-border and domestic transactions in table 7. The value gains for domestic transactions tend to be larger than those for cross-border transactions, and these differences are statistically significant for the (-1,+1), (-2,0), (0,+5), (0,+10), and (0,+15) windows. For example, for the (-1,+1) window, the average abnormal return for cross-border transactions is 5.35 percent compared to 11.88 percent for domestic transactions. Thus, at least with respect to targets, geographically focusing mergers tend to create more value than geographically diversifying mergers. This could be due to the creation of market power, or it could reflect the market's assessment of the friction costs of cross-border operations, due to differences in language, culture, and legal systems.

The average abnormal returns for acquirers are broken into cross-border and domestic transactions in table 8. The results based on transactions involving a change in control are consistent with those based on all transactions; in fact, the conclusions to be drawn from table 8 are stronger than the tentative conclusions based on table 5. The average abnormal returns for domestic transactions are significant and negative in nearly all windows, whereas the average CAARs for the cross-border transactions are mostly positive but statistically insignificant. *t* tests reveal that the differences between the cross-border and domestic CAARs are highly significant for

Table 6. Cumulative Average Abnormal Returns across Event Windows, All Transactions Resulting in a Change in Control for All Years, 1990–2002
Market model, equally weighted index

Type of transaction and event window (days)	Number	Mean CAAR (percent)[a]	Precision-weighted CAAR (percent)[a]	Positive: negative	Patel Z	SCS Z[b]	Generalized sign Z[c]	t test[d]
Acquirers								
(-1,+1)	236	-0.32	-0.21	103:128	-1.523$	-1.221	-0.711	***
(-2,+2)	236	-0.80	-0.58	92:139	-3.040**	-2.501**	-2.147*	***
(-5,+5)	236	-0.78	-0.49	101:130	-1.968*	-1.792*	-0.972	***
(-10,+10)	236	-0.79	-0.21	111:120	-0.917	-0.836	0.334	***
(-15,+15)	236	-1.02	-0.39	106:125	-1.550$	-1.209	-0.319	***
(-1,0)	236	-0.15	-0.03	105:126	-0.436	-0.351	-0.449	***
(-2,0)	236	-0.30	-0.18	105:126	-1.349$	-1.114	-0.449	***
(-5,0)	236	-0.08	-0.06	106:125	-0.658	-0.621	-0.319	***
(-10,0)	236	-0.15	0.06	113:118	-0.187	-0.172	0.596	***
(-15,0)	236	-0.62	-0.35	103:128	-2.261*	-1.449$	-0.711	***
(0,+1)	236	-0.29	-0.24	96:135	-2.009*	-1.650*	-1.625$	***
(0,+2)	236	-0.61	-0.46	95:136	-3.059**	-2.654**	-1.756*	***
(0,+5)	236	-0.81	-0.49	97:134	-2.368**	-2.135*	-1.494$	***
(0,+10)	236	-0.76	-0.33	111:120	-1.324$	-1.128	0.334	***
(0,+15)	236	-0.52	-0.10	108:123	-0.403	-0.324	-0.057	***
Targets								
(-1,+1)	52	9.43	10.20	36:15	26.602***	4.074***	3.430***	
(-2,+2)	52	10.22	10.74	32:19	21.616***	4.202***	2.307*	
(-5,+5)	52	12.91	12.69	36:15	17.020***	4.616***	3.430***	
(-10,+10)	52	14.78	14.66	39:12	13.950***	4.865***	4.272***	
(-15,+15)	52	16.58	15.79	40:11	12.138***	4.743***	4.553***	
(-1,0)	52	8.77	9.66	33:18	30.893***	3.905***	2.588**	
(-2,0)	52	9.54	10.15	38:13	26.456***	4.075***	3.992***	
(-5,0)	52	11.94	11.89	38:13	21.795***	4.477***	3.992***	
(-10,0)	52	13.75	13.69	39:12	18.351***	4.926***	4.272***	
(-15,0)	52	15.44	14.99	38:13	16.493***	4.995***	3.992***	
(0,+1)	52	7.49	8.65	31:20	27.664***	3.701***	2.027*	
(0,+2)	52	7.50	8.70	32:19	22.656***	3.660***	2.307*	
(0,+5)	52	7.79	8.91	31:20	16.327***	3.644***	2.027*	
(0,+10)	52	7.85	9.08	34:17	12.170***	3.497***	2.869**	
(0,+15)	52	7.96	8.90	34:17	9.799***	3.314***	2.869**	

Source: Reports results for all transactions reported in the Thomson Financial SDC database for which corresponding Datastream stock returns data exist, where the acquisition resulted in a change in control. Change in control is defined as a transaction that raised the acquirer's stake in the target from less than 50 percent to 50 percent or greater. Results are for the entire sample period, 1990–2002.
***Significant at 0.1 percent level.
**Significant at 1 percent level.
* Significant at 5 percent level.
$ Significant at 10 percent level.
a. CAAR = cumulative average abnormal return.
b. SCS Z = standardized cross-sectional Z score.
c. Generalized sign Z = non-parametric test statistic.
d. The *t* test is for difference between acquirer and target mean CAAR.

Table 7. Cumulative Average Abnormal Returns across Event Windows for All Target Cross-Border and Domestic Transactions Resulting in a Change in Control for All Years, 1990–2002

Market model, equally weighted index

Type of transaction and event window (days)	Number	Mean CAAR (percent)[a]	Precision-weighted CAAR (percent)[a]	Positive: negative	Patel Z	SCS Z[b]	Generalized sign Z[c]	t test[d]
Cross-border transactions								
(-1,+1)	20	5.35	3.71	11:09	5.533***	1.383$	0.587	$
(-2,+2)	20	5.46	3.73	10:10	4.305***	1.371$	0.14	
(-5,+5)	20	8.39	5.34	12:08	4.092***	1.798*	1.035	
(-10,+10)	20	10.84	7.58	15:05	4.126***	2.225*	2.377**	
(-15,+15)	20	12.33	8.54	16:04	3.739***	2.343**	2.824**	
(-1,0)	20	4.67	3.73	11:09	6.793***	1.421$	0.587	
(-2,0)	20	4.90	3.85	14:06	5.704***	1.450$	1.929*	$
(-5,0)	20	8.04	5.67	13:07	5.913***	1.953*	1.482$	
(-10,0)	20	11.72	8.96	16:04	6.855***	2.719**	2.824**	
(-15,0)	20	12.82	9.95	16:04	6.235***	2.937**	2.824**	
(0,+1)	20	4.10	2.93	9:11	5.378***	1.14	-0.308	
(0,+2)	20	3.97	2.83	10:10	4.229***	1.098	0.14	
(0,+5)	20	3.76	2.62	8:12	2.747**	0.968	-0.755	$
(0,+10)	20	2.53	1.58	9:11	1.201	0.555	-0.308	**
(0,+15)	20	2.92	1.53	8:12	0.964	0.53	-0.755	$
Domestic transactions								
(-1,+1)	32	11.88	13.70	26:6	29.404***	4.041***	4.101***	
(-2,+2)	32	13.15	14.56	23:9	24.101***	4.233***	3.035**	
(-5,+5)	32	15.72	16.72	25:7	18.457***	4.528***	3.745***	
(-10,+10)	32	17.09	18.48	25:7	14.466***	4.542***	3.745***	
(-15,+15)	32	18.96	19.65	25:7	12.442***	4.315***	3.745***	
(-1,0)	32	11.04	12.77	22:10	33.607***	3.762***	2.680**	
(-2,0)	32	12.22	13.50	25:7	28.967***	3.980***	3.745***	
(-5,0)	32	14.25	15.25	26:6	23.015***	4.220***	4.101***	
(-10,0)	32	14.88	16.22	24:8	17.901***	4.276***	3.390***	
(-15,0)	32	16.86	17.66	23:9	16.007***	4.264***	3.035**	
(0,+1)	32	9.58	11.76	23:9	30.931***	3.713***	3.035**	
(0,+2)	32	9.67	11.89	23:9	25.456***	3.682***	3.035**	
(0,+5)	32	10.21	12.30	24:8	18.544***	3.730***	3.390***	
(0,+10)	32	10.95	13.08	26:6	14.426***	3.764***	4.101***	
(0,+15)	32	10.84	12.81	26:6	11.599***	3.531***	4.101***	

Source: Reports results for all transactions reported in the Thomson Financial SDC database for which corresponding Datastream stock returns data exist, where the acquisition resulted in a change in control. Change in control is defined as a transaction that raised the acquirer's stake in the target from less than 50 percent to 50 percent or greater. Results are for the entire sample period 1990–2002.

*** Significant at 0.1 percent level.
** Significant at 1 percent level.
* Significant at 5 percent level.
$ Significant at 10 percent level.
a. CAAR = cumulative average abnormal return.
b. SCS Z = standardized cross-sectional Z score.
c. Generalized sign Z = non-parametric test statistic.
d. The *t* test is for difference between cross-border and domestic mean CAAR.

Table 8. Cumulative Average Abnormal Returns across Event Windows, for All Acquirer Cross-Border and Domestic Transactions Resulting in a Change in Control for All Years, 1990–2002

Market model, equally weighted index

Type of transaction and event window (days)	Number	Mean CAAR (percent)[a]	Precision-weighted CAAR (percent)[a]	Positive: negative	Patel Z	SCS Z[b]	Generalized sign Z[c]	t test[d]
Cross-border transactions								
(-1,+1)	123	0.25	0.16	59:60	0.61	0.487	0.349	**
(-2,+2)	123	0.03	-0.04	55:64	-0.217	-0.174	-0.375	***
(-5,+5)	123	0.04	0.14	59:60	0.137	0.124	0.349	**
(-10,+10)	123	0.41	0.59	64:55	0.721	0.696	1.253	**
(-15,+15)	123	0.04	0.33	60:59	0.251	0.225	0.53	
(-1,0)	123	0.45	0.33	59:60	1.754*	1.355$	0.349	***
(-2,0)	123	0.41	0.22	58:61	0.902	0.761	0.168	***
(-5,0)	123	0.83	0.55	59:60	1.560$	1.586$	0.349	***
(-10,0)	123	0.93	0.60	67:52	1.128	1.104	1.795*	**
(-15,0)	123	0.45	0.24	58:61	0.252	0.234	0.168	**
(0,+1)	123	0.08	0.02	52:67	0.044	0.041	-0.917	**
(0,+2)	123	-0.09	-0.07	51:68	-0.332	-0.311	-1.098	***
(0,+5)	123	-0.51	-0.21	53:66	-0.774	-0.684	-0.736	
(0,+10)	123	-0.24	0.19	61:58	0.331	0.291	0.71	
(0,+15)	123	-0.13	0.29	58:61	0.479	0.409	0.168	
Domestic transactions								
(-1,+1)	113	-0.94	-0.59	44:68	-2.837**	-2.315*	-1.393$	
(-2,+2)	113	-1.70	-1.14	37:75	-4.167***	-3.619***	-2.715**	
(-5,+5)	113	-1.68	-1.16	42:70	-2.986**	-2.781**	-1.771*	
(-10,+10)	113	-2.10	-1.05	47:65	-2.078*	-1.808*	-0.826	
(-15,+15)	113	-2.16	-1.15	46:66	-2.502**	-1.745*	-1.015	
(-1,0)	113	-0.79	-0.41	46:66	-2.460**	-2.128*	-1.015	
(-2,0)	113	-1.07	-0.60	47:65	-2.891**	-2.376**	-0.826	
(-5,0)	113	-1.08	-0.72	47:65	-2.578**	-2.333**	-0.826	
(-10,0)	113	-1.33	-0.50	46:66	-1.447$	-1.265	-1.015	
(-15,0)	113	-1.77	-0.98	45:67	-3.530***	-1.816*	-1.204	
(0,+1)	113	-0.70	-0.51	44:68	-2.950**	-2.219*	-1.393$	
(0,+2)	113	-1.18	-0.87	44:68	-4.074***	-3.352***	-1.393$	
(0,+5)	113	-1.14	-0.78	44:68	-2.615**	-2.419**	-1.393$	
(0,+10)	113	-1.33	-0.89	50:62	-2.258*	-1.874*	-0.259	
(0,+15)	113	-0.94	-0.51	50:62	-1.082	-0.822	-0.259	

Source: Reports results for all transactions reported in the Thomson Financial SDC database for which corresponding Datastream stock returns data exist, where the acquisition resulted in a change in control. Change in control is defined as a transaction that raised the acquirer's stake in the target from less than 50 percent to 50 percent or greater. Results are for the entire sample period, 1990–2002.

***Significant at 0.1 percent level.

** Significant at 1 percent level.

* Significant at 5 percent level.

$ Significant at 10 percent level.

a. CAAR = cumulative average abnormal return.

b. SCS Z = standardized cross-sectional Z score.

c. Generalized sign Z = non-parametric test statistic.

d. The *t* test is for difference between domestic and cross-border transactions mean CAARs.

most of the windows shown in the table. Hence, for the acquirers, geographically focusing mergers tend to destroy value, and geographically diversifying mergers tend to be value-neutral.

On the whole, the results suggest that there is a wealth transfer from the acquirers to the targets, which is larger for domestic than for cross-border deals. Because cross-border M&As appear value-neutral for acquirers and value-creating for targets, such deals appear to be economically viable on average. Whether the value gains for domestic targets are sufficient to offset the losses to acquirers in domestic transactions will be the subject of future research.

Conclusions

During the 1990s, financial markets in Europe were deregulated to pursue the European Union's objective of creating a single market for financial services. The deregulation led to an unprecedented wave of mergers and acquisitions in the financial services industry. This paper analyzes M&As in the European insurance industry over the period 1990–2002. The objective is to determine whether M&As in the European insurance market create value for shareholders. We conduct a standard market model event-study analysis using a sample of insurance M&As selected from the intersection of the Thomson Financial SDC database on M&As and the Datastream database on stock prices. The sample consists of all transactions where either the target or the acquirer is a European insurance company. We analyze all transactions involving the acquisition of a value-stake as well as the subset of these transactions resulting in a change in control, defined as a transaction where the acquirer's stake in the target increased from less than 50 percent to 50 percent or more of the target's shares as a result of the transaction. We analyze 535 acquirer transactions, of which 256 involved a change in control. The total number of target transactions was 165, but only fifty-two resulted in a change in control. The reason for the difference in size between the acquirer and target samples is that many targets were closely held firms, mutuals, or subsidiaries of larger firms.

The results of the event-study analysis show that European M&As created small negative cumulative average abnormal returns for acquirers (generally less than 1 percent) across various windows surrounding the transaction date. Targets, however, realized substantial positive CAARs.

Breaking down the transactions into cross-border and domestic (within-country) transactions, we find that cross-border transactions were value-neutral for acquirers, whereas within-border transactions led to a significant loss in value for acquirers. For targets, both cross-border and within-border transactions created significant value. The value creation tended to be higher for within-border transactions than for cross-border transactions.

Overall, the results are somewhat conflicting with respect to the value of geographically diversifying versus geographically focusing mergers. Geographically diversifying mergers seem to have superior value-related effects for acquirers, but focusing mergers tend to create more value for targets. Given that cross-border transactions are value-neutral for acquirers and value-creating for targets, these transactions seem to produce clear economic gains. Whether the gains for targets in within-border transactions are sufficient to offset the losses sustained by acquirers will be the subject of future research.

Discussion

Robert Litan of Brookings commented on the comparative reforms of the 1990s in the United States and Europe. Much of the activity in the U.S. banking industry had no parallel in the domestic insurance industry. Perhaps a pent-up agenda of mergers due to interstate banking provisions explains the flurry of banking mergers. Dave Cummins responded that Reigle-Neil and similar regulatory change in Europe led to mergers and acquisitions in the banking industry and that the United States never had significant restrictions on interstate mergers. Without closely examining the relative size of European insurers, Cummins did acknowledge the existence of very large European companies due to a precedent of involvement in universal banking activities, which is not the norm for the American market. A cross-Atlantic comparison of firm size would be insightful, both at the level of the mega insurer and of the middle market.

Alan Berger of the Federal Reserve lauded the inclusion of a survey of banking literature. Insurance studies must draw on banking sector research because the empirical work is so much more extensive. Most European banking studies have asked why there have been so few cross-border banking mergers when there have been plenty of cross-border insurance mergers. Future research would do well to examine pairs of countries rather than individual countries. Specifically, what characteristics exhibited by country pairs are common to successful cross-border mergers? This inquiry might support a new trade theory of foreign direct investment in which efficiency gains come from expanding to a country similar to one's own as opposed to traditional theory of comparative advantage, which would encourage mergers across dissimilar countries. The banking industry seems to support this new trade theory; the insurance industry may fit in as well.

Stuart Brahs of Principal Financial Group expressed an interest in case study analysis. For example, Alliance Capital Management had a successful venture in its acquisition of RJF in France, but not in its merger with Dresdner in Germany. Cummins expressed interest in the case study approach and mentioned a banking paper by Stephen Rhoades that examines seven mergers to pinpoint the source of efficiency gains and losses.

Thomas Holzheu of Swiss Economic Research Unit disagreed on what had the greater impact on insurance in the 1990s, pointing to the removal of rate regulation, which increased competitive pressure on small suboptimal insurers, as the reason for the dominance of domestic mergers. Cross-border deregulation had less effect. Freedom of trade eliminated the requirement of holding a subsidiary in the country of business, but in reality doing business effectively requires a physical presence. The wave of mergers occurred before the single market was created, but the machinery of rate regulations imposed severe limitations on doing business. The European deregulation experience of 1994 and 1995 may shed light on the current U.S. insurance market.

Several attendees wanted to discuss the role that nationalism may play in the relative difficulty of banking mergers over insurance mergers. Ulrik Bie of the Royal Danish Embassy and Central Bank of Denmark discussed the recent building of financial conglomerates in Scandinavian countries to keep out Southern European banks, Deutsche Bank in particular. The European Central Bank has encouraged consolidation because working with larger entities is easier than working with small ones, but governments, especially in larger countries, have resisted foreign ownership in the banking sector. This is especially the case when banking is the dominant sector but is famously untrue in the United States and the United Kingdom.

Larry White of New York University discussed several misperceptions that lead to the persistence of mergers in the face of empirical evidence against them. Although economies of scale are exhausted at some modest level, practitioners believe the contrary. First, practitioners may be unduly optimistic about the potential payoff of a merger. Those aware of the likelihood of failure still imagine themselves lucky. Alan Berger of the Federal Reserve added that scale economies exist, but the diseconomies get overlooked; combining two back-office operations may reduce costs, but agency costs, management problems, and the corporate jet increase costs. Finally, improvements in operating costs may come from closing down some operations, leaving higher-interest costs of replacing the funds in a different way.

White also mentioned that foreign bidders benefit the shareholders of the acquisition target by bidding up the price. Shareholders of foreign acquirers, however, see neutral effects, on average. Linking the two to examine net benefit would tell a more complete story.

References

Akhigbe, Aigbe, and Jeff Madura. 2001. "Intra-Industry Signals Resulting from Insurance Company Mergers." *Journal of Risk and Insurance* 68 (3): 489–506.

Beaver, William H. 1968. "The Information Content of Annual Earnings Announcements." *Journal of Accounting Research* 6 (supplement): 67–92.

Berger, Allen N. 1995. "The Profit-Structure Relationship in Banking: Tests of Market-Power and Efficient-Structure Hypotheses." *Journal of Money, Credit, and Banking* 27 (2): 404–31.

Berger, Allen N., J. David Cummins, Mary A. Weiss, and Hongmin Zi. 2000. "Conglomeration versus Strategic Focus: Evidence from the Insurance Industry." *Journal of Financial Intermediation* 9 (4): 323–62.

Berger, Philip G., and Eli Ofek. 1995. "Diversification's Effect on Firm Value." *Journal of Financial Economics* 37 (1, January): 39–65.

Boehmer, Ekkehart, Jim Musumeci, and Annette Poulsen. 1991. "Event Study Methodology under Conditions of Event-Induced Variance." *Journal of Financial Economics* 30 (December): 253–72.

Brown, Stephen, and Jerold B. Warner. 1985. "Using Daily Stock Returns: The Case of Event Studies." *Journal of Financial Economics* 14 (1, March): 3–33.

Campbell, Cynthia J., Lawrence Goldberg, and Anoop Rai. 2003. "The Impact of the European Union Insurance Directives on Insurance Company Stocks." *Journal of Risk and Insurance* 70 (1): 125–67.

Christie, Andrew A. 1982. "The Stochastic Behavior of Common Stock Variance: Value, Leverage, and Interest Rate Effects." *Journal of Financial Economics* 10 (4): 407–32.

Comment, Robert, and Gregg A. Jarrell. 1995. "Corporate Focus and Stock Returns." *Journal of Financial Economics* 37 (1): 67–87.

Cowan, Arnold R. 1992. "Nonparametric Event Study Tests." *Review of Quantitative Finance and Accounting* 2 (December): 343–58.

Cummins, J. David, Martin F. Grace, and Richard D. Phillips. 1999. "Regulatory Solvency Prediction in Property-Liability Insurance: Risk-Based Capital, Audit Ratios, and Cash Flow Simulation." *Journal of Risk and Insurance* 66 (3): 417–58.

Cummins, J. David, and Christopher M. Lewis. 2003. "Catastrophic Events, Parameter Uncertainty, and the Breakdown of Implicit Long-Term Contracting: The Case of Terrorism Insurance." *Journal of Risk and Uncertainty* 26 (2-3): 153–78.

Cummins, J. David, and María Rubio-Misas. 2004. "Deregulation, Consolidation, and Efficiency: Evidence from the Spanish Insurance Industry." Working Paper. University of Pennsylvania, Wharton Financial Institutions Center.

Cummins, J. David, and Anthony M. Santomero. 1999. *Changes in the Life Insurance Industry: Efficiency, Technology, and Risk Management*. Boston, Mass.: Kluwer.

Cummins, J. David, Sharon Tennyson, and Mary A. Weiss. 1999. "Consolidation and Efficiency in the U.S. Life Insurance Industry." *Journal of Banking and Finance* 23 (2-4): 325–57.

Cummins, J. David, and Xiaoying Xie. 2003. "Mergers and Acquisitions in the U.S. Property-Liability Insurance Industry: Productivity and Efficiency Effects." Working Paper. University of Pennsylvania.

Cybo-Ottone, Alberto, and Maurizio Murgia. 2000. "Mergers and Shareholder Wealth in European Banking." *Journal of Banking and Finance* 24 (6): 831–59.

DeLong, Gayle L. 2002. "Stockholder Gains from Focusing versus Diversifying Bank Mergers." *Journal of Financial Economics* 59 (2): 221–52.

Dravid, Ajay R. 1987. "A Note on the Behavior of Stock Returns around Ex-Dates of Stock Distributions." *Journal of Finance* 42 (1): 163–68.

Estrella, Arturo. 2001. "Mixing and Matching: Prospective Financial Sector Mergers and Market Valuation." *Journal of Banking and Finance* 25 (12, December): 2367–92.

Group of Ten. 2001. *Report on Consolidation in the Financial Sector.* Basel, Switzerland: Bank for International Settlements.

Lepetit, Laetitia, Stephanie Patry, and Philippe Rous. 2002. "Diversification versus Specialization: An Event Study of M&As in the European Banking Industry." Working Paper. University of Limoges, Centre de Recherche en Macroéconomie Monétaire.

MacKinlay, A. Craig. 1997. "Event Studies in Economics and Finance." *Journal of Economic Literature* 35 (1, March): 12–39.

Ohlson, James A., and Stephen H. Penman. 1985. "Volatility Increases Subsequent to Stock Splits: An Empirical Aberration." *Journal of Financial Economics* 14 (June): 251–66.

Patel, James M. 1976. "Corporate Forecasts of Earnings per Share and Stock Price Behavior: Empirical Tests." *Journal of Accounting Research* 14 (2): 246–76.

Pound, John, and Richard Zeckhauser. 1990. "Clearly Heard on the Street: The Effect of Takeover Rumors on Stock Prices." *Journal of Business* 63 (3): 291–308.

Rhoades, Stephen A. 1998. "The Efficiency Effects of Bank Mergers: An Overview of Case Studies of Nine Mergers." *Journal of Banking and Finance* 22 (3): 273–91.

Scharfstein, David, and Jeremy Stein. 2000. "The Dark Side of Internal Capital Markets: Divisional Rent-Seeking and Inefficient Investment." *Journal of Finance* 55 (December): 2537–67.

Schwert, G. William. 1981. "Using Financial Data to Measure the Effects of Regulation." *Journal of Law and Economics* 25 (April): 121–45.

Swiss Re. 2000. *Europe in Focus: Non-Life Markets Undergoing Structural Change.* Sigma 3.